THE LIFE AND THOUGHT OF ALBERT SCHWEITZER

(*By permission of Karsh, Ottawa*)

THE LIFE AND THOUGHT OF ALBERT SCHWEITZER

BY

WERNER PICHT

TRANSLATED FROM THE GERMAN
BY
EDWARD FITZGERALD

HARPER & ROW, PUBLISHERS

New York and Evanston

ALBERT SCHWEITZER: THE MAN AND HIS WORK
Translated from
ALBERT SCHWEITZER: LEBEN UND BEDEUTUNG

Library of Congress catalog card number: 65-10373

PRINTED IN GREAT BRITAIN
for
HARPER & ROW

CONTENTS

ILLUSTRATIONS

INTRODUCTION

Whoever proposes to add to the vast number of books which have been written about Albert Schweitzer is obviously under some obligation to justify his intention.

The man whose work and significance this book proposes to analyse has probably had a greater influence and been more widely recognized than any other of the great men of our time. A little more publicity can hardly add anything to his stature, but a man's spiritual significance can be eroded by too much talk. The fame and genius of a Napoleon cannot be affected by a hundred more books, good, bad, or indifferent. However, one of the fatal tendencies of our civilization is to seize on any elemental spiritual phenomenon when it appears amongst us—which it does all too infrequently—and grind it away in an involved and anonymous mechanism of criticism and interpretation.

Against his own inclinations, and at the cost of his peace of mind, Schweitzer has submitted willingly to publicity in order, like the philosophers of the Enlightenment in the eighteenth century, to encourage men to think, and to benefit mankind by the spread of his own ideas. Is he aware of the daemonism inherent in that process, which gives itself out as the handmaid of the spiritual, and yet compromises all spirituality? Is it our task to revere him silently, and passively to allow the spiritual strength of this extraordinary man to flow to us?

But, above all, is there really anything further to be said about him? With that great gift of graphic communication which is peculiarly his own, Schweitzer has given us himself in a self-portrayal. In consequence his biographers have had a relatively easy task: their material was not only lying ready to hand, but it had already been formed for them by the hand of a master. Schweitzer's personality lends itself to anecdotal portrayal. All you have to do is to turn to his own youthful reminiscences, to his own accounts of his hospital in the African jungle. And if you want to know about his aims and his achievements from the beginning of the thirties, embracing all the important phases of his activities, there it is in his own book *My Life and Thought.* In his own words, and written with his own inimitable graphic power, there is almost all you need to know about the tremendous phenomenon of his existence. And should anything still be lacking—perhaps biographical details relating to a later period—it is readily obtainable in other publications. So what gap, if any, remains to be filled?

And yet this simple question misses the point, for the task this book sets out to perform lies elsewhere. It does not propose to add to what Schweitzer himself and his followers have already written. And it is certainly not another attempt at a biography. It is instead an attempt at an adequate elucidation of the phenomenon Schweitzer, which has only too often been sentimentalized and obscured by uncritical affirmation. A lifelong close personal association with Schweitzer has confirmed the author's conviction that reverence is not incompatible with criticism. The revelation of true greatness is the result of the concerted action of both. The book does not entirely lack chronological order, but it does not feel bound to it. Where chronological happenings are dealt with the aim is solely to reveal the essence and significance of Albert Schweitzer's personality.

The analysis of the phenomenon is much more difficult than would appear at first sight. To begin with it is impossible for any one man to master thoroughly the various spheres of Albert Schweitzer's many-sided productivity: theology, philosophy, music, and so on. That is a difficulty which must be accepted as inevitable, and the author has no intention of seeking the easy way out with quotations and excerpts. But the real difficulty lies even deeper; it is inherent in the paradoxical nature of Schweitzer's personality, a fact which will be referred to repeatedly during the course of this book.

Schweitzer's personality is unpretentious, but it is not simple. And it is this which explains why, despite the existence of authentic documentation readily available in large editions on an unusually wide scale, he has nevertheless been the victim of the grossest misinterpretation. How can we reconcile the 'heroization' with the, sometimes simultaneous, creation of a devotional atmosphere which suggests that everything is immediately understandable, consistent in itself, and readily acceptable without question to any properly constituted person?

The tremendous impression created by the moral personality has obviously paralysed and confused judgement on the phenomenon as a whole. In addition, the latter is difficult to appreciate as a whole, and still more difficult to grasp. The result is that, generally speaking, uncritical admirers regard it as sufficient to speak in terms of respect and admiration, whilst the experts, though also deeply respectful, adopt an attitude of reserve, if not of indifference. There are, of course, exceptions to this latter attitude, for example the work of the Basle theologian Fritz Buri, and the religio-scientific analysis of Pastor Rudolf Grabs in his book *Albert Schweitzer, Denker aus Christentum*.[1] But these studies did not set out to deal with the problem as a whole, or to clarify the indistinct reflection in the mirror of public opinion.

Thus a situation has developed which is as strange as it is unsatisfactory. An incalculable influence is acknowledged, but at the same time there is great confusion as to its spiritual origins. The veneration accorded to Schweitzer is genuine, but it is thoughtless. There is no obligation to rack one's brains over a fool in Christ, but when thought is demanded, and when, as is the case here, it is invested with a positively redeeming power, then that obligation must be taken fully into consideration. Even more, one must grapple vigorously with it and not be intimidated by the fear of encroaching too closely on an awe-inspiring personality. On the contrary, it would be truly disrespectful to ignore the difficulties Schweitzer presents to those who are ready to let themselves be carried along by the thought processes of his own passionate spirit.

The decision—taken only after long hesitation—to tackle the present task, no matter what the consequences, and, above all, without false piety (in short, the attitude which inspired Schweitzer's own investigation into the problem of Jesus), was determined to some extent by a realization that only in this way would it be possible to counter a certain danger which is becoming more and more obvious the longer it persists.

Albert Schweitzer is a divine gift in troublous times. But unless the blessing it represents is to run away like sand between our fingers that gift must be cherished with a feeling of the utmost responsibility. It is now being endangered in a very special way.

In both theology and philosophy Schweitzer is 'a highly disputed and isolated phenomenon'.[2] Despite his firmly established fame, doubts are beginning to arise as to whether his work amongst the natives of equatorial Africa is entitled to be rated any higher than that of innumerable other though lesser known servants of humanity. No sooner had he made himself politically embarrassing by his public stand against nuclear warfare than his jungle hospital became the target of denigrating criticism. Jealous rivalry also raised its head. Schweitzer is still with us today, and the powerful impression of his personality on the world is sufficiently strong to hold such criticism in check; in fact his influence is still growing.[3] Nevertheless, despite its tremendous impact, the popular image of Schweitzer rests on insecure premises. In his daring advances in the world of the spirit, Schweitzer has never bothered to adopt the precaution, usual in the world of scholarship, of, as it were, protecting his flanks when adopting a position which is in the nature of an advanced post. He has always refrained from making any reply to attacks made on him. Circumspect in the world of action, Schweitzer has always rejected anything which smacked of what might be called spiritual strategy. His allies are never chosen because of their strength or their immediate usefulness, and they are not deployed at strategically dominating points. Even his own performance is treated with the generous unconcern of genius. Work to which a great deal of his already very limited time has been devoted will suddenly be abandoned before completion. Key positions are not consolidated, whilst outworks of secondary importance are erected. On the whole one receives an impression of heart-warming and yet dangerous generosity.

It is even not easy to know quite what to make of Schweitzer's intellectual and spiritual position. Is it still possible to call it Christian?[4] What is the relationship between his theological and his philosophical thought? And what relationship do both bear to his actions? Has he really advanced the interpretation of the New Testament? Which of his achievements is likely to be permanent? And what is his abiding spiritual signifiance? The descriptions we have of his life and work cannot be said to provide us with completely satisfactory answers to these questions. What can the theological layman make of a summary of studies on the historical Jesus if their significance is not brought into relief against the framework of corresponding research before and after? What is the reader to make of the rendering—however conscientious—of an ethical teaching if its obvious contrast with the teachings of Jesus is not felt as a difficulty—if it is even regarded as being on all fours with the Christian mysticism of an Ignatius Loyola and a Francis of Assisi, whilst at the same time being presented as a more effective remedy for the ills of the world than all the recommendations of the theologians?[5]

The questions which inevitably arise out of any objective and unprejudiced attempts to understand Schweitzer demand an answer with increasing urgency. Unless these answers are provided an impression of uncertainty will remain. And things will be made worse if instead of answers we are fobbed off with uncritical affirmations—the kind of thing which in his struggle for truth Schweitzer himself has always rejected.

Thus if we are to clear up the doubts now being cast on Schweitzer and his work then we must do our best to see him not only in his greatness, but also in his limitations; we must see him both in his errors and in his achievements. In short, we must see him as he is; and in attempting to do so we can be quite certain that we are acting in his own true spirit.

The obligation of truth prohibits all tendentiousness. So far Schweitzer has been presented to the world almost exclusively by the representatives of an enlightened, liberal Christianity, who claim him for their own. And certainly Schweitzer himself feels that this is where he really does belong. However, on closer examination there is more than a suggestion that this attempt to classify him securely tends to distort his real significance, since the particular characteristic of his nature has always been its capacity to embrace contradictions readily, so to speak in peaceful co-existence, and to leave many problems in abeyance. In fact in this sense not only his outlook but his world of ideas is not complete in itself; it is '*unabgeschlossen*', and represents a strange and rare mingling of rigidity and mobility, of bond and free. No religious doctrinal authority has ever imposed more binding limits on the human spirit than the self-confidence of enlightened thought. Now although Schweitzer never questions this obligation, his need for freedom of thought, and at the same time for spiritual freedom—that is to say, not freedom 'from', but freedom 'to'—is so elemental that it finds ways and means of transcending those limits without the thinker Schweitzer's being untrue to himself. Thus when later on in this book we shall be led to say things which seem to contradict not only the usual interpretations (particularly with respect to his religious views) but even some of Schweitzer's own statements, the intention is not to 'save' him in the interests of a positive theology—which would certainly be a hopeless undertaking anyway—but purely in order to underline the uniqueness of a nature permanently poised in extreme polarity. Understanding will not be easy, and it will demand patient effort on the part of the reader.

The polymorphic nature of Schweitzer's thought is closely related to the spirit of his age. It has developed in a period of spiritual upheaval, and it contributes in its turn to the fulfilment of that period. As a New Testament scholar Schweitzer appears as the liquidator of both liberalism and historicism, whilst nevertheless remaining indebted to both. His greatest scientific task was the search for the historical Jesus, but once satisfied that he had succeeded in finding him, the question lost its formerly central significance for him. It is nothing at all unusual for pioneers like Schweitzer to be called upon to sacrifice their singleness of outlook.

To classify Schweitzer in his historical spiritual context relativizes his importance without diminishing it. It demonstrates that he has made history in his own sphere. In addition it underlines his actuality.

A superficial judgement might suggest that Schweitzer in our time has little more to tell us beyond the timeless validity of his humanity. New Testament scholarship has not adopted his formulation of the problem. The particular affinity of his thought to that of the eighteenth century would seem to exclude any fruitful relationship to contemporary spiritual problems. Nevertheless such a relationship does exist and in a very urgent and important respect.

Schweitzer's life is dominated by two impulses. One is a form of the ethic of love or charity, based on will-power, which is timeless. This has found its expression in the jungle hospital of Lambaréné, and it culminated in the belief in the Kingdom of God. The other impulse, whilst rooted in rationalism, is not dominated by it. Schweitzer stands out in our time as the last great embodiment of the passion for truth which produced what has been called the quest of the historical Jesus. With this—its 'greatest achievement'[6]—German Protestant theology made a very determined and systematic attempt to resolve the conflict between belief and knowledge: the actual crux, the true cross, of Europe's sickness.[7] Nevertheless, this conflict is just as much a problem for theology today as ever it was—as witness the debate on the 'de-mythologization' of the Christian Gospel, an attempt to cure a long-seated disease by a resort to the scalpel—namely by removing the troublesome 'mythological growths' altogether.

But a comparison of *Der alte und der neue Glaube* (*The Old and the New Belief*) written by David Friedrich Strauss in the year 1872 (and translated into English by M. Blind in the following year) with the publication of *Die Zukunft des Unglaubens* (*The Future of Unbelief*) by Gerhard Sczesny[8] creates the impression that there has been no advance towards a solution of the problem in almost a century.

The fact that in the meantime disbelief has wormed its way unobtrusively into the religious beliefs of all denominations, thus making the dividing line between belief and disbelief less clear than it was before, and the further fact that there seems less inclination on both sides to wage the disputes with the passion of former days, both get us no farther—and neither does the dogmatic rigidity of the ecclesiastical authorities. All this merely underlines the seriousness of the situation.

Belief cannot be produced to order. And putting it on short rations doesn't help either, because that is equivalent to retreating from the field of conflict. It does not even help to preserve what still remains; on the contrary, it exposes it to even greater danger. The attempt to rehabilitate the events described in the gospels by depriving them of their 'factuality' where they seem to conflict with modern scientific thought merely evades the issue and does nothing to strengthen their credibility.

Unless the question of truth is accepted frankly as the point of decisive importance, and answered as such, it becomes impossible to invalidate the objection that 'the old beliefs contradict the new scientific truths', or to reply to the assertion that for Christianity 'any spiritual wrestling for truth is absurd and dangerous', and that, in fact, its defenders 'regard the claims of scientific truth as a direct threat' to their positions.[9] The fact that the concept of truth put forward here is contestable does nothing to rebut the charge that Christianity is 'the prototype of an anti-philosophic world outlook'[10] any more than that the lack of knowledge on the part of those who make it deprives it of validity. Belief must lose the day if it fails to convince us that unflinching truthfulness is an essential part of real religion.[11] 'I am not a hero of faith', says Schweitzer of himself.[12] It is the right and the duty of theologians to decide the limits of his belief, but in so doing let them by all means acknowledge the strength of his belief that, in the words of Saint Paul (2 Cor. xiii. 8.), 'we can do nothing against the truth, but for the truth', and that Christianity has nothing to fear from the truth—not even when the search for truth makes many a detour and takes many a wrong turning.

In his *Quest of the Historical Jesus*, Schweitzer summed up an epoch of Protestant theology, a saga of the will to truth that imbued one generation in order that later generations should experience it again and rekindle their belief from it. The fact that this new voyage of the Argonauts in search of the golden fleece did not achieve—or has not yet achieved—its direct aim (an aim which necessarily remained unattainable in so far as these adventurers after truth cherished the illusion that their discoveries would lead them to the actual essence of belief) does not diminish the significance of the example they have given, a significance which, incidentally, extends far beyond the limits of mere scholarly investigation. However, fascinating though Schweitzer's description of this spiritual historical process is, it is hardly readable for any but the cognoscenti; at least, not since the second edition of the book, which extended it from 418 to 659 pages.

In order to preserve its original intention of achieving a broader effect the appendix at the end of the book attempts to provide a general outline even though the abridgement involves a considerable loss. The extension of this historical survey to the present day was intended to allow the theological layman to recognize the author's position in the general stream of New Testament research. It is hoped that critical theology will seriously consider the reference to the decisive importance for the future of the quest for the historical Jesus of the philosophical criticism of the concept of truth. This sketch should not be judged too harshly. It is the fate of theology that it may not withdraw into the citadel of a scholarly research. In so far as it has to do with ultimate realities it is subject to a supra-scientific authority. Whoever, without being particularly interested in theological questions, seeks information about Schweitzer's personality, may well ignore this appendix and concentrate on the chapter dealing with Schweitzer's quest for Jesus (which may show even the theologian its essential characteristics more clearly than they have been revealed up till now); on the short excerpt from Schweitzer's *Life of Jesus*; and on the sermons dealing with Jesus the master and Paul the liberator, now published for the first time.

This study, which aims at establishing the essence and significance of Schweitzer, is not meant to be a hymn of praise. The man who, as a youth, sat at the feet of the preacher of St. Nicholas' Church at Strassburg, who sat at his side at the desk in Günsbach when *Bach* was written, who drew the stops for him at the ancient Silbermann organ of St. Thomas's in Strassburg, who was with him when his decision to go into the wilderness was first conceived, and who accepted it at once as a matter of course, and who in the subsequent years followed the difficult path of 'the prisoner of Jesus' from stage to stage, was faced with no light task when he undertook to present the balance of a lifetime. He can no longer hope for the unqualified approval which met his first attempt at presenting Schweitzer to the world:[13] 'you see me as I see myself'.[14] The general picture aimed at in this book is obtainable only from a vantage point beyond its subject. Of course, to interpret the will and the achievement pre-supposes that the interpreter can see both from within; so to speak with the eyes of Schweitzer himself. But this is not all. If the interpretation and assessment are to have even an approximate validity, if the book is to achieve its aim and illuminate the significance of its subject and make clear its abiding importance for the contemporary world and for posterity as well, then a certain independence of judgement is essential.

No man is in a position to see himself as he really is, and certainly not a man like Schweitzer, whose nature is little given to introspection. Thus an objective estimate of his work must necessarily be different from his own. If this were not so then its personal and time involvement would make it a doubtful venture from the start.

The most difficult task which any admirer can be called upon to perform is to lay hands on a beloved image, since its features are threatened by every stroke of the chisel. Let this work therefore be regarded as the deepest possible expression of both gratitude and attachment. The greatness of Schweitzer can only be enhanced by such an approach.

Before me lies the page-proof of his work on Johann Sebastian Bach. In conclusion there stands in Schweitzer's own hand: S.D.G.

SOLI DEO GLORIA

In the last resort the whole being of Albert Schweitzer and the solution of all the paradoxes it raises, is summed up in those words.

WERNER PICHT

Hinterzarten, Schwarzwald, in July 1959
Altbirklehof

THE MAN AND HIS WORK

I

FUNDAMENTALS

Every valid utterance concerning Albert Schweitzer, whether in approval or disapproval, must proceed from, or at least lead to, a realization that, one way or the other, a tremendous personality is involved. His very existence is a fact of elemental force. Like every other phenomenon of human greatness in our midst, Schweitzer's, in its turn, changes the picture of our world.

Since this statement is intended not as an expression of uncritical admiration, but as an objective presentation of an existing fact, proof of the rightness of this estimate is required, and will, of course, be given. The aim of the present book is not merely to add another voice to the thousandfold chorus of praise with which public opinion in the Western World identifies itself with this philanthropist and upholder of humanitarian ideals—thereby placing itself, so to speak, on a level of familiarity with him, whilst at the same time not bothering its head about whether it has the right to do so or not. On the contrary, the claim made on Schweitzer's behalf here protects him from any over-hasty familiarity. It demands the proper distance of awe. It also raises the question of whether the contact with him sought in the following pages is likely to be a merely edifying and quite harmless experience by means of which the well-meaning seeker will find his own feelings happily confirmed, or whether, on the contrary, it involves the risk of his finding himself suddenly face to face with a disconcerting personality which contradicts traditional standards and values; even a personality whose authority may call the very mode of thought and way of life of the seeker himself into question.

An understanding of a great personality presupposes that human greatness is recognized and accepted in its true essence. The excessive alacrity with which Schweitzer's contemporaries have applauded him as 'the greatest man in the world'—to use a phrase adopted and used with sickening regularity by American popular journalism whenever Schweitzer is mentioned—suggests that in his case this has not been so. The presence of an unusual power is certainly recognized; nevertheless the spirit of the age—to which, incidentally, Schweitzer has declared himself in complete disagreement[1]—has not squarely faced its challenge. How otherwise would it be possible for such a unique and unconditional phenomenon to be accepted without question, for all the world as though it were a matter of course and needed neither proof nor a decision—and that not only by a spiritually-minded inner circle, but by the leading spokesmen of the day, and by the great ones of this earth, who join forces to load him with honours? Only when the voice which sounds from the African jungle dared to speak out against the atom bomb was a discordant note temporarily introduced into the unanimous chorus of approval. Many broadcasting stations refused to disseminate the message, and slanderous attacks sought to turn friends and contributors against the jungle hospital. The great man had broken the unwritten rules. So long as he confined himself to publishing philosophical works proclaiming the ethic of reverence for life, and to making atonement by his own behaviour for the crimes of the civilized world, there was not a jarring note in the unconditional paean of praise. After all, what better justification could a civilization of crumbling ideals expect or hope for? This unanimous celebration of a personality which had become a symbol offered a cheap and yet at the same time impressive collective excuse —provided, of course, that the much lauded idealist showed sense enough to mind his own business, and made no attempt to meddle with the affairs of those who wield temporal power!

The incident was very illuminating. It demonstrated the real relationship to human greatness in an age when mediocrity rules the world. That relationship undoubtedly reflects a secret longing. A great action is welcomed eagerly by a parched conscience, like water struck from the barren rock by the staff of a prophet. But should the prophet at the same time set himself up as a law-giver, then the people, whoring after a false freedom, will turn away from him. They are willing to let themselves be vaguely edified, but they are not prepared to be told what to do. Both in thought and action, however, Schweitzer belongs to an ordered world, a world regulated by commandment and obedience. He represents this ordered world by a life in which every gesture is obedience, a life which by that very fact itself becomes an imperative commandment. In consequence Schweitzer is really a stranger in a world which praises him to the skies but avoids looking him in the eye for fear of what it might find there, for fear that it might thereafter be unable to interpret his image and his teaching according to its own interests and desires.

To begin this study with a preliminary assessment of its subject demands a comment. It is a challenge to the reader who is not one of the many thousands who have been impressed by even a superficial acquaintance with Schweitzer's powerful personality.

In applying the term 'greatness', which represents a standard of measurement, to a phenomenon which is not objectively measurable, there is clearly a risk of building our edifice on the disputable basis of a purely personal opinion. And an even greater cause for misgiving is that in aligning Schweitzer with the master spirits of humanity there is a danger of finding ourselves at odds with the man himself.

A biographer as such has an easier task. He lays brick upon brick until the resultant pile speaks for itself. But the interpretation of the human problem attempted in this book necessarily proceeds from the attribute of greatness as an *a priori*, and from there it must go on to the inner definition which must prove its validity. Only in this way can both essence and influence be comprehended. Attributes and achievements, and even the aberrations and limitations, of this great man, reveal their actual shape only by first being traced within this framework. A mere summary of qualities will not lead to comprehension. It is obviously not so much the objective achievement in itself—as extraordinary as that may be—which represents the significance of this particular life and gives it its dramatic character; it is even more the impetus imparted by the personality itself which gives each of its manifestations its particular, not always rationally explainable, impact. The explanation is to be found in the secret of greatness as such; it is this which puts its unmistakable seal on the work of the theologian, the moralist, the doctor and the artist alike.

Schweitzer rejects any attempt to link him and his work to the idea of greatness. In his autobiography *My Life and Thought* he describes himself as 'a man of individual action', and in the same breath he insists that 'there are no heroes of action—only heroes of renunciation and suffering. Of such there are plenty. But few of them are known; and even these not to the crowd, but to the few.'[2] Obviously he does not reckon himself amongst them. Referring to his decision to become a doctor in the African jungle he says in the same place: 'only a person who feels his preference to be a matter of course, not something out of the ordinary, and who has no thought of heroism, but just recognizes a duty undertaken with sober enthusiasm, is capable of becoming a spiritual adventurer such as the world needs.' He is not impressed by Carlyle's *Heroes and Hero Worship*, and he points out—quite rightly!—that it is 'not a profound book'. Schweitzer's attitude is in accordance with the tendency of ethical humanism towards 'de-heroization'; and where it is combined, as it is here, with a Christian outlook, it finds no difficulty in turning to the teachings of Jesus for support. As with Jesus, so also with Schweitzer there is a particular sympathy with the lesser ones of this world, with the poor in spirit and with the materially poor. Both Schweitzer's simplicity and his humility make him at home with them.

Thus the question arises whether for him too the lesser has become the expression of real greatness. This is not the case. His ethic of reverence for life requires no such justification for its benevolent attitude towards what is small, since it is an attitude which equally embraces every living thing. It is individualistic. It demands that the individual should 'rise ever higher'. The ultimate aim of human civilization is 'the spiritual and moral perfecting of individuals'.[3] But Schweitzer's vitalistic philosophy cannot set up a standard of values within the various manifestations of life; and here, in fact, lies one of its greatest difficulties, though it is not one we propose to discuss now. The valid equation is life = life. The 'truly ethical' man does not ask how far this or that life deserves his sympathy as being valuable—life as such is sacred to him.[4]

From this it follows that 'ethics are responsibility without limit towards all that lives'.[5] Thus the small is not regarded as great, and, conversely, the great is not reduced to the stature of the small. The question of the value of any particular living phenomenon is excluded from ethical thought. However, at the same time the capacity for judgement retains the liberty to distinguish between what is great and what is small.

Here, for the first time, we come across one of those inconsequential devices by which Schweitzer's thought is enabled to escape from its own noose. If every living thing has an absolute right as such to respect, then, one would suppose, all its manifestations ought to be regarded as being on the same level. But whatever Schweitzer's philosophy of life may have to say on the point, Schweitzer himself is a born 'heroizer', and the fact that he constantly expresses his own loathing of any false heroism, and his own determined opposition to any attempt to 'heroize' his own person, makes no difference to this whatever. From Jesus to Paul and from Goethe to Bach, Schweitzer's life and work stand in the service of the great personality; his own nature, directed to greatness, turns to great personalities as to affinities in whose sphere of influence it finds itself at home and under whose guidance it fulfils itself.*

The spiritual phenomenon which is Schweitzer bears the unmistakable mark of that hour in German spiritual history when '*Grosses wiederum gross ward*' (Stefan George)[6]—when 'greatness once again became great'. Schweitzer was himself greatly influenced in his formative years by Nietzsche—from that solitary thinker he received 'all that he had to give to the world'.[7] The capacity to appreciate and accept greatness was in the air. It was equated with the heroic. Schweitzer's Jesus expresses himself in imperative words.[8] Against the humanization of Jesus at the hands of liberal biblical research, which reduced his figure to a commonplace level, Schweitzer stresses his 'greatness'.[9] There is, of course, no suggestion that Schweitzer's conception of Jesus is taken from any mundane sphere.[10] All the same, the colours he uses are taken from the palette of an era which preceded the age of world wars, an era in which the human spirit anticipated 'an end and a beginning', an era in which many long-forgotten truths were re-discovered, and many things revealed themselves in a new light.

According to Schweitzer himself, a preliminary 'real appreciation of unique greatness' is essential before any human being can enter into the sphere of influence of a great man.[11] Thus anyone who prefaces an exposition of the personality and work of Schweitzer by an assumption of greatness may well appeal to this. The distance from the examples makes no difference, nor the acknowledgement of errors, nor the admitted limits of insight. 'The greatest human beings are not those who err the least, but those who can—indeed, must—commit the greatest errors without at the same time losing their own value.'[12] Greatness is not rationally demonstrable, but it is instinctively appreciable. It can be made evident. The reference to it sets the key in which the symphony of this life is written.

Before one proceeds to assess a personality its place in the world must first be established. If it has 'roots', if it is deeply attached to a particular countryside and founded in some spiritual mother soil, formed by it and nourished by it, then these are factors which go to determine its character. Where Schweitzer is concerned the situation

* Just as his early Christian relationship to 'the Master' cannot be traced back to the re-discovery of Friedrich Gundolf's *Gefolgschaft und Jungertum (Followers and Apostles)*.

in this respect is paradoxical, as it is in so many others. He is unquestionably a 'citizen of the world', and as such he is claimed by all countries as one of their own, though he denies himself to each and every one of them. He is a writer whose books have been translated into innumerable languages and published all over the world; and his fame is no less amongst the Anglo-Saxons than it is amongst the Germans, no less in France than in Switzerland or the Scandinavian countries. As an organist he is as much at home with the Spanish as the Dutch organ. As a philosopher he occupies himself no less intensively with the thinkers of India and China than with Kant. And, finally, he is the jungle doctor of Lambaréné who, in order to maintain his independence, will accept no formal help from any government, and whose work is financed by contributions from the 'Brotherhood of those marked by suffering' all over the world. At first sight it could hardly appear helpful to go back to its origin in order to explain a phenomenon incorporating so many diverse aspects. For a time those who were not close to him were even under the impression that they had to do with a plurality of personalities, all bearing the unmistakable stamp of genius. However, it is now generally known that the theologian, the philosopher, the preacher, the musician, the master of graphic narrative, the doctor, the organizer and the colonizer are all one and the same man. But his many-sided nature has tended to become a stumbling-block for judgement, and Schweitzer has been compared in colourful confusion to Beethoven, Michelangelo, Rembrandt,[13] and to the founder of the Salvation Army, William Booth.[14] Some have even gone so far as to compare him to a Goethe-like Vincent de Paul.[15] The manifest richness of his personality has led some to place him on a par with the universality of a Leonardo or a Goethe, but both comparisons are beside the point. The vessel of this tremendous and embracing power is neither a Renaissance spirit nor an all-embracing Goethean nature. The spirit of investigation is quite foreign to him, and so also is any urge to embrace a whole world in himself or to create a whole world out of himself. According to his own account, he is creative only in musical improvisation: 'my delight was to improvise'.[16] Despite his profound appreciation of Nature he is not fascinated by the wonders of creation, nor is it in accordance with his temperament to apprehend men and things in the same way as Goethe did, in their essential particularity. 'The children of his mind have all a strong family resemblance.'[17] He is certainly tolerant—if only out of respect for the spiritual nature of others, and because of his firm belief in freedom, but his outlook is determined by his own firmly fixed vantage point. The origin of understanding is the *ratio* not the intuition. Even 'the non-rational conviction', which is allowed a central position in his world outlook, results from 'thinking experience'.[18] However, where Schweitzer is concerned, reason is not harnessed in the service of any urge to knowledge for its own sake. His temperament knows nothing of that insatiable curiosity which urged a Leonardo through all the spheres of creation—that same insatiable curiosity which is at the basis of all modern science. Schweitzer's motivation is an ethical impulse. When as a theologian he seeks for 'truth' he is following a moral imperative. When as a philosopher he seeks to found an ethic based on thought, the same is true. Precisely because of this, his knowledge is turned immediately into action. The identity of thought and action is complete.

Those characteristics, which are immediately revealed by even a superficial glance at the spiritual physiognomy of Schweitzer, suggest a oneness and an accumulated energy of character which are plainly not consonant with any unsystematic richness either of gifts or activities. One feels at once that there is no room for chance, no room for anything of an arbitrary nature. We sense instead the operation of an absolute law, a predestination from the beginning.

This impression is not deceptive. The apparently disparate elements assume their proper order and slip into place when they are traced back to their origins. What those who attempt to describe the man and his work usually present as an unsystematic juxtaposition becomes understandable as an organic whole, as a simple and necessary developmen from one common root. Simplicity and necessity are the guiding laws of Schweitzer's life.

Albert Schweitzer was born in a parsonage in Günsbach in the Münster valley of Alsace,[19] and all his life he has remained loyal to this origin. The Goethe Prize awarded to him in 1928 by the town of Frankfurt was used to build a house according to his own plans in his own birthplace—not set back in a garden, but facing on to the street; because any suggestion of isolation from his fellow-men is abhorrent to him, and below the mountain ridge—'as a protection from the guns of the next war'. The chosen site has justified itself in both senses, and the place is his home when he is in Europe. And even when the host himself is absent, it is a centre which attracts innumerable friends and admirers. Even in the permanent splendour of the primeval forest, which knows no changing seasons, the spring in Günsbach is not forgotten; and, in fact, no landscape is more in accordance with the character of the man than this valley in the Southern Vosges with its striking mingling of gentle peace and gaunt greatness, revealing itself to the deeper searcher, after an unexpectedly tranquil introduction of foothills, as something overwhelmingly elemental. There is no type of human being with whom Schweitzer is more at home than these Alleman peasants, to whom he has been a familiar figure from childhood as 'our Albert', with whom he chats in the local dialect, whose cares and pleasures he knows and shares, and who daily place little gifts—pears, eggs, grapes, vegetables, raspberries and mushrooms—on the window-sill of his modest study.

And thus past and present come together. The past is not only treated with piety, it remains present. The traditional Sunday walk is a repetition of the Sunday walk his father was accustomed to make with his five children. And in memory of his mother, Schweitzer still makes the same pilgrimage she made with her family and her guests to the hillside on the farther side of the valley to picnic. The simple food taken along is exactly the same now as it was in those far-off days. In the account given to us by an Englishwoman who is his friend[20] we see him even in the thirties going to morning service, wearing his father's old black gown and Geneva bands and the biretta-like cap of his maternal grandfather.

Schweitzer's father was a parson who actively exercised his ministry until his ninety-seventh year (the Schweitzers are made of iron, they say in the Münster Valley). His mother was the daughter of another parson. This man's name was Schillinger and he lived in the upper part of the same valley. The mother's brother, after whom she named her son Albert, was also a parson—of the Church of St Nicholas in Strassburg, at which Schweitzer himself was locum tenens from his twenty-fourth year until he left to go to Africa; and once again during his involuntary stay in Europe at the end of the First World War.

Without giving us any detailed picture of his mother, his youthful memories pay her the deepest and most beautiful homage in the simple sentence: 'We understood each other without using words.'[21] She was the mother soil of human greatness, whilst the outstandingly amiable and benevolent character of the father, who delighted himself and others by the composition of village stories and by his improvisations on the cottage piano in his spare time, was the embodiment of capable activity and sensitive humanity—though without suggesting the likelihood of anything out of the ordinary in his progeny.

It is when we turn to Schweitzer's maternal grandfather, Parson Schillinger, that we find—in moderation certainly—a 'dominating personality'. There was a passion for the organ and for organ building;

and a profound and ardent nature, which Schweitzer's mother inherited and passed on to her son. And finally, as the particular and determining heritage for the grandson, whom, incidentally, he never knew, old Schillinger passed on the spirit of the eighteenth century. Parson Schillinger was an enthusiastic adherent of the Enlightenment movement; and Schweitzer himself had the impression that in his fourteenth year the spirit of enlightenment inherited from his maternal ancestor awoke in him never to leave him again: 'Actually I have remained what I became at that time.' He might well have written: 'what I was by origin: the son of the Günsbach Parsonage'. Whatever this 'spiritual adventurer' was to undertake in his life, in whatever way he was to surprise the world, his whole activity was no more than the administration of inherited talents. No theme ever arises which is not clearly adumbrated in advance. Despite a completely natural lack of conventionality there is never a word or gesture which runs counter to the inherited way of life. The carpenter at work in his shirtsleeves in Lambaréné, and the preacher with open shirt and cork topee may outwardly appear as different as possible from those ancestors with their neck-bands of fine lawn, but fundamentally they are one and the same stock.

Schweitzer's background is the religious ambient of the parsonage, the seat at the organ, and the pulpit. His personal relationship to this background is of unusual fervour. When he went off to school in Mühlhausen he suffered much from a homesick longing for the church at Günsbach, and he greatly missed his father's sermons, and the familiar church service. It was from this atmosphere that he drew 'with me into life a feeling for what is solemn, and a need for quiet and self-recollection'.[22] He rejected 'the sermonizing church'. 'A church is something much more than a place in which you listen to a sermon. It is a place of devotion.' This need was particularly encouraged in Günsbach by the circumstance that the church there was both Catholic and Protestant by turns, so that during the Protestant service the lad looked into a Catholic chancel, which, for his childish fantasy, was the embodiment of everything wonderful. 'There was first an altar painted to look like gold, with huge bunches of artificial flowers upon it, then tall candlesticks of metal with majestic wax candles in them; on the wall above the altar and between the two windows, was a pair of large gilt statues, which to me were Joseph and the Virgin Mary; and all these objects were flooded with the light which came through the chancel windows. Then through the windows themselves one looked out over trees, roofs, clouds and blue sky on a world which, in short, continued the chancel of the church into an infinity of distance, and was, in its turn, flooded with a kind of transfiguring glory imparted to it by the chancel. Thus my gaze wandered from the finite to the infinite, and my soul was wrapped in peace and quiet.'[23]

It was chiefly the organ Schweitzer had to thank for the innumerable hours and days he spent in lonely communion in churches, so that whether it was Sunday or weekday, he became, so to speak, a dweller in the church.

Just as the organ was 'in his blood' (despite his inherited musicality he did not find the tone of the violin beautiful at first, and had to get used to it gradually) so also was preaching. It was on this account that he decided to enrol in the theological rather than the philosophical faculty, because the Strassburg professor of philosophy, Theobald Ziegler, under whom he graduated, gave him to understand that it would be frowned upon if, as a lecturer in philosophy, he also preached. 'But to me preaching was a necessity of my being. I felt it as something wonderful that I was allowed to address a congregation every Sunday about the deepest questions of life.'[24] During the long years of his activity at St Nicholas he was in the pulpit every Sunday, sometimes both morning and afternoon. And even when the simultaneous demands of his medical study, his lectures at the university, his theological research and his organ concerts threatened to exhaust even his almost superhuman energies, he did not abandon his preaching.

To the memories of his youth—which he had an opportunity to set down owing to an illness which kept him in bed for a while in Berlin—he adds in 1924, before his second departure for Lambaréné, meditations which recall the sermons delivered at St Nicholas. His exposition of the ethic of reverence for life, in which the second part of his philosophy of human civilization culminates, is, despite its theme and despite the place at which it was given, more a sermon than a lecture on philosophy. Schweitzer proposed to go to Africa as a doctor and not as a missionary so 'that I might be able to work without having to talk'.[25] Unquestionably this impulse to serve the religion of love 'by an actual putting of it into practice' has continued to determine the whole of his subsequent life. However, for an understanding of his character it is important to know that because the missionary society operating along the Ogowe River looked askance at his liberal theology, Schweitzer gave an assurance that he would serve as a doctor only, and otherwise remain '*muet comme une carpe*' —as mute as a fish. But he had been in Africa only a few months when the missionaries on the spot asked him to undertake preaching as well, and to this request he joyfully acceded. The heavy burden of silence had been taken from his shoulders.

When you consider the spiritual world of the Protestant parsonage, and Schweitzer's role in the history of German spiritual thought in the nineteenth century, then the theologian, the preacher, the philosopher, the Goethe and Bach scholar and the organist Albert Schweitzer, can be seen as an intensification of the typical elements contained *in nuce* in the former. As a variant of the missionary—his father held a missionary service in Günsbach on the first Sunday in every month—the jungle doctor is of the same origin. Thus the homogeneity of the phenomenon, and the subordination of its components under a central law, is preserved by the attachment to the original source.

The suggestion that this attachment should have had so much to do with determining the stamp of so original a personality may seem a contradiction in itself. But originality, in the true sense of the word, is that which relates to the origin. To regard the exception, the apart (*à part*, that which is to one side), that which contradicts the rule, as the original is an individualistic misconception. Thus even in this, its pre-condition, the existence of Schweitzer represents a correction of contemporary thought.

But the effectiveness of this predestination presupposes a character which is able and willing to subordinate itself to the law according to which it began, and to the early lessons of its life. It presupposes not only the ability to experience, but also the ability to make use of experience. In Schweitzer's case what has once been recognized can never be lost but remains an abiding possession. The memories of his youth provide some impressive evidence of this.

Once when he was stung by a bee as a very small child (he was not yet breeched at the time) he naturally screamed, but then, as is the way with children, when he noticed that this made him the centre of general attention and sympathy, he went on screaming. It was not his feeling of honour which afterwards revolted against this behaviour, the feeling perhaps that he had not shown sufficient manly restraint. No, it was the prick of conscience. 'I felt that I had behaved very badly, and it made me unhappy for days. How often in after life, when assailed by temptation, has this experience warned me against exaggerating, or making too much of whatever had happened to me!' His first experience of going to school similarly helped him afterwards: 'it has always been without illusions that I have entered on the Unknown'. The memory of the Jewish cattledrover Mauschel smiling tolerantly at the mockery of the village boys still 'compels' Schweitzer to exercise patience when his first impulse is to lose his temper. During his first year at school another boy blabbed to the teacher about a thoughtless gibe Schweitzer had made against her. This 'first experience of betrayal' shattered all his preconception and expectation of life up to then. 'I had now learned about life'. And again, when he was about seven or eight a companion tempted him into catapulting birds. But as he drew back the elastic the church bell rang. The 'Voice from Heaven' ordered him to throw away his catapult, and to shoo off the birds to safety, even at the cost of being teased as a namby-pamby. 'From that day on I dared to liberate myself from the fear of what my fellow human beings might think.'

A characteristic feature of these anecdotes is the mingling of strength and gentleness in Schweitzer's feelings, and this has remained true of him both as boy and man. As far back as his memory reaches, Schweitzer's nature always reacted strongly and often vehemently to every stimulus. There is something more than mere sensitiveness here. Each happening is experienced in its full magnitude and significance, and then added as a permanent part of his inner possessions. And each happening becomes an experience. There is never a superficial, half-hearted, indifferent or self-indulgent reaction to the demands of life. Nothing is ever lost which might contribute to the development of his inner personality.

Two things in particular give this disposition its general form and shape: will and the moral sense.

At no stage would the inherited capacities of Albert Schweitzer have developed in the way they did but for the added presence of a truly extraordinary will-power. Although thought occupies such a central position in his own consciousness, nevertheless the dominant factor in his existence is the will. In this respect the suggestion of 'a very persistent' influence on the part of Schopenhauer[26] is an error. In fact, Schweitzer himself denies it, but apart from this it is obvious that such a character trait can hardly spring from philosophic thought —and certainly not from philosophic thought at second hand—but must be inborn. There is also some early evidence for this. The lad who has grown up in obedience to his parents nevertheless refuses to wear a winter coat because he doesn't want to be different from the other village boys, who don't wear winter coats. The lad fights a long and hard battle over the issue, and punishment makes no difference. 'I stood firm.'

Extraordinary will-power is not conceivable without an extraordinarily passionate nature. Like a wrestler, Schweitzer develops

2. Schweitzer at the age of thirty
(By permission of C. H. Beck Verlag, Munich)

his character in a struggle with this his strength. When he was nine or ten he struck his sister because she played a game with so little interest that her indifference gave him too easy a victory. 'From this time on' he began to feel misgiving because of his own passionate intensity in games, and finally he gave them up altogether—never daring, for example, to touch a card again. And because smoking had developed into a passion with him he gave that up too. That was on January 1, 1899, and he has never smoked since. At one time his handwriting was so bad as to be almost illegible. By his own decision he set out to make it legible, and it has remained so since despite a tremendous amount of written work and frequent attacks of writer's cramp. The simultaneous exercise of four or five different professions was made possible by night work, copious draughts of strong black coffee—and by keeping his feet in cold water.

This combination of will-power and rational determination has caused his life to develop along predetermined lines. In 1895 at the age of twenty-one he decided that until he was thirty he would devote himself to preaching, scientific research and music; after that to the direct service of mankind. Thenceforth it was inconceivable that there should be the slightest deviation from the path so laid down. Whether experience or decision, 'for good and all' has always been the motto of Schweitzer's life.

The all-important question as to what tasks this extraordinary power should be set to was basically settled even before it arose.

Predestination to scholarly research into the life of Jesus became evident in his eighth year when, at the boy's request, his father gave him a copy of the New Testament. From then on it was zealously studied. However, its contents were not accepted without critical examination. 'Amongst the stories which interested me most was that of the Three Wise Men of the East. What did the parents of Jesus do, I asked myself, with the gold and other valuables which they got from these men? How could they have been poor after that. That the Wise Men should never have troubled themselves again about the Child Jesus was to me incomprehensible. The absence, too, of any record of the shepherds of Bethlehem becoming disciples gave me a severe shock.'

Schweitzer's musical talent also showed itself quite early on. During a singing lesson in his first year at school his teacher played the music of a chorale with one finger, note for note, on the harmonium, after which the usually rather shy boy sat down at the instrument and played the whole thing through again from his head, adding the appropriate accompaniment.

His 'enthusiasm for the true and the serviceable'[27] made itself felt in Schweitzer's fourteenth year. It determined his attitude towards Christian belief and urged him on beyond theology to ethical philosophy. Whilst still being prepared for confirmation, Schweitzer quietly rejected the suggestion that all thought should cease in the face of belief. 'I was convinced, and I still am, that the truth of the fundamental ideas of Christianity must justify themselves above all in thought. The ability to think, I said to myself, has been given to us so that by it we can understand even the most lofty truths of religion. And this certainty filled me with joy.'

Now all these impulses could have found fulfilment within the framework of a normal, ordinary life. What then shattered this framework and led finally to a breach with normal life and ordinary professional behaviour, and thus to the construction of a very different and unique personal framework in the African jungle, were two 'profound youthful experiences'.

The first was Schweitzer's deep personal suffering at the misery of the world around him. 'The early influence upon me of the commandment not to kill, or to torture other creatures is the great experience of my childhood and youth. By the side of that all others are insignificant.' 'The terrible thought that out of carelessness we kill others and make them suffer' tortured him as far back as he can remember. And so, despite his own happy youth, he tells us that he never really knew the natural, ordinary, carefree, youthful joy in life. His compassion went out to animals in particular. The sight of a man dragging a lame old horse to the knacker's yard whilst a second man brought up the rear thwacking its bony rump with a stick, would haunt his memory painfully for weeks. And it was just inconceivable for him that he should remember only human beings in his evening prayers. 'So when my mother had prayed with me and had kissed me good-night, I used to add silently a prayer I had composed myself for all living creatures. It ran "O heavenly Father, protect and bless all things that have breath, guard them from all evil, and let them sleep in peace!"' Gradually in this way the 'unshakable' conviction was borne in on him 'that we may bring neither death nor suffering to any living thing without unavoidable necessity'.

The other experience was connected with the problem of justice and happiness. His deep emotion at the misery of the world could have led, as it so often does, to a thoughtful and considerate attitude to others, to the classic pity of the Samaritan; and to the development of a charitable disposition reacting automatically with the helping deed whenever it came into contact with suffering. However, deliberately to seek this contact with misery and suffering is not essential even for the sympathetic heart. But with Schweitzer the emotional experience joins forces with the moral idea, and from this results the absolute necessity for charitable action. Once sympathy reveals a solidarity with the life of another, a shared responsibility for that life develops as a logical consequence. With the boy Schweitzer the idea went even further, and he became more and more convinced that whoever had been given beauty and happiness in life must give proportionately in return. This irrational view arose from an instinctive knowledge of the mysterious law of moral economy which prevails in Creation. The recognition meant a break-through to the 'mysticism of Reality'.[28]

These two fundamental experiences gradually merged into one, and 'with this my attitude to life and to the destination of my own life was determined'. This decision was brought about by no outward influence and by no spiritual encounter, as one might have expected of a man whose spiritual life developed in a passionate concern with the thought of mankind. 'The ideas which determine our characters and life are implanted in a mysterious fashion.'[29] The untenable generalization reveals the profundity of the personal experience.

But in order that these inborn ideas should develop the force necessary to sustain the life of the individual and make him capable of any achievement and any sacrifice, and at the same time radiate through him into the world around him, something else is necessary as well. 'The power [of these ideas] becomes effective only when they are embodied in a purified man.' Repeatedly Schweitzer—whom one would have supposed it impossible to influence in personal relationships—records that he is under the compulsion of such men who, without knowing it perhaps, and perhaps without even having exchanged a word with him, have, as a result of something they gave him, or as a result of something they were, became part of the forces at work within him. It is, in fact, an outstanding characteristic of this powerful, original and independent nature that it does react to related power, that strong affinities can operate effectively within him. Thus the idea which had force over him needed the seal of a personification. The knowledge which arose in him did not remain isolated; it developed into an understanding of the words of Jesus that we may not keep our lives to ourselves: 'For whosoever will save his life shall lose it; but whosoever shall lose his life for my sake and the gospel's, the same shall save it.' (St Mark viii. 35.)[30] Thus confirmation was available from the ultimate authority. The demand first arising in the moral conscience now took on the form of a commandment. But in the words 'for my sake' it establishes a connection with the person of the law-giver. A will seeking its own way is now embraced by a stronger and taken into its service. Albert Schweitzer had found his Master.

Once you have recognized the nature of the unusual forces wrestling for expression in the spirit and character, first of the child and then of the youngster, you begin to wonder what will happen when the days of schooling are over and the young man comes to grips with the things to which his spirit impels him. From the earliest days each experience has been an emotional event leaving ineradicable traces behind and continuing to operate further; in particular, each contact with material appropriate to this nature has produced a fundamental reaction, so that one may expect that deliberately sought contact with such material will from the very start result in something more than mere receptive comprehension, namely in a creative process. And, in fact, hardly has this force entered into action independently than the expectant observer witnesses something like a volcanic eruption. What has happened (first of all in the private thoughts of a young man who has heard his first course of theological lectures) is that the interpretation of the life of Jesus put forward by the dominant school of critical theology at the time has been completely upset. How did this come about?

Even when, as here, there is no biographical intention, the phenomenon of Schweitzer's existence can be presented and interpreted only in the chronological sequence of the happenings. In the life of this man whose thought not only transforms itself into action with inevitable necessity, but whose thought itself is action, everything which happens, whether it consists of secluded research, or a venture in practical charity such as took shape in the jungle hospital at Lambaréné, has a dramatic character—despite the fact that any stressing of personality is foreign to Schweitzer's character. Everything combines into one tense action, and to understand it one must see it as a whole. It is, however, one of the paradoxes of Schweitzer's nature that his life, regarded from within, flows peacefully and regularly, and nevertheless goes forward in a positive whirl of activity, proceeding, so to speak, in a charmed area of imperturbable serenity, from which, whenever necessary, the essentially serene and composed personality can emerge to express itself in word or deed. Thus the personal accompanying circumstances of his creative work are important although in general they do not contribute a great deal to the understanding of spiritual achievements. Schweitzer himself certainly felt he had a very good reason for weaving them into the description of his life and thought. It is from this description that we learn how this first independent move in the theological sphere actually came about.

In the autumn of 1893 Schweitzer went to Strassburg University. His first term there was devoted chiefly to preparing for 'the Hebraicum', the preliminary examination in Hebrew. However, he also found sufficient time to listen to the lectures of Wilhelm Windelband and Theobald Ziegler on philosophy, and also to take a course of lectures on the synoptic Gospels by Heinrich Julius Holtzmann, who was at that time regarded as the leading exponent of the liberal school of research into the life of Jesus. Schweitzer chose this very theme for the examination he had to take at the beginning of the winter term of 1894 to obtain a stipendium. However, his one-year period of compulsory military service began on April 1st of that year. Incidentally, Schweitzer has always recalled his short period of military service with pleasure.

The young recruit was very anxious to pass his examination under his highly-respected teacher Holtzmann with credit, so when he set off for the Autumn manœuvres there was—not a marshal's baton but a Greek Testament in his knapsack. Tiredness was unknown to him, and so after a gruelling day in the field on manœuvres he was still able to study in the evening.

He grappled at once with the central problem of liberal theology, and took the first step into the scientific sphere by broaching the fundamental theme of his theological life's work: a study of the life of Jesus.

His reading, whose preliminary objective was to obtain material for further study, led right away to some exciting results.

Holtzmann had secured general recognition in scholarly circles for the Marcan hypothesis; that is to say for the claim that this Gospel is the oldest, and was taken as the basis for the Gospels of Matthew and Luke, and that therefore the information it contained regarding the life of Jesus was sufficient for its interpretation. But then—'with astonishment and pained misgiving'—the young student was forced to the conclusion that the x and xi chapters of Matthew, which contain information not to be found in the Gospel of St Mark, were of decisive importance for an understanding of the words and acts of Jesus. Schweitzer tells us in his own words how he came to make his fundamental discovery, and reading what he says we can sense the dismay this new view caused in him, and the first inkling he had of its importance:[31]

'In Matthew x the mission of the Twelve is narrated. In the discourse with which He sends them out Jesus tells them that they will almost immediately have to undergo severe persecution. But they suffer nothing of the kind.

'He tells them also that the appearance of the Son of Man will take place before they have gone through the cities of Israel, which can only mean that the celestial, Messianic Kingdom will be revealed while they are thus engaged. He has, therefore, no expectation of seeing them return. . . .

'I was dissatisfied with Holtzmann's explanation that we are dealing not with an historical discourse of Jesus, but with one made up at a later period, after His death, out of various "Sayings of Jesus". A later generation would never have gone so far as to put into His mouth words which were belied by the subsequent course of events.

'The bare text compelled me to assume that Jesus really announced persecutions for the disciples and, as a sequel to them, the immediate appearance of the celestial Son of Man, and that His announcement was shown by subsequent events to be wrong. But how came He to entertain such an expectation, and what must His feelings have been when events turned out otherwise than He had assumed they would! Matthew xi records the Baptist's question to Jesus and the answer Jesus sent back to him. Here too it seemed to me that Holtzmann and commentators in general do not sufficiently appreciate the riddles of the text. Whom does the Baptist mean when he asks Jesus whether He is the "one who is to come"? Is it then quite certain I asked myself that by the Coming One no one can be meant except the Messiah? According to the late Jewish messianic beliefs the coming of the Messiah is to be preceded by that of his forerunner, Elijah, risen from the dead, and to this previously expected Elijah Jesus applies the expression the Coming One, when he tells the disciples (Matt. xi. 14) that the Baptist himself is Elijah who is to come. Therefore, so I concluded, the Baptist in his question used the expression with that same meaning. He did not send his disciples to Jesus with the question whether he was the Messiah; he wanted to learn from Him, strange as this may seem to us, whether He was the expected forerunner of the Messiah, Elijah.

'But why does Jesus not give him a plain answer to his question? To say that He gave the evasive answer He did give in order to test the Baptist's faith is only an outcome of the embarrassment of the commentators, and has opened the way for many bad sermons. It is much simpler to assume that Jesus avoided saying either Yes or No because He was not yet ready to make public whom He believed Himself to be. From every point of view the account of the Baptist's question proves that at that time none of those who believed in Jesus held Him to be the Messiah. Had He already been accepted in any way as the Messiah, the Baptist would have so framed his question as to imply that fact.

'I was also driven into new paths of interpretation by Jesus saying to the disciples after the departure of the Baptist's messengers, that of all born of women John was the greatest, but that the least in the Kingdom of Heaven was greater than he. (Matt. xi. 11.)

'The usual explanation that Jesus expressed in these words a criticism of the Baptist, and placed him at a lower level than the believers in His teaching who were assembled round Him as adherents of the Kingdom of God, seems to me both unsatisfactory and crude, for these believers were also born of women. By giving up this explanation I was driven to the assumption that in contrasting the Baptist with members of the Kingdom of God, Jesus was taking into account the difference between the natural world and the supernatural messianic world. . . .'

It is not within the scope of this book to attempt an exhaustive account of the theological work undertaken by Schweitzer, any more than his philosophical work or his Bach research. Nevertheless, his, so to speak, spiritual 'handwriting' must be traced, and its unmistakable characteristics can be identified from the beginning.

The way of thought is already fully fashioned; even more, it is finally determined. Subsequently the forces will strengthen and knowledge will increase, the methods will develop and the sphere of work will widen, but nothing completely new or different will ever be able to penetrate into the already clearly formed substance of this spirit, which is essentially foreign to all Faustian vacillation.

Just as in Schweitzer's private life his contemplative absorption in the closely familiar and the loyally cherished is characteristic, just as the total intensity of his being remains concentrated on apparently unimportant events, pictures and customs preserved unchanged through decades, so the thinker and investigator remains similarly bound to the thing once taken in hand. His thought develops and proliferates, but it does not change its position. Each subsequent 'idea' is only a confirmation and an extension of the original substance. Continuance in one stay is a fundamental characteristic of his nature.

Just as his activities all over the world make no difference to the fact that Günsbach remains his home, just as he succeeds in reproducing the atmosphere of home even in the African jungle, and—within the given limits—even succeeds in reproducing his own particular and appropriate style of life there, so the same is true of his stability in the spiritual sphere.

It was in accordance with this particular characteristic that, on a rest day during the autumn manœuvres, spent in the Alsatian village of Guggenheim, the nineteen-year-old theological student, temporarily a raw recruit, discovered the golden key to 'eschatological interpretation'. With its aid he was to attempt during the course of the subsequent years, either directly or indirectly, to resolve the riddles left unresolved by modern critical research both in the life of Jesus and in the teachings of St Paul. This also sets the theme for his later, uncompleted, theological work dealing with the Mystery of the Kingdom of God.

One would hardly find a case of so early and so definite a determination of theme and central thesis of a scientific life's work in all the history of the moral sciences. The unchanging features of Schweitzer's spiritual physiognomy are clearly discernable very early on.

What impelled the young apprentice to reject the teachings of his masters? And what gave him the strength to go even beyond them? From the text we have quoted we can draw a fourfold conclusion.

First of all: greater critical acumen. Wherever the general sense of a passage indicated a weakness in the current textual interpretation it was pounced on immediately and pursued with logical clarity *ad absurdum*.

This intellectual acumen is reinforced by a quite unacademic quality of common sense; a capacity to look at things and to judge them with the natural directness of a man of the people. Just as Schweitzer is able to talk to the peasants, labourers and workmen of Günsbach as one of themselves about all the problems and difficulties of their simple daily lives, so in his biblical criticism he seeks to put himself in the position of those simple fisherman of Lake Gennesareth and their Master, and in this way to find a natural explanation for their behaviour.

This is in accordance with Schweitzer's down-to-earth way of thought, for which the simple explanation is always the more likely. Schweitzer's reasoning sparkles with intelligence, but it is not 'intellectual'. There is none of the sophisticated subtlety which often plays such a role in liberal biblical criticism.

At the same time this simplicity of thought is thoroughly radical.

It seeks for truth unconditionally and without qualification. As Schweitzer himself says in one of his more recent theological utterances, his way of thought stands *per se* under this 'compulsion'.[32] Schweitzer's very first independent venture shows us very clearly that a desire to know and recognize the truth is the only motive which impels him. No obstacles of rigid dogma are allowed to stand in the way; and no axiom of theological research, however apparently well established, is accepted without critical scrutiny—no matter how great the authority which propounds it. Whatever Schweitzer takes in hand is thoroughly examined as though it were being considered for the very first time; and nothing whatever is allowed to come between the object examined and the mind examining it. In particular, Schweitzer's attitude has absolutely nothing of that constant urge of liberal theology to use the methods of modern critical research in order to bring the figure of Jesus 'nearer' to the people of our own day. And later on, when the need to bring critical research into harmony with pastoral guidance became evident, it was satisfied in a quite different fashion.

Thus the outlook is not entirely uninfluenced, but in place of dogmatic prejudice there stands enlightened thought, which, however, remains open to the unusual, the unexpected, and even the untimely. There is nothing whatever to hamper recognition of the completely different, the astonishing, even the violence of the world of ideas of Jesus, which so greatly exceeds the proportions of our own.

II

KANT

Before Schweitzer turned to the preparation of his licentiate and thus to theological research he decided, on the advice of his teacher Theobald Ziegler, to choose philosophy for his doctoral thesis. One day, whilst they were sheltering under an umbrella on the steps of Strassburg University, Ziegler proposed that Schweitzer should tackle Kant's philosophy of religion. The advice was not as casual as the extraneous circumstances of its giving might suggest. A Tübingen man, Ziegler's own background was theology, and ethics and the philosophy of religion were his main interests. Thus the choice of the theme was a compliment for the young undergraduate and at the same time an indication that Ziegler understood the young man's spiritual position on the dividing line between the philosophical and theological faculties. Schweitzer needed a philosophical basis for his thought. His life's work shows the unusual, and in this form probably unique, need to go forward to the secret of existence along two separate paths. With his own particular instinct for what was necessary, he immediately adopted the suggestion, and at the end of October 1898 he went to Paris to devote himself to this task at leisure, whilst simultaneously taking philosophy at the Sorbonne and continuing his study of the organ under the famous organist Widor.

Schweitzer's tremendous achievement in the following winter was an earnest of the forces residing in the now twenty-three-year-old, and an indication of their nature.

He found the 'old-fashioned methods' of study at the Sorbonne irritating. 'Four- or five-hour summarizing lectures such as I was used to at Strassburg did not exist here. The professors either gave lectures relating to the examination schedule or they read about quite specialized fields.' In consequence he often skipped the lectures altogether. However, he certainly studied intensively under Widor, and, in addition, he took piano lessons both from a professional teacher, and from the pupil and friend of Franz Liszt, Marie Jaël-Trautmann, who was, like himself, a born Alsatian. It was to her he owed his training in touch. Widor and an uncle, one of his father's brothers, introduced him to intellectual Paris, a new world in which he soon felt himself at home.

This might have been thought quite enough to occupy the time and attention of any ordinary young man, but Schweitzer had gone to Paris to do scholarly work, and it had to be done quickly, particularly as his finances were very limited. His first intention was to concentrate on the Bibliothèque Nationale to find out what work had already been done on the subject. But there too he found the reading-room system clumsy and time-wasting, and he soon decided to give up going there altogether. Instead he bought himself an oil lamp, got hold of the works of Kant, withdrew from the scholastic world into a student's attic in the Latin Quarter, and bothered no more about 'the literature on the subject'; since his declared aim was, 'apart from the works on his philosophy of religion, to secure a hearing for the man himself once again'.[1]

The idea will sound familiar to those who know Schweitzer. 'Jesus himself speaks again' he says in the final lecture on his investigations into the life of Jesus.[2] And, as we shall see later on, Bach is made more understandable by interpreting the Choral Preludes (which completely puzzled even Widor) with the aid of the accompanying texts.

Schweitzer does not think much of 'Lectures on . . .' He is always anxious to make the subject with which he is dealing speak for itself; and this applies both to historical research and to the world of ideas, and is a logical conclusion from his own analytical nature. He is the opposite of an intellectual. At its best his work provides brilliant examples of his own peculiar power to express himself in words—and yet all forms of literary extravagance are foreign to him. His great literary ability, something rather unusual amongst scholars, never lets pass a careless, self-satisfied or incautious use of words even in a single line. He wrestles tirelessly to formulate an idea accurately, and each sentence must be 'solid', a favourite word of his. That is to say, it must stand four square; and if necessary he will go back to it again and again until it finally meets with his approval. It must provide the exact expression required by the subject itself, and it must at the same time be simple. In fact everything he turns out is 'solid' in this sense, whether it is a scholarly investigation, a factual report, a sermon, a dissertation on Goethe, or a warning on the dangers of nuclear warfare.

The work on Kant was ready by the middle of March 1899, and it met with great approval at once. A short dissertation? No, it was a very thorough work of 325 pages entitled *Die Religionsphilosophie Kants von der Kritik der reinen Vernunft bis zur Religion innerhalb der Grenzen der blossen Vernunft* (*Kant's Philosophy of Religion from the Critique of Pure Reason to Religion within the Limits of Reason Alone*).

It was of fundamental importance for Schweitzer's own thought which found itself clarified and confirmed in the critical treatment of the Königsberger philosopher's work.

Schweitzer's spiritual affinity with the 'all-destroyer who has brought all dogmatism and all dogmatic metaphysics to an end'[3] is immediately obvious. Like Schweitzer, Kant bases religion on ethics and for Schweitzer Kant's greatest achievement lies in the fact that: 'He is the first since Plato to feel, like him, that the ethical is the mysterious fact within us.'[4] 'In the ultimate analysis it has its origin in the compulsion which men experience to strive for self-perfection.' The originality and grandeur of the moral law prevails only when it appears to us as an end in itself, and never when it appears as a means to an end. Utilitarian ethics must necessarily give way to the ethics of direct and absolute obligation. This is the meaning of the categoric imperative. It proclaims the unconditional nature of ethics. The moral perfection of mankind it demands is identical with the fulfilment of the Kingdom of God. Kant's religion of reason is moral theology. Schweitzer is heart and soul in favour.

Their agreement finds its limits in Kant's postulates of *a priori* belief: God, liberty, immortality. Kant's 'pure moral theology' contains the essential features of Christian belief in a new interpretation. Practical reason is given superiority over theoretical reason. Ethical consciousness demands the reality of the highest good. The 'postulates' are the conditions of moral life, and their reality, although it is not theoretically recognizable, must equally be accepted.

Schweitzer comes to the conclusion that with Kant a critical and an ethical philosophy of religion go side by side, and that he seeks to reconcile and harmonize them. At the same time Schweitzer feels that the attempt is not successful, because Kant progressively intensifies the idea of the moral law as presupposed by the transcendental dialectic of the *Critique of Pure Reason*. This 'religious philosophy of the profounder moral law' drops the postulate of immortality and turns the idea of God into an auxiliary notion. Not only had ethics become unconditional; they were based on themselves alone.

Schweitzer now had only four months in which to prepare for his doctoral examination, a very short interval in which to make up for lost time where philosophy was concerned, since—apart from music—he had occupied himself primarily with theology, having passed his theological examinations in May 1898, only a few months before he left for Paris. But what did Schweitzer do with the summer of 1899? He went to Berlin; listened to numerous lectures, some on theology, some on philosophy; read 'the main works of old and new philosophy'; and, in addition to regular organ playing, devoted a great deal of time to following the psychological studies of Karl Stumpf on tonal perception. It is therefore not surprising to learn that in the viva voce he rather disappointed the expectations his dissertation had aroused. As in his study of Kant, we see once again, right from the beginning, his tendency to go his own way, to think his own thoughts, not to attach himself to any established school of thought, and to treat the textbooks with indifference. In this respect he is rather like Nietzsche. However, he was not greatly disturbed by the result of this examination, which in any case did not prevent his being subsequently invited to join the philosophical faculty.

III

THE QUEST OF THE HISTORICAL JESUS

Schweitzer's contribution to Kantian studies was the first, brilliant proof of his ability to conduct original scholarly research, and particularly that of a textual critical nature. This contribution occupies an important place in the economy of his spiritual household, because it was the starting point of his own ethical philosophy. However, this excursion into philosophy as such remained a digression. Schweitzer is never concerned with knowledge for its own sake and without any particular purpose. Speculative thought does not suit his intellectual make-up. His own philosophy avoids abstractions and concerns itself with what can be directly experienced, what can be applied, what has a 'purpose'. It demands 'elementary', even 'naïve' solutions. As he once declared bluntly to friends: 'I never could understand anything over-spiritualized. . . . And as for the transcendental I've never been able to understand it at all.'[1] Thus his rejection of Theobald Ziegler's suggestion that he should seek admission into the philosophical faculty was not merely due to the difficulties that would arise if as a lecturer on philosophy he were also active as a preacher.

Schweitzer's main intellectual interest is theology, and his ethical philosophy begins where theology no longer serves him.

His basic theological theme is research into the life of Jesus. From his very first term as a university student it has represented the most exciting element in his intellectual life. His interest was again turned towards it by the thesis of his first theological examination: 'Schleiermacher on the Last Supper compared with the New Testament version and the conclusions of Theology.' His greatest scholarly and literary work is devoted to the same subject: *Von Reimarus zu Wrede, Eine Geschichte der Leben-Jesu-Forschung* (*The Quest of the Historical Jesus*—whose later editions bore the title *Geschichte der Leben-Jesu-Forschung*). The subject of considerable dispute, it is now, after half a century, recognized as classic.[2] His investigations into the Last Supper,[3] and within this framework the draft of 'a new interpretation of the Life of Jesus', was the preliminary, the Pauline investigations the culmination. The question of the role of eschatology in the Pauline teachings on Christ derives from the eschatological interpretation of the Life of Jesus.

What is the aim of these utterly undogmatic textual critical investigations into the life of Jesus? And what caused Schweitzer to undertake them? We may reasonably assume that with a temperament such as his, always avid of spiritual action, it was from the beginning something more than a desire to launch himself into a scholastic career, to enter the ranks of a body of scholarly investigators by means of an academic problem which fascinated him and seemed to promise new results. Schweitzer's is not, in fact, a professorial nature, and therefore, looking back, we cannot say that Lambaréné cost him a university career. He has not the slightest inclination to contribute to the store of scholarly learning. When a naïve theological colleague expressed the hope that his voyage to Africa and his work amongst the Negroes there would soon produce scholarly results, the idea was merely amusing for those who really knew Schweitzer.

A glance at his *Quest of the Historical Jesus* immediately reveals a style which is most unusual in scholarly literature, a combination of enthusiasm, and sometimes even vehemence, with the strictest objectivity. It is not difficult to realize that Schweitzer is writing in the moving consciousness that he is daring to tackle the supreme subject of all historical investigation. 'We are dealing with the most vital thing in the world's history.'[4] He is not so much interested in adding to historical knowledge as in influencing the world, and changing the spiritual life of his time. Later on, in his ethical philosophy, he frankly admits the impulse that is at work here: a nature whose deepest urge is to attach itself to Jesus determines the subject of investigation in advance.

Schweitzer's mode of thought was formed at the end of the heroic epoch of Free Thought. The theological pathos of the world into which he was born is hardly understandable today because the questions which thrilled that world no longer excite our generation. We must therefore recall it to memory.

Historicism and scientific thought were confidently engaged in a concentric attack on the fortress of belief. It is true, of course, that by the end of the century materialism in the moral sciences had been largely overcome, but this did not upset the dominance of that mode of thought to which the age owed the civilizatory progress that had revolutionized all the conditions of life. Similarly, it was still generally accepted—in fact the conviction can still be met with even today—that 'historical thought has made any metaphysical understanding of belief impossible.'[5] The clash between the spirit of the age and belief in revelation expressed itself in a controversy between 'Science and Faith'. Its origins went back to the Reformation, and it was carried forward on a broad front by eighteenth-century Rationalism, which was dominated by scientific thought. The controversy is by no means at an end even in our own day: the vehemence of the conflict between 'Reason' and 'Belief in Revelation' goes to show that powerful forces were at work on both sides. Our generation looks back with some astonishment at the passion expended to defend positions which are 'held' today without any violent clash; and because there is no heat now we find it difficult to understand it, because what was at stake in this 'struggle for truth' gave rise to the whole research into the life of Jesus, and thus led at the same time to Schweitzer's whole scholarly life's work.

'Ultimate things' are truly at stake here. The most elementary urge of the human spirit seeking to raise itself above the mere struggles for existence is the effort to understand the significance of being. It is unhappy and rootless without a haven in the innerness of truth, or what it conceives as truth. From this it follows that the urge to truth is, like all other spiritual movements, of variable intensity, and not attached to any definite ideology or any definite period in history. The Enlightenment Movement was deceiving itself when it supposed that in the Middle Ages the Church deliberately prevented the recognition of truth because, in Haeckel's words, it 'contradicted science and reason on principle', and that the recognition of truth was revived by Rationalism from the days of Descartes on. To show how mistaken this view is, all we need to do is to recall the impressive achievement of Alberto-Thomism with its rational penetration of mediaeval thought, which derived from Albert Magnus (1193–1280), himself a considerable natural scientist, and Thomas Aquinas (1225?–1274). In fact, 'A powerful urge to truth informed the mediaeval mind. Hardly ever—with the possible exception of classic Chinese culture—did the man of knowledge, the scholar, enjoy such prestige as he did then.'[6] To live, to fight and if necessary to die for the recognized truth largely determined the character of this particular epoch of European history.

There was a fundamental difference, of course, in that the mediaeval

3. On the edge of the primeval forest
(By permission of Marie Waytt-Secretan, Strasburg)

way of truth went through Revelation, whereas for the newer age the basis of truth was the 'Cartesian amalgam of truth and knowledge'.[7]

'Objective science' was now established as the only legitimate method of arriving at truth; and its supreme law was that nothing might be admitted as knowledge unless its truth could at any time be tested and demonstrated. In the new age man sought to find in demonstrable knowledge that certainty which belief had once given him. A belief in objectivity became the hidden theology of the age. Natural science persuaded itself that it possessed an objective knowledge of the forces and matter of the universe, and in the historical sphere man sought to use science as an instrument to extend the horizon of objectivity. All authority that could not demonstrate its validity before the court of critical reason was summarily dismissed.

It was therefore only logical that a scientific mode of thought that regarded itself as the champion of truth must needs feel itself under an obligation to destroy the superstition of pseudo-truths. In consequence the urge to truth expressed itself above all in a determination to expose the illusions of that thought which had been led astray by belief. It was under this banner therefore that 'the both splendid and barbarous fight against deception'[8] was waged, inspiring Kant's doctrine of transcendental appearance, and, a hundred years later, Nietzsche's attack on Christianity. In theology it finds its most vigorous expression in the investigations into the life of Jesus—'the most tremendous thing religious consciousness has ever dared and done'.[9] The scientific method now sought to apply its criteria unconditionally to the origin of Christian belief, and to demonstrate their validity in the most secret recesses of the fortress of faith.

This break-through of the Enlightenment Movement into Protestant theology was begun by Reimarus, the 'Wolfenbüttel unknown' (who died in 1768). Fragments of his work were published after his death by Lessing: this marks the real beginning of the historico-critical investigations into the life of Jesus. But, in fact, Rationalism lacked the strength not merely to negate the spiritual world but even to oppose it effectively in its own sphere. It has no relationship at all to spiritual reality and therefore in any discussion of it it must inevitably stumble. (Hase, Schleiermacher.) The consistent distinction between the historical and the mythical in the Gospels was therefore not made under its aegis, but under the influence of Hegel. The mythical explanation (the use of mythos in Gospel exegesis) results from a synthesis of supernatural explanation and rationalist interpretation, and its guiding principle is the conviction that the validity of the idea is not affected by critical investigation. The historical investigation conducted by David Friedrich Strauss proceeded from the assumption that the belief in Jesus as the creator of the religion of man would not be affected. This was the basis of its courage to accept its own conclusions.

Strauss's *Life of Jesus* (1835–36) was like a liberating gesture for those engaged in the struggle between 'Science' and 'Belief'. Strauss felt himself to be a prophet and he is so regarded by Schweitzer. His aim was to give the thinking man access to the Gospels. Our own age has lost belief in the saving power of science, just as it has lost the ability to take the teachings of the Church seriously. In consequence it can no longer understand the passion with which in those days educated men plunged into the battle between 'the old' and 'the new' belief. Nowadays a new interpretation of the Gospels would have no more hope of becoming a best seller than a book on the essence of Christianity.[10] But the dynamic tension between Enlightenment and Belief that existed in those days can be measured against the vehemence with which thought, on the basis of Christian civilization, turned against its religious past—a unique spiritual spectacle. According to Haeckel, whose *Riddle of the Universe* (1899) established with complete confidence on the basis of scientific investigation that Christian belief could not be reconciled with man's reasonable knowledge of nature, the contradiction between science and Christianity is the outstanding feature of the nineteenth century. As Schweitzer points out, the best lives of Jesus were inspired by hatred. Man's belief in progress sought its confirmation on the highest level. At the same time the conviction of its own superiority over all previous Christian thought, and in particular that of the Middle Ages—the 'most deplorable period in human history' (Haeckel)—was absolute. The criteria of spirituality were ignored, lying, as they did, outside the scope of the new religion of reason. It appeared urgently necessary to restore the pristine figure of Jesus, which had been buried under lies and deceit since the days of early Christianity.

The historical Jesus finally brought to light would, it was hoped, prove a powerful ally in the liberating struggle against dogmatism. Quite clearly, a task conceived in this spirit necessarily inflamed men's minds. The moral courage of German Protestant theology in applying the criteria of the scientific method to the truths of belief canvasses our admiration. 'The investigations into the life of Jesus represent a blow for truth delivered by Protestant Christianity.'[11]

The undertaking did not produce the expected results. Attempt after attempt was made to seize the 'real' figure of Jesus, but, like a *fata morgana*, it continued to evade man's grasp. Not that the investigations made no progress at all: the problems involved were formulated, and some were actually solved, whilst others were eliminated. However, two things made ultimate success impossible. First of all, and almost as though under compulsion, each new generation of investigators introduced its own ideas, and so it seemed impossible ever to arrive at an objective viewpoint from which the subject could be seen as it really was. Such results as were obtained proved ephemeral, and so before long they were swept away in the whirlpools of spiritual history. But another circumstance proved even more disastrous: as the investigations proceeded so their subject-matter seemed to disintegrate more and more. Nowadays any unprejudiced observer cannot help but be shocked at the arbitrary treatment of the New Testament sources by textual criticism proclaiming itself to be scientific. Those who used it ruthlessly discarded everything that did not suit their general book, and so 'in the end only a hopelessly mangled text was left, and nothing could be done with it any more'.[12] All this search for the 'real' Jesus provided was a changing and constantly disputed picture whose features bore a strong resemblance to those of nineteenth-century man. After a century and a half of agonizing effort 'there is nothing more negative than the result of the critical study of the Life of Jesus'.[13]

As a young theologian, Schweitzer witnessed the certainty of historical theology that it had discovered the historical Jesus dissolve into doubt and confusion. The whole investigation ground to a standstill as its rationalistic predecessor had done. From the start the investigation sickened of an internal contradiction. The historian was anxious to discover history; the liberal theologian was anxious to find a Jesus who would fit into the modern age. Lacking the support of historical science the investigations were left to themselves, and unconsciously the theological tendency tipped the scales. The founder of Christianity was robbed of all his glory, and the attempt to fit him into the age only made him infinitely smaller.

At first glance it may have seemed an easy triumph for dogmatic theology, but merely to register the failure of a daring undertaking on the part of emancipated thought was not enough. Biblical criticism had to be taken seriously. To ignore the historical and textual critical problems raised by the Gospels—an easy enough matter for Martin Luther in his day[14]—would have meant a breach between Christianity and the development of human thought and have laid theology open to a well-founded charge of lacking courage to face the truth. In answer to a summary condemnation theological liberalism could claim the justification of a higher ethical attitude. The liquidation of liberal investigation into the Life of Jesus had to take place on its own ground. And it was at this point that Albert Schweitzer's achievement began.

Schweitzer developed from the school of liberal theology as a pupil of Heinrich Julius Holtzmann. The historico-critical attitude to biblical texts and Church dogmas is common to them both, and Schweitzer adopted Holtzmann's formulation of the problem. The method too is fundamentally the same. And the aim with both is the 'liberation' of Jesus from the bonds of Church dogma in the name of truth. At the same time, in accordance with contemporary thought, the conception of truth as held by the exact sciences is taken as a basis. Schweitzer himself stresses the great influence his preoccupation with the natural sciences at the beginning of his medical studies exercised on him.[15] There is as yet no inkling of the fact that the assumption of unconditional certainty for scientific knowledge is based on a philosophical prejudice, and so whenever the evidence of the sources conflicts with this particular conception of truth then it is dismissed without more ado. As this premise is tricked out with dogmatic authority, this inevitably means that not unimportant parts of the Gospel texts are *ipso facto* excluded from the investigation. If a thing is *a priori* impossible there is no need for any critical examination. Quite generally it must be said that one of the characteristics of liberal theology is that it tends to ignore any fact which is uncongenial to it. Neither liberalism nor the scientific method guarantees an unprejudiced examination of the whole body of evidence. For example, the Middle Ages are dismissed *in toto*.[16] Dogmatic theology is reproached with prejudice, but those who make the reproach are themselves no less prejudiced—even though in their case the characteristics are of a negative kind.

Schweitzer, too, is the product of his intellectual environment, and all his life he has remained rooted in it. His world of ideas is completely stable. The plan of his life was laid down very early on with remarkable finality; after which all his energies were bent to building a monumental edifice whose ground plan was never subsequently called into question.

Thus Schweitzer never leaves the basis of liberal theology, but with him the climate is completely different. The vehement nature of the ethical impulse gives an altogether missionary ardour most unusual in the academic sphere to that urge for truth which is the motive force of theological liberalism. It takes on an uncompromising quality, and there is no room at all for those ifs and buts that usually play such a role in Jesus research. Here for the first time, without hostility to others—indeed, with a deep respect for every true form of Christian belief—the historical Jesus is subjected to a thoroughly objective investigation. The apotheosis of this daring undertaking of Protestant theology takes place in an altogether unexceptionable atmosphere. In so far as they were really seeking the truth, his predecessors are treated with respect, even when their shipwreck on the corner-stone of Christianity is clearly recognized and uncompromisingly recorded. At the same time the theological misgivings which so often barred the way to their critical achievement are consumed in the flames of his passion for truth. The belief in reason, which must take the place of belief in revelation if the biblical criticism which negates it is not to degenerate into scepticism, is far more profound in this eighteenth-century intellect, than in the representatives of liberal theology whose background was the historical, scientific and psychological thought of the nineteenth century. It has the true quality of belief. Schweitzer is firmly convinced that the free play of the intellect represents a religious advance, and that the clearing away of 'externals' can only spiritualize the positive dogmatism of the Gospels. Thus—in significant agreement with David Friedrich Strauss—he wins through to a position from which a radical investigation into the life of Jesus may be dared—always in the conviction that the spirit of Jesus, which is the spirit of truth, must operate in it.

Methodologically two possibilities present themselves: the literary-critical method adopted by Wrede, and the eschatological-historical method. Only the latter comes into question for Schweitzer. The 'tortuous construction' (Kaehler) of an allegedly reliable portrait of Jesus with the help of detailed source criticism does not suit his temperament, and none of the attempts to arrive at it really satisfy him. 'All rules for the separation of the true from the false in the two oldest synoptic Gospels are fundamentally meaningless.'[17] It is impossible to find a reliable criterion for such a separation, and therefore in the last resort the basis of all such attempts is subjective and arbitrary.[18] The more one eliminates from the Gospel accounts the less significant Jesus becomes—and the less vital, until finally he means nothing for religion, or, in the best case, no more than a host of other outstanding personalities.[19] Such a pseudo-scientific procedure must therefore be discarded.

There can be no doubt that early Christianity greatly influenced the accounts of the public life of Jesus. But early Christian belief cannot have introduced any new facts, since the life as such was regarded with indifference. There was absolutely no such thing as an early Christian conception of the life of Jesus, and the Synoptic Gospels contain nothing of the sort.[20] The Gospel accounts, and in particular the messianic secret, cannot therefore be explained either as an interpolation of the evangelists or as a product of tradition. Tradition operates in a fashion very different from the account we find in Mark. A creative tradition would have carried out the theory of the messianic secret in the life of Jesus much more boldly and logically, that is to say, at once more arbitrarily and more consistently.[21] Christian theology has no obvious interest in pre-dating the messianic nature of Jesus into his earthly activity.

Modern theology had abandoned the attempt to attach credence and importance to the order in which the events of the public life of Jesus are recorded. It also disposed of everything it regarded as unexplainable: either by eliminating it altogether, or by ascribing it to the 'mythological' distortions of tradition. With this it barred the way to an historical solution, which presupposes the exclusion of any natural-psychological interpretation, and of modern ethical criteria. The texts must be allowed to stand as they were written. Certainly, there was something mysterious about the public life of Jesus even for those who were his contemporaries. Thus all vital accounts of Jesus can be no more than hypothetical constructions. Their scientific value is measured by the extent to which they reveal the inner relationships of the reported words, acts and events, and are able to explain the greatest possible number of details according to consistent criteria. Schweitzer himself utters a warning against dismissing the unexplainable and the miraculous as due to later tradition. Such an assumption is tenable, but it cannot be proved. Further, the miracles are not something accidental, and it must not be assumed that they are of no importance for the investigations into the life of Jesus just because the scientifically-thinking man takes exception to them. Generally speaking it is not a question of occasional healings or the subsequent mythologization of natural events. On the contrary, those who witnessed them were fully aware that Jesus was leading them into an age of miracles as a proof of the imminence of the Kingdom of God. Further, it is wrong to dismiss certain prophecies out of hand on the ground that they are unhistorical. 'The surprising fulfilment of this or that prophecy is no certain evidence, that it must have been subsequently edited *ex eventu*.'[22] How readily one is inclined to dispute the historicity of such a phrase as: 'Thou art Peter, and upon this rock I will build my church'! Though so far 'no one has been able to show convincingly how it could have been interpolated into the Gospels in order to justify Petrinian or Roman claims.' It is quite another question, namely one of interpretation, whether the 'church' is not to be understood here as the pre-existent Church which was to appear in the last days and is thus synonymous with the Kingdom of God.

Whereas in its investigation of the sources critical theology tended more and more to place the onus of historical proof on each pericope, Schweitzer reversed the process: for him the texts (of the two first Gospels) are valid as historical sources so long so they are not proved to be unhistorical. However, he regards their unhistoricity as established where any of the circumstances conflict with natural laws (the awakening of the dead, the empty grave), and where the historical interpretation does not follow from the context. Thus for him the feeding of the multitude and the transfiguration, both of which left rationalistic criticism helpless, become milestones in historical development. The rationalist Schweitzer discards rationalistic criticism of the Bible by rejecting both the rational psychology and the natural explanation of the miraculous. He is facilitated in this by his freedom from prejudice in judging the account, and he does not, as is almost the fashion in critical theology, contemptuously discard even such things as the fulfilment of prophecies, which, outside the theological field, are, though not scientifically explainable, accepted as facts of experience. Furthermore, the thoroughgoing eschatological interpretation produces a radical change of perspective. Whereas previously what accorded with the modern outlook, or was acceptable to it, was regarded as historical, now, the contrary proceeding was adopted: 'The want of connexion, the impossibility of applying any natural explanation, is just what is historical, because the course of the history was determined, not by outward events, but by the decisions of Jesus, and these were determined by dogmatic eschatological considerations.'[23]

By comparison with previous investigations into the life of Jesus, Schweitzer's work is revolutionary in a twofold sense: because he recognizes the texts of the first two Gospels as an historical source, and because he interprets the words and actions of Jesus as being rooted in Jewish ideology, whilst taking their own line in the creative development of eschatological dogmatism through the amalgamation of prophetic and Daniel-apocalyptic eschatology, and in the identification of his own person with that of the Messiah. In effect this is a liberation from literary scepticism as well as from the tendency to turn Jesus into a modern man. All modern ideas, even in the subtlest form, must be eschewed. Historical investigation must not allow itself to be sidetracked by contemporary religious interests. It must reject all attempts to interpret the sermons of Jesus as though they were not, in fact, conditioned by the ideas of the time.

According to Schweitzer, Jesus lives only in dogmatic history; he even succeeds in turning his own dogmatism into history. Eschatology itself is nothing but dogmatic history forcing its way into ordinary history and thereby negating it. 'The thoroughgoing eschatological school says they are dogmatic, and therefore historical.'[24]

The figure of Jesus, which liberal investigation since the eighteen-sixties had reduced to contemporary criteria 'unconsciously under the influence of an imposing modern-religious nationalism in art'[25] and decked out with features of contemporary appeal, appears great, strange and mysterious in this interpretation. It thus differs in three respects from the life of Jesus according to the liberal school. And this threefold difference is what Schweitzer is aiming at. To what extent he is right in detail in his interpretation of the texts does not worry him a great deal. Exegetic detail is open to discussion, though he rejects the assumption that his simplification of the literary problem derives from a naïve attitude towards the texts. It is based on the insight—obtained from a detailed exegetic study—into the laws according to which the early Christian conception and estimate of the personality of Jesus subsequently conditioned the story of his life and works.

The outstanding characteristic of the historical Jesus as Schweitzer sees him is his greatness. He tells us that his own 'realistic' account of the life of Jesus, aims expressly at presenting the 'overwhelming heroic greatness of Jesus to the modern age and to modern theology.'[26] He is quite willing to submit his work to the judgement of the critics though he knows in advance that in accordance with their own dogmatic, historical and literary standpoint they will not be sparing of criticism, but just this one thing is sacrosanct. Such an attitude is unusual in the world of scholarship. But here Schweitzer feels himself secure in the possession of knowledge which cannot be rebutted by any scientific objections, because in the last resort it is based on personal experience. However he is not merely making a confession, whose appropriateness within the framework of a scholarly investigation might be queried. He is raising a question which juts out like a salient rock in the course of the investigations into the life of Jesus, a rock on which the barque of investigation has suffered shipwreck again and again. And he answers it.

The greatness of Jesus is unique not only in that it manifests itself in an historical personality but also in that this personality claims itself to be supernatural. Whether one assumes that Jesus appeared as the Messiah all along, or that he kept his 'Messianic secret' and revealed it only to his closest confidants, and then only towards the end of his life, does not lessen the difficulty which arises when any attempt is made to understand and represent him as a man 'like any other'. And it does not alter the fact that his own understanding of himself is the central problem of those investigations, and that without a satisfactory solution every attempt at an historical interpretation of the phenomenon of his existence must fail. And yet no one is able to solve it.

Even David Friedrich Strauss, who was the first to go straight to the historical material, found himself at the end of his psychological tether when faced with the disconcerting idea Jesus had of himself; namely that as the expected Messiah he was destined to appear very soon on the clouds of heaven, surrounded by unearthly glory, to be escorted by angels to the last judgement; after which the Kingdom of Heaven would come. Strauss tries to extricate himself from this embarrassment by saying on the one hand that from our point of view Jesus must certainly be described as a visionary, and on the other hand that he was nevertheless 'a sensible man' whose extraordinary ideas can be explained from the messianic views of neo-Judaism. But this is very far from explaining how it came about that, on his own authority, a man should declare himself identical with the Messiah, behaviour which would necessarily be regarded by all Jews living in and accepting those views as a blasphemy worthy of death. Thus Strauss was being quite consistent, when, thirty years later, in his second life of Jesus (1865), he describes the messianic ideas of Jesus as 'very close to madness', and therefore pays little attention to them.

In this respect, as in so many others, subsequent investigation did not go beyond David Friedrich Strauss—until the advent of Schweitzer. It was inclined to judge the claim of messianic dignity without any real feeling for the enormity of its 'arrogance'; even to dispute it altogether as unhistoric; or to explain it away as mere pathological extravagance. So when Schweitzer actually stressed this messianic consciousness and acknowledged its central position in the outlook of the Nazarene, his teacher Heinrich Julius Holtzmann, and others, warned him that he was picturing Jesus as a man whose ideology was akin to lunacy. They also considerately drew his attention to medical investigations which purported to prove the 'paranoia' of the Jewish Messiah. But this made no impression on Schweitzer, who was able to dismiss these objections of the theologians with the authority of an expert, because he was studying medicine at the time in preparation for his work as a doctor in the African jungle. In fact he actually took the psychiatric judgement passed on Jesus as the theme of his doctoral dissertation[27] and demonstrated the baselessness of the psychopathic interpretation of the apocalyptic visions of Jesus. He was aware to a much greater extent than his critics of the 'infinite self-assurance' which lay behind the words and actions of Jesus, and for him it was not a source of misgiving. It strikes him as both pointless and historically false to attempt to explain—to speak of judging—a person psychologically, who, 'in the given form of his own day knows that with his actions and his death he is creating a moral world which will bear his name'. The history of the past two thousand years has proved how well founded that knowledge was.

The sphere of the supernatural is not accessible to Schweitzer the thinker. In his view he was waging a struggle against dogma in the name of truth. This attitude was modified later, but never entirely abandoned. The result of his investigations into the life of Jesus is therefore all the more remarkable: 'This Jesus is far greater than the one conceived in modern terms: he is really a supermundane personality.'[28] His words are reminiscent—though certainly unconsciously—of those uttered by the Roman Centurion at the foot of the Cross: 'Truly this was the son of God!' (Matt. xxvii. 54.) In other words, this was the Messiah. Once Schweitzer had obtained this result, the problem of the messianic self-knowledge of Jesus which so troubled anti-dogmatic Jesus research, presented no further difficulty for him. This puts an end to all attempts to 'understand' Jesus and thus provide a coherent and psychologically based picture of his personality and actions. The critical examination of the Gospel texts is still a task of theological science. The Appendix on the quest of the historical Jesus indicates the lines on which it proceeds. The 'Life of Jesus Movement' however—an expression Schweitzer himself uses to describe the century and a half of persistent efforts to provide a biography of Jesus—is exposed as hopeless; not only on account of the inadequacy of the available sources, which have been variously interpreted down to our own day, but chiefly because of the incomprehensible nature of its subject. Schweitzer's attitude to the messianic self-knowledge of Jesus involves a realization that in this unique case historical investigation is faced with something incomprehensible. We may not dare 'even to wish to understand his nature'.[29] The real difficulty which cannot be disposed of by any method of critical Gospel research does not lie in the miracles recorded in the Gospels, but in the miracle of Jesus Christ himself. It represents the limit of scientific knowledge.

So far Protestant theology hardly seems to have noticed the importance of the fact that this conclusion was arrived at on the basis of the Enlightenment by a spirit guided by the strictest obedience to truth. The significance of this divination of the greatness of Jesus as the result of historical critical research into His life—the consequence of a great spirit's meeting an even greater—is none the less remarkable on that account. But the Jesus of Schweitzer is difficult to 'grasp', not only on account of this greatness, but also because of its strangeness. A psychological understanding is not only rendered *a priori* impossible because the greatness of Jesus exceeds all human criteria (Schweitzer describes His personality as 'superhuman'),[30] but by the abyss between our outlook and that of the world in which He lived and worked. With this thesis Schweitzer erects another milestone along the road of Jesus research, and it is immovable unless one is prepared to abandon the historical Jesus altogether.

Schweitzer sums up the quest for Jesus: 'It set out in quest of the historical Jesus, believing that when it had found Him it could bring Him straight into our time as a Teacher and Saviour. It loosed the bands by which He had been riveted to the stony rocks of ecclesiastical doctrine, and rejoiced to see life and movement coming into the figure once more and the historical Jesus advancing as it seemed to meet it. But He does not stay; He passes by our time and returns to His own. What surprised and dismayed the theology of the last forty years was that despite all forced and arbitrary interpretations, it could not keep Him in our time, but had to let Him go. He returned to His own time, not owing to the application of any historical ingenuity, but by the same inevitable necessity by which the liberated pendulum returned to its original position.'[31]

The validity of this summary does not depend on whether Schweitzer is right in his assumption that logical eschatology resolves all the riddles of the Gospel account. His technique is deliberately black and white. For him Jesus 'thought either eschatologically or uneschatologically'. Every significant word uttered by Jesus and handed down to us must be interpreted against his objective vision of the end of the world and the coming Kingdom of God. Every form of eschatological sublimation is rejected. The texts are either historical or unhistorical.

'Either the Marcan text as it stands is historical and therefore to be retained, or it is not, and then it should be given up.'[32] 'There is, on the one hand, the eschatological solution, which at one stroke raises the Marcan account as it stands, with all its disconnectedness and inconsistencies, into genuine history; and there is, on the other hand, the literary solution, which regards the incongruous dogmatic element as interpolated by the earliest Evangelist, into the tradition and therefore strikes out the Messianic claim altogether from the historical life of Jesus. *Tertium non datur.*'[33]

Here we are faced with an obvious 'violation of truth', such as, according to Schweitzer's own words, frequently accompanies the discovery of a true principle. His passionate temperament tends to drive things to extremes. But in so doing he lowers his guard and makes it easier for New Testament research to evade a detailed discussion of his own interpretation of the texts. He is not worried at the thought of providing cheap pretexts for the rejection of his 'solution', pretexts which are all the more tempting because his solution involves theological difficulties. But the results of this historical-critical method are necessarily 'inconvenient, because they do nothing to bring the New Testament within the orbit of modern humanitarianism or humanistic teaching'.[34]

Theologically speaking something else is even more awkward. If the eschatological solution is right, if the sources correspond only in essentials with the historical facts, then Jesus was not only embedded in the thought of his day, but in consequence He was also subject to error. He expected the imminent coming of the Kingdom of God. Attempts to interpret the messianic prophecies in such a way that the actual time of the beginning of the last days is left open, break down against the clear and definite words at the sending out of the apostles: 'For verily I say unto you, Ye shall not have gone over the cities of Israel, till the Son of man be come.' (Matt. x. 23.) The parusia of the Son of man, which is logically and in point of time identical with the coming of the Kingdom of God, is to take place before they have hurried through the cities of Israel with their message. How a theology which believes in the texts can accept them as they stand and nevertheless still believe in the infallibility of Jesus is its own affair. The procedure arouses misgivings, and it is questionable whether belief is well served. If the utterances of Jesus are to be regarded as untouchable then there is no room for any unprejudiced examination of the sources, because then every utterance of Jesus which has been passed down to us must be accepted as authentic, even when it is in itself unlikely, or when it stands in an obviously unhistorical relationship, which would similarly be removed from any critical examination. Thus the conflict with truthfulness arises. This unwillingness to admit the possibility of an error on the part of Jesus is even more deep-rooted than the fear of venturing on the thin ice of source criticism without the reinsurance of unconditional respect for 'the word of the Lord'. Here we must ask ourselves whether orthodox theology has exhausted the paradox of 'true man and true God', or whether it has not, recoiling from the full consequences of the 'like us' as though from a blasphemy, toned it down. But not to take these words literally would be equivalent to toning down the Act of Love represented by the Divine self-sacrifice. The 'without sin' in connexion with the susceptibility to temptation grants the humanity of Jesus even if it simultaneously underlines His uniqueness amongst men; for man is more or less subject to sin, and he is fundamentally free to choose in the face of each temptation. But ideological involvement is a constitutive characteristic of man, a circumstance from which he is unable to free himself. It results from his existence in time. He is an historical being. And only as such is he a human being. Thus the idea of a Jesus whose ideas are independent of time and place, and who is yet true man, is untenable. It was conceived at a time when historical thinking was still undeveloped, and it becomes illusory as soon as man realizes that His existence is historical.

The awe at the prospect of encountering an 'all-too' historic Jesus is so deep-rooted that even liberal Jesus research, which set itself the task of discovering the historic Jesus, instinctively avoids fixing his spiritual place in history. But it fails to realize that its own modernization of Jesus also means a relativization in time—and an objectively unjustifiable one at that. It has no objection to a violation, a sentimental and commonplace retouching of the portrait of the Saviour such as is carried out in all innocence even by dogmatic Christianity; there, however, under the control of Christology. But where its own technique of textual criticism comes up against the definitely unfamiliar it is at a loss, and it casts around for excuses. The sending out of the disciples becomes an 'obscure tradition' (Bousset). The prophecies of suffering and the prophecies relating to the coming of the Son of man are eliminated altogether, relegated to the final 'gloomy epoch' of the life of Jesus, or dismissed as due to early Christian theology, though there seems no obvious reason why this latter should subsequently have invented prophecies which remained unfulfilled.

Schweitzer's procedure is radically different. He suffers from no theological inhibitions. The magnetic needle remains unswervingly pointed to the recognition of historical truth. The half-measures of biblical research, the waterings and tonings down, are just as firmly rejected as the arbitrariness of textual criticism. As an historian he is keenly aware of the role which both the one and the other play in the quest for Jesus. One even has the feeling that in the last resort it might well be his loathing of both which has driven him to adopt extreme positions. For example, he regards the words sending out the apostles as 'historical as a whole and down to the smallest details, precisely because according to the view of modern theology it must be judged unhistorical'.[35] They are eschatologically dogmatical and thus in the description of what is going to happen to the apostles necessarily unempirical. The tribulations announced to them are no more historica than the parusa of the Son of man.

It is not necessary to describe the eschatological interpretation of the Gospel accounts here; it is set out in Schweitzer's own 'Sketch of the Life of Jesus'. What matters here is its significance for the struggle to obtain an idea of Jesus.

The unfamiliarity of the historical Jesus is recognized, and accepted, and the great adventure of the quest for the historical Jesus is carried out with previously unexampled logic: namely to seek frankly to understand 'the Lord' as an historically conditioned phenomenon, without at the same time prejudicing His sovereign dignity. The consequent tension between historical distance and present immediacy is developed with a courageous loyalty to truth and followed through to the end. The loss of intimacy is counterbalanced by the gain in clarity of outline. The Gospel accounts are taken at their face value: 'Jesus talks again'—in his own language. The happenings and events which accompany his appearance, and which had faded in the hands of critical investigation, now stand out in glowing intensity. His Baptism and the Last Supper are comprehended as eschatological sacraments and thus recover their real sacramental significance. The transfiguration on the Mount, which leaves liberal investigation completely at a loss, is a revelation of the messianic nature of Jesus, i.e. in truth a 'transfiguration' of his appearance in the eyes of his disciples. His death is vicarious atonement. 'Jesus did actually die for the sins of men.'[36] The stark outlines of a heroic mountainous landscape now arise out of the mists in which the critically dissected texts threatened to disappear altogether, and the profile of Jesus to lose itself in vague, devotional interpretations. But whoever dares to venture into this landscape is taking a great risk. He abandons himself to the storms of the 'last

Days'. Everything is put to the final test. The world-rejection of eschatology is of course not the last word. The 'Kingdom' has not come about in the expected form of a cosmic happening. Even after the turning point of history men are once more called upon to live their lives in this world and to fulfil the Kingdom of God on earth in the spirit of Jesus; that is to say, to accept the life here below as a form of existence in accordance with the will of God. But for Christians the way to this acceptance of the world leads through the purgatory of the world—rejection of the eschatological Gospel of Jesus. This —according to Schweitzer—is the path of his followers.

The objections have resulted in a failure to recognize the true significance of Schweitzer's discovery of both the greatness and the unfamiliarity of the phenomenon Jesus for the investigations. This discovery is of lasting importance. It has put an end to the attempts to modernize the image of Jesus. Where they still survive they need no longer be taken seriously. Schweitzer's blunt conclusion is: either there is no historical Jesus at all, or he is a man of his own time. Nowadays this may sound like a statement of the obvious. But what efforts and what circumlocutions were necessary before it was arrived at!

The personal components of the eschatological solution are recognizable. It suits Schweitzer's own nature because of 'the intrinsic impulse of eschatology towards an immediate and absolute ethic'.[37] According to the evidence of the Gospel accounts the message of Jesus relates 'with utter concentration to the coming Kingdom of God'.[38] Its leitmotif is eschatology. Thus eschatology must stand in the central point of historical Jesus research, and its task is to discover to what extent the eschatological thought of Jesus is determined by his environment, which is filled with eschatological expectations, and to what extent it transcends it.

The third feature of the historical Jesus in Schweitzer's interpretation is that he appeared as an unknown who did not wish to be recognized. 'Jesus was a Messiah who during his public ministry would not be one, did not need to be, and might not be, for the sake of fulfilling his mission.' 'The faith which he required had nothing to do with his person, but it was due only to the message of the nearness of the Kingdom.'[39]

The particular, even unique, quality of this personality appears in a twofold antinomy: a will which sets out in full consciousness of its authority to violate the course of history, is joined by an endeavour to withdraw from the people. No one else has ever intervened in history with comparable claims and success; so much so that since then history can be understood only as *ante* or *post Christum natum*. But this highest measure of historical effectiveness, unlike any other intervention in history, was aimed at and achieved together with a deliberate restraint from any attempt to secure public recognition. On the contrary, the master of history sought seclusion. He needed no other followers beyond the twelve apostles, i.e. an innermost circle of witnesses and preachers of his Gospel; they were supers in a supernatural drama which was being played out by one actor only. But this actor appears neither as a teacher of morals, nor as a founder of religion; had he done so he would have had to work as a missionary on a big scale, converting and convincing. Not only does he disappoint the expectations of those who looked to him for political action, but he obviously does not regard it as his task to lead humanity along the path of moral improvement towards a more perfect state. Where the idea of a development arises in the interpretation it has been interpolated into the words of Jesus by modern thought. On only one occasion does he charge his disciples to carry his Gospel out into the cities of Israel, and even then it is made quite clear that he is not interested in the spread of any 'teaching'. (The instructions of the resurrected Christ: 'Go ye therefore, and teach all nations' (Matt. xxviii. 19) would be unthinkable in the mouth of the historical Jesus.) The only exhortation is contained in the cry of atonement: 'The Kingdom of Heaven is at hand.' It is to be fortified by wonders, since the immediately pre-messianic period is an age of miracles. These signs are a gift of God by which He shows men that the hour is at hand. It is thus no more than a quick warning to prepare for the imminent coming of the Kingdom. But the Kingdom is not of this world. It does not arise out of any human testing and it is not founded on power and influence. To strive for either therefore would be more than unnecessary, it would be senseless. It is true that atonement and moral renewal herald the coming of the Kingdom, and so the corresponding exhortation by Him who knows He is the Messiah is the preliminary to His appearance on the clouds of Heaven. He is the precursor of the Kingdom. But its coming is the work of God. It is independent, not of the appearance of the messenger, but of his success; and whether this messenger is recognized or not is immaterial. Jesus is aware that His appearance in the world is an event which carries its own significance irrespective of the attitude of men towards it.

There is thus no reason for Jesus to make the people recognize Him. With this we encounter the second antinomy of His appearance:

4. Schweitzer as a civilian internee during the First World War

despite a self-confidence transcending all human criteria there is no attempt to secure acknowledgement. Even present-day opponents of consistent eschatology stress the 'very strange', and 'very extraordinary' circumstance that Jesus made no claim to be the Messiah and even went out of his way to disappoint the messianic expectations which his advent and his activities had aroused.[40] He keeps his messianic dignity a secret. Consistent eschatology explains this by its character of futurity, and it is in agreement here with the old synoptic tradition and with the views of early Christianity. 'Jesus of Nazareth, a man approved of God among you by miracles, and wonders and signs.' (Acts ii. 22.) 'This Jesus hath God raised up, whereof we all are witnesses.' (Acts ii. 32.) 'God hath made that same Jesus . . . both Lord and Christ.' (Acts ii. 36.) Only in the Gospel of St John does the Messiah appear in the flesh and demand that men shall believe in him.

The indifference to any inner-worldly success and the concealment of his identity with the Messiah are both explained by the eschatological-dogmatic thought of Jesus. The significance of his appearance on this earth, his life and his death, is a secret between him and God. Whether he ever intended to tell even his disciples is not certain. According to the synoptic versions it was wrung from him by the events themselves.

No attempt at an historical interpretation of the many riddles and apparent contradictions in the life of Jesus has any hope of success unless it starts with this question. It is therefore no accident that Schweitzer's study of the life of Jesus bears the title *The Secret of Jesus' Messiahship and Passion.* As his life was obviously not determined by external events, but, including its end, by a will directing events, so its significance can be understood only by some divination at least of its content. It circles around an unexplainable secret but one which can be recognized in outline.

In a detailed investigation Schweitzer demonstrates that no one could possibly have guessed from the behaviour or the utterances of Jesus that he regarded himself as the Messiah. The revelation of the messianic secret invariably takes place in circumstances of ecstatic emotion. At Baptism the secret of his personality becomes known to Jesus himself in a state of ecstasy, at the transfiguration on the Mount to the three intimate disciples Peter, James and John. It takes place on the mount on the north shore of the Lake of Gennesareth where Jesus had prayed when he came to Bethsaida (Mark vi. 46). It precedes the happening at Caesara Philippi. Afterward it would have been insignificant and incomprehensible. Literary reasons also favour this course of events. At Caesara Philippi the twelve apostles also learn the messianic secret, but it still remains hidden to the people. The entry into Jerusalem is certainly a messianic action on the part of Jesus, but the ovations of the multitude are for 'he who should come', the prophet, and Elias, whose coming presages the imminence of the Kingdom. In answer to the question: 'Who is this?' (Matt. xxi. 10) the people answered: 'This is Jesus the Prophet of Nazareth of Galilee' (Matt. xxi. 11). There is no mention of the Messiah either here or in Mark's description of the entry into Jerusalem. In fact, the treachery of Judas consists in the betrayal of the messianic secret to the High Priests. But as Judas is the only available witness to the charge, an admission by Jesus himself is necessary for court proceedings. Jesus provides this admission at once and refers to his imminent parusia as the Son of Man. This is the blasphemy for which he is then condemned to death.

The secret of the passion is closely connected with the messianic secret. It was the general opinion, and it was firmly underlined by Jesus himself, that the coming of the Kingdom would be preceded by a time of great tribulation. The Messiah would be born out of these tribulations, which he must suffer with his disciples. According to Schweitzer, the secret of Jesus consists in the fact that during the final period of his life, when the expected time of tribulations did not come about, he came to the conclusion that he must take on himself vicariously the atonement which must precede the coming of the Kingdom. And this he did (Mark x. 45). He identifies his condemnation and crucifixion with the prophesied pre-messianic tribulations, and thanks to his authority to bring this about, he projects an eschatological happening into history. He sets off for Jerusalem in order to die there, and to die alone; and against all likelihood he succeeds in turning this dogmatic decision into history.

The magnificence and logic of this attempt at an interpretation of the 'hidden' Jesus stands out in impressive contrast against a background of the modernization fashionable at the time. The latter approach assumes that throughout the greater part of his life Jesus did not think of his passion, and suggests that the idea came only when it was forced upon him by the hostility of the Scribes. From this angle his messianic mission takes on an ethic-idyllic character in the first period, and a modern-resigned character in the second. The popularization of Gustav Frenssen[41] who has studied Holtzmann, Weinel, Jülicher, Bousset, P. W. Schmidt and Harnack, shows clearly what sort of a picture then emerges. The first act: 'It was a great age. A spring storm swept through the little land. He carried the storm and the storm carried him. It was clear that the whole people would be conquered.' Act 2: 'All his jubilation was now gone. A terrible, oppressive fear lay heavily on his soul . . . the harsh, mocking attack and the sudden desertion of the people, had struck him a heavy blow.' But as 'things can no longer go on in this way with humanity,' the 'pure, good and holy man' goes southward to the capital in order there to proclaim the Kingdom of God. Everything goes off very nobly, very humanly and very understandably. In fact any soul, provided it is sufficiently naïve, can readily appreciate the whole thing.

Schweitzer's method of investigation objects to this humanization of Jesus. He set out with the aim of advancing inquiry along the lines of the life of Jesus movement, and to correct such errors as he had recognized. At the same time he felt himself at one with the motivation of that investigation. As we already know, the investigations desired to serve truth. The historical Jesus was to take the place of the Jesus of Church doctrine. But once the work began the accent changed. What happened did not involve any theological shift, and probably even Schweitzer did not quite realize what was happening. Nevertheless it soon became unmistakably clear. The thing which was to be opposed was no longer, as it had been with David Friedrich Strauss, a creation of dogmatic 'superstition'. Making every allowance for the radicalism of enlightened thought, the procedure both towards the tests and in many other questions (the real significance of the sacraments and the serious historical analysis of the most important miracle stories and of the prophecies) was restorative as against the critical extravagance of those who had gone before; certainly not out of sympathy with any of the beliefs they may have been attacking, but from critical insight. The vehemence—and vehemence is at work here as never since the days of Reimarus—was differently directed. It no longer confidently aimed at overthrowing some bogey set up by Church dogma. Frenssen, particularly because of his lack of intellectual independence, is a reliable witness to the great role played by resentments even in the liberal period of the investigations. It entered the lists in the service of 'the Lord', whose essence had revealed itself to Schweitzer during the course of his investigations in all its immeasurable greatness and with all the inexplicability of its seclusion. 'Renan desecrates him [Jesus] and reduces him to the level of a sentimental figure; pusillanimous spirits like Schopenhauer dare to appeal to him to justify their own enervating ideas; and our own age has modernized him, by attempting a psychological interpretation of his maturing and development.' Schweitzer not only condemns this attitude towards Jesus as unhistorical, but he regards it as impermissible; above all because it arrogantly dares to treat an absolutely superior being beyond all human criteria as though he were on its own level. For Schweitzer this betrays a lack of respect, a lack of feeling for the scale of values, which must cause historical understanding to go astray, since it is essential that it should know its own limits: 'Before that mysterious person . . . we must be forced to lay our faces in the dust, without daring to wish to understand his nature.'[42]

Schweitzer's quest for Jesus has the courage and the logical consistency to negate itself in an admission which has no equal in critical theology. Its concluding observations end in the words: 'He comes to us as One unknown, without a name, as of old, by the lake-side He came to those men who knew Him not. He speaks to us the same word "Follow me!" . . . He commands. And to those who obey Him, whether they be wise or simple, He will reveal Himself . . . and as an ineffable mystery they shall learn in their own experience Who He is. . . .'[43]

Here Protestant rationalism is carried to its uttermost conclusion. It ends on the one hand in a radical abandonment of all the standpoints of belief, and on the other in an unconditional surrender to Jesus as the unfathomable Lord of the World. Such paradoxes arise when a figure stands at a turning point in history, when, in fact, it incorporates this turning point.

Thus Schweitzer's investigations into the life of Jesus do not culminate in the historical Jesus, as one would expect, but in a 'Jesus mysticism'.[44] Prepared for any sacrifice he has travelled the Golgotha of truthfulness: 'I find it no light task . . . to put pressure on the Christian faith to reconcile itself in all sincerity with historical truth.'[45] But when he seemed to have discovered the historical Jesus, he found that He was still, and more than ever, an 'unknown', to whose secret neither knowledge nor wisdom could provide the key, but only the act of surrender. In his efforts to penetrate into the heart of the secret he did not hesitate to take this difficult path. No third person can look into this sphere of the 'unutterable'. In so far as it can be experienced, but not articulated, as something which cannot be thought, it cannot be understood even by him who experiences it. But it is possible, and for the solution of our task even necessary, to attempt to discover the truth about this strain of irrational experience which runs through the middle of unprejudiced and reasoning thought; and is—obviously in Schweitzer's view too—immeasurably more valuable and illuminating.

What are we to understand under Schweitzer's Jesus mysticism? And what place does it occupy in his religious life?

Schweitzer is rooted in a Protestant tradition described by Goethe in a keen generalization committed to his diary on September 7, 1807: 'Protestantism stands for the moral training of the individual, and thus its first and its last interest is virtue, virtue which also plays a role in our earthly everyday life. God retires into the background, Heaven is empty, and the talk of immortality is purely problematic.'

It is clear that from the start God has no very strong position, and even then it is endangered from two sides in Schweitzer's theological thought: the idea of God is emptied by rationalism, and at the same time narrowed down by voluntarism. Schweitzer's forerunner here is not, as has been supposed, Schopenhauer, but Augustine, who was, like Schweitzer, an impulsive and strong-willed nature, and who in the investigation of his own personality, came upon will as its deepest essence. Thus in all the states and movements of the soul he sees in the last resort nothing more than the urge of the will (*voluntates*), and from this standpoint he seeks to form an analogous idea of the nature of God, though this certainly does not mean a denial of its character as an absolute personality. It remains the sum of all truth. On the other hand, because of its fundamental denial of any source of comprehension of a personal God beyond the 'experience' of God in his own inner life, Schweitzer's theism is completely subject to the primacy of will. 'The ultimate and most profound knowledge of things comes from the will.'[46] However, for Schweitzer this is identical from the beginning with ethical will. Thus God too can be grasped only as an ethical personality. God is a will powerful in being and capable of changing it. We enter into relationship with God when we allow this ethical will to operate in us. 'The ultimately important thing is to be possessed by the ethical will of God.'[47] This is the sum of religious experience in so far as it can pass through the filter of thought. The sphere in which it moves is not extended by Schweitzer's 'mysticism of reality'. For reasoning thought the *cognitio experimentalis Dei*, the comprehension of the 'abstract' in experience as against his 'living' mysticism, has not the quality of authentic knowledge. As with contemplation, there is no room within the framework of ethical voluntarism for the spirituality associated with it.

Schweitzer's philosophy of civilization tells us something about his philosophical conception of God, and we must therefore turn to it in advance.

Schweitzer sees the Godhead operating in the world as 'a universal will to life', as a creative force which compels our awe, but which at the same time troubles us with the terrible riddle that its creation is not 'good'. This is the pantheistic aspect of his experience of God. A relationship to this God who stands beyond good and evil would contradict the identification of religion and ethics. In addition, the individual is unable to enter into a relationship with the totality of being. The surrender to the absolute is 'a purely intellectual act'. Why? Because 'the motives of action are not present' in it. The living quality of a man participates only in a spirituality which 'carries the urge to action elementally in it'. Thus the pantheistic way of a life in God is barred.

Now paradoxically God is at the same time comprehended as a will which aims at negating the self-alienation of the will to life which we experience in the world. As such it takes on the character of a personality. Only a personality can be the vessel of a clearly directed will in conflict with the natural state of the world. I can let myself be 'possessed' by this will to love. But though personal, it remains anonymous. It is not prepared to answer any of my questions. It is certainly not an abstraction as the absolute is, but, astonishingly, it is brought no nearer by my perception of it in me. Its personality is an intellectual necessity but nevertheless inconceivable. This absolutely formulated ethical activism, this will to love which intervenes in creation only through the medium of the human personality, has the reality of an inner operating force, but nevertheless no personal reality capable of experience. As it takes no part in man's personality, needs and troubles, merely compelling him to work against the incomprehensible self-alienation of creation, man can therefore attain no relationship to its person. Though constantly experienced, it remains in the inadequate sphere of the (for man) unreal. 'It is only through the manifestations of Being, and only through those with which I enter into relations, that my being has any intercourse with infinite Being.'[48]

The appearance form *kat exochên* of the ethical God personality is Jesus. Thus a religiosity which seeks communion with the Divinity must turn to Him. 'In Jesus Christ God is manifested as Will of love. In union with Christ, union is realized in the only form attainable by us.'[49] 'Our religion is Christ mysticism.'

With this, religious life would seem to be reduced to its simplest possible formula. The complications and puzzles of Church dogma are eliminated. The intellectual conscience is satisfied. One can ignore the religiously unhelpful God idea in its constant pendulum movement between Pantheism and Theism, and its (despite all its attempts at a real content) abstract vitalism. 'What matters, and all that matters, is that a man can say: "I believe in Jesus as my Lord and Master." And then in this belief he has all belief.'[50]

This belief is, however, subject to doubt. The 'New Protestantism' in which Schweitzer feels at home by origin and by outlook, has a tendency to 'translate' the events between God and man which constitute the subject of Christian faith, into general truths of reason (Troeltsch). At the same time it falls back upon Jesus, his person and his teachings as on one of the 'founders and heroes' of religious life in whom the ubiquitous divinity operating in the human soul was particularly pure and powerful.[51] In the circumstances it is theoretically possible to do without this person, should historical research fail to prove his existence. This looks like a real gain, because modern Christianity must always reckon with the possibility of an eventual abandonment of the historicity of Jesus. Schweitzer does not doubt this historicity, and those who deny it, and with whom he disputes, in detail, are not in a happy position. But as a true son of the Enlightenment he does not think in historical categories. When he talks of the 'historicity' of Jesus he means the fact that Jesus once lived, and it is true that he has consistently interpreted the thought of Jesus against the background of his environment. But with this, and even allowing that he made history, Schweitzer has not granted Jesus an absolutely unshakeable place in history. Indeed, Schweitzer's own theological thought insists on the independence of religion from any history. 'Religion must have a metaphysic, that is to say, a fundamental idea concerning the nature and significance of being, which is completely independent of history and verbal tradition, and can be created afresh at any moment and in respect of any religious subject. If it does not have this direct and inalienable possession then it is the slave of history and must live in the spirit of a slave fearing itself constantly endangered and threatened.'[52]

The conviction of the uniqueness of Jesus of Nazareth, not as a historic Jesus, but as the vessel of salvation, whose message represents the content of the Gospels, is not rooted in Schweitzer's theological thought. And thus it may well lose sight of the fact that the revelation of God in Jesus has the character of an historical event. When Schweitzer delivers lectures on Christianity and world religions to missionaries with the intention of helping them in their work amongst non-believers, he does not indicate with a single word that the aim is any different today from what it was in the time of Paul, namely to spread the Gospel of Jesus Christ; he merely seeks to demonstrate the ethical superiority of Christianity. The thing that counts is 'to possess the spirit of Jesus', to radiate 'the truth of Jesus'.[53] And so, concludes liberal theology, referring expressly to Schweitzer, 'we may speak of the reality of Christ when being enters a crisis because the radical question of the significance of life arises in the human spirit, and when the ethical attitude of respect for life arises as a consequence of thinking the question through to its logical conclusion. With this we are freed once and for all from the problem of the possible unhistoricity of Jesus', because if the latter were proved by historical research 'we should lose only an historical illustration of the idea of Christ, though, admittedly, a very valuable one'.[54]

Though this may seem to follow logically from certain of Schweitzer's theological utterances, the language in which it is couched is certainly not his, nor is it an interpretation of his Jesus mysticism. What is actually happening here—and not altogether without his fault—is that the importance of the decisive and the lastingly valid event which determines everything else in his life—the encounter with Jesus of Nazareth—is being disputed.

Towards the end of his history of the investigations into the life of Jesus, Schweitzer introduces the idea of the Jesus mysticism in direct relation to the profession of his own discipleship towards Jesus as Lord and Master. This is to be taken very literally. 'Thus Jesus also creates community amongst us. He does not do it as a symbol or as anything of that sort',[55] that is to say, not as an illustration of the idea of Christ.[56] 'Belief can remain indifferent to a Jesus who, in the last resort, is a "symbol" with more or less reality. . . . An inwardly healthy religiosity will be warned by its instinct for truth against committing itself to any such idea and what it involves. Should it nevertheless succumb it will perish inwardly in consequence.'[57]

In his sketch of the life of Jesus (1901) we read: 'The Christian religion is founded upon the messianic consciousness of Jesus. . . . If Jesus did not take himself to be the Messiah this means the death blow to the Christian faith.'[58] And again the second edition of his history of the quest of the historical Jesus (1913) bears witness to the fact that Jesus rules in the world as 'the alone great and alone true'.[59] 'The new world began with the death of Jesus, a world to which the old law no longer applied.'[60] This testimony, which could be repeated *ad lib*, tells us that Schweitzer's belief in Jesus Christ is not a belief in an idea but in an historical superhistorical personality.

The relationship to Jesus is greatly intensified by the unsatisfied longing for an approach to belief in God. The capacity for love and the need for surrender, which can find no access to 'God's throne', are concentrated on Jesus. The impervious cupola of Heaven throws all the rays of religious life back to this one focal point. The reality of the earthly life of Jesus justifies the relationship to him before a court which recognizes no transcendent reality.

Schweitzer is frankest of all about his belief in Jesus when speaking to his congregation. The voice of a preacher who could say the most intimate things with such discretion still echoes in the memory after many years. It is the voice heard by hundreds of thousands since 1957 in the film made by Erica Anderson, a somewhat dry and unpathetic delivery but with the precision of a man striving for objective expression; sometimes it even sounds a little weary, but it is always deeply impressive. Let us hear what it has to say about belief and disbelief:

'. . . Ultimate belief has nothing to do with anyone or anything but Jesus, and with Him it is not a matter of any kind of knowledge, but only with what lies in the words: "Dear Lord, help us!" Our religion is the religion of the infinite become flesh. A man can be mistaken about what lies above the clouds, about what is above our knowledge and understanding. But if he recognizes the whole spiritual, divine world just at that point where it approaches him tangibly in the shape of our Lord and Master Jesus, then he has and holds it; and what is more, he has everything, even those things to which his spirit cannot raise itself and which he is unable to believe. If you think profoundly on this, the divine made flesh becomes a compassionate act of the divine spirit. Who can measure what it means for us that our religion is concerned with a man who loves and has his being, whose words we still possess, and whose being represents the eternal and the true for us. . . .'[61]

Jesus 'speaks' to us. He is not only representing the eternal and the true for us, but we possess his words. And compared with this it seems quite unimportant to Schweitzer that perhaps this or that utterance could be questioned by biblical criticism: ' . . . leave the individual alone'[62] with the sayings of Jesus. And it is not only in the Gospels that He speaks to us. Schweitzer insists that we 'must obey the voice of Jesus'. Asked how one can hear it he replies 'You must keep your ears open for it all your life'.

This Jesus is set above us as our Lord and Master. ' "Lord and Master" are the fundamental words of Christianity.' 'For me belief in Jesus means that He rules us more than we could confess to anyone. Something no one can put into words for himself, something he cannot describe in words to others . . . but something you can hold in your hands all your life long.'[63]

From the testimony of later years we can see that these words have retained their validity. In his autobiographical work *Aus meinem Leben und Denken* (1932) (*My Life and Thought*) we read: 'Anyone who ventures to look the historical Jesus straight in the face, and to listen to what He may have to teach him in his powerful sayings, soon ceases to ask what this strange-seeming Jesus can still be to him. He learns to know Him as one who would have sway over him.'[64] Finally, abiding things are said in Schweitzer's theological swan song (1950). He tells us that he 'suffered severely through the compulsion which truth laid upon us to put forward something which was bound to offend faith' namely that the eschatological outlook of Jesus was conditioned by His time. 'To me, however, Jesus remains what he was. Not for a single moment have I had to struggle for my conviction that in Him is the supreme spiritual and religious authority. . . . He remains our spiritual Lord.'[65]

Thus Schweitzer himself makes clear the nature of his Jesus mysticism, and he does so unmistakably and with great emphasis, though now and again his liberal theology spoils the picture. His Jesus mysticism neutralizes 'disbelief'. And what is the situation with regard to disbelief? Does it have the last word?

'Disbelief does not come from any brooding, from any false desire to know. It is there; it is there of itself.'[66] In other words, it is given with the spirit of the age.

The philosopher Schweitzer is an agnostic.

It was the Prague professor of philosophy Oskar Krauss, the follower and literary executor of the philosopher Franz Brentano, who first pointed to the metaphysical agnosticism in the religious philosophy of Schweitzer. His attempt to provide an analysis of Schweitzer's character is a combination of the determinist assumptions of the author, biographical information and philosophical analysis, the whole informed by respectful admiration, and it adds up to one of the most valuable and unusual critical efforts of scientific philosophy to deal with Schweitzer's ideology.

Rudolf Grabs, Schweitzer's German biographer, refers to Krauss, and also points to Schweitzer's 'stressed agnosticism', but rightly qualifies the expression by saying that Schweitzer's agnosticism is not sceptical but humble.[67] He does not specify just what this means.

The Basle professor of theology and interpreter of Schweitzer, Fritz Buri, has taken a rather closer look. His verdict also finds agnosticism, but he regards Schweitzer's speculations on God and Christ as a dissolution of philosophic rationalism which contradicts his agnosticism. Grabs had already pointed out that the figure of Jesus was 'numinously determined' in the experience of Schweitzer,[68] whilst Buri is seriously disturbed by Schweitzer's offences against liberal dogmatism. Schweitzer must obviously be called to order. His thought must 'be freed from the armour of ideology in which, despite his hostility to metaphysics, it occasionally parades', so that like David after discarding Saul's armour, he can appear as the true David. This friendly service is due to Schweitzer. His 'mythological and speculative utterances must not be taken in their objectivity'.[69] Belief must remember the merely symbolic significance of all his utterances, which must be regarded as nothing but an expression of an attempt at self-knowledge. It is only too obvious here that the author is inspired less by the wish to understand Schweitzer's religiosity than by a desire to see his own opinions confirmed.

Two things must be taken into account.

The philosophical diagnosis is correct in its approach. Under the influence of Kant agnosticism holds that the human understanding can embrace nothing definite about supernatural things. Schweitzer thinks so, too. But in his work on the religious philosophy of Kant Schweitzer himself has already pointed out that the profounder conception of the moral law at which Kant gradually arrived, involved religious demands beyond what critical idealism according to the Kantian conception can admit. In satisfying the demands of his ethical philosophy, Schweitzer's 'thought mysticism' goes beyond the limits of metaphysical agnosticism. Ethical personality, the form in which he becomes conscious of God, is definite experience, even when he cannot harmonize it with the 'creative will beyond me', and must thus be content with 'an incomplete ideology'. This willingness to be content with less certainly means the rejection of revelation in written and Church tradition and also of spiritual contemplation as sources of perception. 'Only the will contemplates life from within.' But this 'unassuming thing' allows a living experience of God to arise from the basis of being and to survive the court of reason as a supposed 'logical experience of thought'. It withdraws itself from the tyrannies of 'unconditional reasoning thought' without the latter involving itself in conscious inner contradiction.

This is one of the essential corrections which must be made in the usual interpretation of Albert Schweitzer's utterances about God.

A second point is even more significant. It relates to the inner secret of personality and evades all rational analysis. The God experience of Schweitzer does not stop at a dawning consciousness of an 'ethical will in me'.

Schweitzer's critical thought does not negate his roots in Christian tradition. The 'out-dated' original or ur-picture, shimmers through the rationalistic overpainting, and gives it depth. It stands under the protection of the *docta ignorantia*, the knowing unknowingness. In this connection Schweitzer is not afraid to borrow an expression from mediaeval mysticism.

Buri feels that he must rebuke Schweitzer for such 'defects' in his theology. Schweitzer adopts mythological ideas which tend to a formulation of Christian belief which cannot be reconciled with his own ideas of religion and philosophy.[70] There is in fact a disagreement between religious utterance and rationalist philosophy, and Schweitzer is mistaken when he thinks that the content both here and there is 'absolutely the same'.[71] But the source of this disagreement is not 'the adoption' of 'ideas'; that is to say, a sort of intellectual slovenliness. The thing is of more than personal significance. In the unique amalgam of scientific superstition which regards truth as a subject of objective perception and enlightened rationalism, which is characteristic of Schweitzer's thought, reason has erected a double barrier against the 'supernatural', equipped with the armour of passionate conviction, and always so to speak on the alert. In no period of his life has he ever abandoned it. But in moments of elementary religious experience a hardly conscious belief passes through it like the Resurrected one through closed doors. Neither the claim of scientific thought to universal validity nor the denial of a transcendent being by the theory of knowledge is philosophically overcome. But this theoretically unshaken position has, so to speak, ceased to be impervious.

The decisive steps forward in the history of thought are usually undertaken naïvely. In the last resort Schweitzer's theological historical significance probably lies in the fact that he, a son of the Enlightenment, and unshakeably rooted in its thought, being conscious of the inadequacy of man's ability to know, is content where the deepest secret of being is concerned to leave its results in the balance, and leave his mind open to the revelation of elementary religious experience; and by virtue of this 'incompleteness' of his theological thought, gains access to transcendent reality, under the gentle, unnoticeable but irresistible compulsion of a power which allows him to be conscious without conflict of its presence. Intensively stressed elements of the antagonism between belief and knowledge exist side by side in peaceful coexistence in Schweitzer's spiritual world—a highly unusual, even unique phenomenon. On the face of it this is both theologically and philosophically untenable. But what seems to be a weakness of his position between two frontiers turns out to be unexpectedly fruitful. By virtue of his religious personality it allows him—a spiritual historical anticipation—to leave behind the dispute between belief and knowledge.

In his *Mitteilungen aus Lambaréné* (*Notes from Lambaréné*) Schweitzer describes the evening after the move into the new hospital building: 'For the first time since I have been working in Africa my patients are housed like human beings. How much I suffered in those years because I had to herd them into airless gloomy places! Full of gratitude I raise my eyes to God, who has allowed me to experience such joy.'[72] No theological or philosophical artifice can identify the God to whom this wordless evening prayer is said with the God of Schweitzer's Philosophy, the 'ethical personality which makes itself conscious in me as ethical will'. The 'union with God', which comes to pass in 'union with Christ'[73] lies beyond all ethical voluntarism.

Rationalism usually appears in the form of rational hubris. The peculiarity of Schweitzer's rationalism is its modesty. On no account would it deny itself anything either Heaven or earth could offer. But it is quite prepared for self-sacrifice—which is something quite different.

It is not only Schweitzer's ideology which is incomplete ('*unabgeschlossen*'), but also his belief. In the last resort it does not depend on knowledge, and therefore not on any theology either. It goes its own way. It is the life of a soul which surrenders itself to God. In consequence despite all 'disbelief' it does not experience doubt in the way that a believer does when he feels his beliefs wavering, and this is the compensation for the lack of religious certainty—disbelief is *a priori* here. The pious soul is safe.

All Schweitzer's theological utterances contain the reservation: 'I can go no farther.' Humility and intellectual honesty forbid his theology to proceed from the nil point of unconditional reasoning thought to valid utterances concerning the transcendent. Its guiding principle is: 'The deeper piety is the humbler are its claims with regard to knowledge of the supra-sensible. It is like a path which winds between the hills instead of going over them.'[74] Thus the existence of these 'hills' is not disputed, but even underlined. Schweitzer's religiosity does not allow its wings to be clipped by critical thought, whilst the latter refrains from attempting to embrace the sum of religious knowledge attained by experience, in the consciousness that it cannot hope to embrace the highest reality.

IV

PAUL

Albert Schweitzer took two great themes as the subject of his theological investigations: Jesus and Paul. His work began with an investigation of the Last Supper, and ran counter to the generally accepted opinion of critical theology up to the end of the nineteenth century by deciding that it was a sacramental act and not merely a symbolic action, so also with the baptism of John, so also with Jesus and Paul; the Kingdom of God theology was its crowning achievement. In the centre stand the two dominating figures of early Christianity. Christianity is summed up for Schweitzer not in a doctrine and not in metaphysics, but in these historical personalities.

Those who have followed us thus so far and so become acquainted with Schweitzer will find nothing surprising in this. But his preoccupation with Paul, which produced two scholarly works, although the circumstances seemed impossibly unfavourable, requires some explanation. In dealing with the biography our intention is not to provide a further illustration of his phenomenal will and working capacity, which need no further proof, but to indicate the importance Schweitzer himself attached to this undertaking.

The decision to leave for the Congo and work there as a doctor was taken in 1904. The necessary medical study began in the autumn of 1905. And now, as Schweitzer himself puts it, began a wrestling with fatigue which lasted for years. This was primarily due to the fact that he could not make up his mind to give up his theological teaching or his preaching. And so whilst he was a student of medicine he continued to give lectures which needed very careful preparation because he was dealing for the first time with the problems of Paul's teachings. Almost every Sunday saw him in the pulpit. And as organist of the Paris Bach Society he took part in concerts several times every winter for years, and he also played the organ at the Bach concerts of the Orféo Català in Barcelona. In addition, the first few months of his medical studies saw his treatise on the reform of organ building, which we shall discuss later, and also the final chapters of his history of the investigations into the life of Jesus. 'During the two last years of my medical course [he obtained a first in his final], and the period I spent in the hospitals as house physician, I found time, by means of serious encroachment on my night's rest, to bring to completion a work on the history of scientific research into the thought-world of St Paul, to revise and enlarge the *Quest of the Historical Jesus* for the second edition, and together with Widor to prepare an edition of Bach's Preludes and Fuges for the organ, giving with each piece directions for its rendering.'[1]

As with his investigation into the Last Supper and the life of Jesus, Schweitzer once again felt the need to write a history of the whole problem first. 'That I three times brought myself to follow such a laborious by-road [The procedure was adopted for a fourth time in connection with the philosophy of civilization. W. P.] is the fault of Aristotle. How often have I cursed the hour in which I first read the section of his *Metaphysics* in which he develops the problem of philosophy out of a criticism of previous philosophizing! Something which slumbered within me then awoke. Again and again since then have I experienced within me the urge to try to grasp the nature of a problem not only as it is in itself but also by the way in which it unfolds itself in the course of history.'[2] This method gives Schweitzer both scholarly and artistic satisfaction.

The *Geschichte der Paulinischen Forschung* (*Paul and his Interpreters*) was first published in 1911, and its preface announced the imminent publication of the main work *Mystik des Apostels Paulus* (*The Mysticism of Paul the Apostle*). But in 1913 he left for Africa. The money for the journey and for the founding of his hospital had to be raised somehow, and one of the ways was by giving concerts. Schweitzer completed the revision of his history of the investigations into the life of Jesus whilst he was already packing for his journey. 1913 to 1917 were the first years in the African jungle. Then the First World War put a temporary end to his work in Africa and incarcerated him in an internment camp in France (1917–18). After release came a serious illness in Alsace as a result of dysentery, which made two operations necessary. When he recovered he was penniless and he started again as an assistant at Strassburg Hospital (Bürgerspital), whilst simultaneously serving as locum tenens at St Nikolai, where

5. Schweitzer the builder
(By permission of Erica Anderson, New York)

for a while after the armistice he was without any help. The years 1920–23 were filled with journeys, lectures and organ recitals, and, above all, preparations for reopening his hospital at Lambaréné. His philosophy of civilization was presented in lectures at Uppsala, and in this period his Pauline investigations receded into the background. By 1924 he was able to go to Africa again and open his hospital on a bigger scale than before. By 1927 he was in a position to pay a visit to Europe, but it was filled with concert and lecture tours in Sweden and Denmark, Holland and England, Switzerland, Germany and Czechoslovakia in order to raise funds for his work in Africa. New doctors and nurses had to be recruited, and even during his absence he did not relinquish control over the hospital. Yet despite all this work, this period saw the completion of his *Mysticism of Paul the Apostle*, a work of 407 pages. The last chapter was written on the return voyage, on board ship travelling from Bordeaux to Cape Lopez, at the end of 1929. The author's preface was written on the river steamer which took the jungle doctor up the River Ogowe to Lambaréné, i.e. in the last few hours before the jungle swallowed him up once more.

It is clear that this was an act of obedience to an inner necessity. Schweitzer was now fifty-five years old, and his resignation from the *civitas academica* lay far behind him. He was no longer in its service, and the struggle against human suffering now occupied his time. Accordingly his spiritual productivity now changed direction and the development of his ethic of reverence for life was the result. In this connection he had felt as long ago as 1919 a desire to examine the world religions, and in particular Chinese and Indian thought, to discover their ethical content. The determination with which he nevertheless completed his Pauline research is therefore all the more remarkable. The impelling force was a double one: it was both scholarly and personal.

First of all it was the fulfilment of an obligation he had imposed on himself as a young student—and we already know the binding force of those early decisions! During his student days Schweitzer had decided to interpret the spiritual development of Christianity in its early stages on the assumption that the teaching of Jesus on the Kingdom of God was completely eschatological and that it was understood as such by those who heard it.

His own investigations into the life of Jesus sought to prove the eschatological character of the teachings. But 'anyone who deals with the teachings and life and work of Jesus, and offers any kind of new reading of it, ought not to stop there, but must be held under obligation to trace from the standpoint at which he has arrived, the pathway leading to the history of dogma. Only in this way can it be clearly shown what his discovery is worth.'[3] Schweitzer's Pauline research was therefore not an end in itself; he owed it to his quest for Jesus.

Since Strauss and Renan, no one who had occupied himself with the life of Jesus had felt such a necessity. Scholarship had arranged the history of spiritual development in early Christianity into neat compartments: the life of Jesus, the Apostolic Era, and the History of Dogma. Even with Harnack the history of dogma began only after Paul. The master of dogmatic historical research comes to the conclusion that there is no bridge leading from the Pauline teachings to the beliefs of the early Christian Church.

As against this, Schweitzer proceeds from three fundamental theses: Pauline teaching belongs to the history of dogma, because its formation begins immediately after the death of Jesus.

The Apostle of the Gentiles did not develop his system from the teachings of Jesus, and it stands towards the latter as something completely on its own. It is a re-creation of the Christian idea.

The question of the Hellenization of Christianity represents the basic problem of the history of dogma. The apostle did not hellenize Christianity. His ideas are different from those of Greek philosophy and the Greek mysteries. Pauline Christianity and the Greek philosophers have a religious language in common, but not ideas. Paul belongs to early Christianity. His teachings are to be understood exclusively from Jewish early Christian thought. But in his eschatological mysticism of the being in Christ he gave Christianity a form in which it could be hellenized.

Schweitzer begins by examining previous Pauline research, intending it as the introductory chapter to his *Mysticism of Paul the Apostle*. This investigation of the history of scholarly interpretation of the epistles of St. Paul particularly attracted him because it had not been done before. The chapter developed into a book. A brilliant analyst once again had an opportunity of trying out his abilities on a great subject. His work is all the more valuable because it summarizes a literature which is not only difficult to obtain, but is available only to very few on account of its vast extent; because it brings order into chaos—the situation he found was no less—and arranges the material according to subjects; and because it communicates the essential results of the works it deals with. When the *Mysticism* was first published, the preface promised an extended second edition to include the literature published in the past twenty years. It is impossible to read this promise without being moved. At the time, in 1929, Schweitzer had not realized that in the future he would be unable to carry on any such specialized scholarly work, or indeed any theological work at all which was not imposed on him by a higher necessity. The second edition, which appeared in 1933, was unchanged.

The main work also ran into a second, unchanged, edition as late as 1954. Scholarship tends to withdraw if it is disturbed. The publication of *The Quest of the historical Jesus* created a sensation. It brilliantly illuminated a theological sphere which had long attracted lively interest both inside and beyond specialist circles. It was the history of a movement whose aim was to reveal the historical Jesus. A great part of the literature involved was written for a wider public. People were prepared to tolerate the 'logical eschatological solution' even though they rejected it, and even though the whole presentation was directed towards it, but with the Pauline research the situation was different. It dealt with a specialized problem of scholarship which went beyond the understanding and—despite its importance for Christian thought—interest of the non-theological reader.

Paul is a theologian. The teaching of the Apostle of the Gentiles was developed in dispute with Jewish Christianity, and it bears the mark of a theological situation which is unknown to a present-day Christian and does not affect him. Paul's teaching is made still more difficult to understand because, according to Schweitzer, it has a double aspect: a juridical aspect based on the idea of justification, and an ethical aspect dominated by the idea of salvation. And, for Protestant Christians, it is still further complicated by Reformation exegesis, which fought and was victorious in Paul's name. It put its own ideas into Paul's teaching and received them back equipped with apostolic authority. The doctrine of righteousness by faith was central for Luther but for Schweitzer it is only 'a subsidiary crater, which has formed within the rim of the main crater—the mystical doctrine of redemption through the being-in-Christ'.[4] It is 'the fragment of a redemption doctrine', although it became the most effective part of the teachings of Paul. Paul needed this 'subsidiary doctrine' in order to deal with the law through the scriptural evidence from the standpoint of the traditional idea of the atonement. He preached freedom from the Jewish law and its works, not the unimportance of good works as such. He is not worried because justification by belief cannot logically arrive at an ethic, since in his mystique the ethic is naturally associated with the idea of the forgiveness of sins and the Atonement in general.

These few indications will suffice to convey some idea of the difficulty and complication of the subject. To attempt to explain in a few pages the problems themselves, and how Schweitzer dealt with them, to anyone not already well versed in the subject-matter would be hopeless. Summaries with the use of numerous quotations have already been attempted more than once, and the prospect of attempting another one is not attractive. Statements are made and no proof is provided, and even then their scope and bearing cannot be understood without a detailed knowledge of the epistles of St Paul and their effect on two thousand years of Christian thought. Interested readers will find a summary of Schweitzer's Pauline investigations in his own autobiographical work *My Life and Thought*. The theologian will have to consult the sources and judge for himself. Further, what Schweitzer said of the Pauline investigations of the 'Ultra-Tübinger' group is true of his own work: even if his hypothesis were proved untenable 'this is by no means to get rid of it, as accredited theology wished to persuade itself. A few squadrons of cavalry which were skirmishing in the open have been cut off. The fortress has not been taken, indeed the siege has not even been laid.'[5]

Schweitzer's Pauline investigations are a direct continuation of his investigations into the life of Jesus. Both have the same broad perspective, the same logical consistency, the same freedom from theological prejudices, the same determination to resist modernizing tendencies, the same knowledge of all the methods, both right and wrong, of previous research, and in consequence the same incisive formulation of the problems involved. And in each case the 'solution' has the same radical exclusiveness and at the same time indicates a certain family likeness of the hero with Schweitzer. 'The unfamiliar, abstruse, systematizing, antinomist, predestined' are seen as characteristic of the early apostolic Pauline. But how easy it all is for an investigator to accept when at the same time he discovers so many characteristics related to his own nature!

After only a few hours' stay with the then eighty-three-year-old a visitor to Lambaréné came away with the impression that Jesus and Paul were the two figures to which his attention and thought were directed. All his life they had been his guiding stars, showing him the way and shining down on him. Jesus is the Lord and Master to whom one hardly dares to raise one's eyes. But to Paul a relationship is established which, with all due respect, one can only term intimate. This is the second pillar which supports Schweitzer's Christianity, a Christianity which, with all the insistent stressing of the fundamental importance of the act of thought, is very personally based. He himself bears witness to this in the second of a series of sermons on St Paul delivered at St Nicolai Church and reproduced in the appendix. Paul is the 'Christian brother who is at our side when we are heavy burdened and despairing . . . who takes us by the hand . . . and frees us from those things which oppress us, making us serene and happy'.

And how sympathetic Schweitzer finds Paul's liturgical simplicity![6] Is it not reflected in Schweitzer's own religious services, which eschew 'all solemn apparatus'?

Paul's religion: 'His faith, hope, and fear all revolve about one centre: the abolition of corruption and the bestowal of incorruption. His religion is a "will to live" in a large elemental sense.'[7] And thus a bridge to Schweitzer's own vitalistic definition of human existence is built: 'I am life which wills to live, in the midst of life which wills to live.'

And then: Paul is the patron of freedom of thought. 'In Paul, the first Christian thinker set himself against the authority of the Church, and shared the fate of those who have since made the attempt.'[8] The age has changed, and therefore the teachings of Jesus are no longer authoritative, so Paul is compelled to stand creatively beside Jesus. He does not fall away from Jesus, but merely develops his teachings. As far as possible he avoids bringing forward anything from the Gospel of Jesus—even avoiding all mention of it. Where he frees himself from the authority of the historical Jesus he appeals to the idea of spiritual revelation. Because he is spiritually inspired direct from Christ, he can ignore the traditional teachings of Jesus of Nazareth. 'Paul vindicated for all time the rights of thought in Christianity. Above belief which drew its authority from tradition, he set the knowledge which comes from the spirit of Christ. There lives in him an unbounded and undeviating reverence for truth. He will consent to a limitation of liberty only if it is laid on him by the law of love, not imposed by doctrinal authority.'[9] Thus Schweitzer is able to appeal to the authority of Paul in his struggle for truthfulness in religious thought, for he believes that 'the truth which came into the world with Jesus did not immediately possess its full spiritual stature, but developed it only in the course of time under the influence of the spirit of Jesus'.[10]

The moralist Schweitzer also finds his confirmation in Paul. Paul's teaching of freedom from the law clears the way for the inherent urge of eschatology towards a direct and absolute ethic, such as the Baptist and Jesus both demanded. His messianic-eschatological mysticism is an expression *per se* of religious mysticism which has penetrated to the living truth. Through it we experience that engrossment in the love of God which seeks to fulfil itself in us. 'The messianic eschatological world-view is an overcoming of dualism, arrived at by bold and vigorous thinking through the victorious arising, within the belief in the infinitely enigmatic Creator God, of a belief in the God of love.'[11] Pauline theology is thus brought into harmony with the ethic of reverence for life.

For Schweitzer, to believe in the Gospel means to make the belief in the Kingdom proclaimed by Jesus live in the belief in him and in the salvation experienced in him. But it was Paul in his Christ mysticism who first fulfilled this. His achievement is that he formulated the evangelical, early Christian belief in salvation through Christ, in the coming of the Kingdom, and in the belief in Jesus as the future Messiah 'and thinks it out so thoroughly that it becomes freed from its temporal limitations and becomes valid for all time.' With his Christ mysticism Paul 'thus solves in a definitive fashion that pressing problem of the Christian faith, namely, that although Jesus Christ has come His Kingdom is still delayed. He does not admit that, because God has tried us by not causing them to coincide temporarily, the two events are no longer to be connected practically in Christian belief; but he makes Christian belief capable of holding together in thought in their original integral connexion, these two realities which have become separated in time.'[12] Thus the belief in the Kingdom of God, in the overcoming of the spirit of this world by the spirit of God, which is an uncompromising article of faith for the 'Agnostic' Schweitzer, and the thing from which this champion of Christ draws his unshakable confidence, is rooted in the teachings of Paul.

But the greatest achievement of this 'greatest teacher of all times' is that he comprehends the essence of being a Christian in the experience of communion with Christ. With Paul, Schweitzer regards Christianity as the Christ mysticism; that is to say, as communion with Christ as our Lord and Master, comprehended in thought and realized in experience. 'By simply designating Jesus "our Lord", Paul raises Him above all the temporarily conditioned conceptions in which the mystery of his personality might be grasped, and sets him forth as the spiritual Being who transcends all human definition, to whom we have to surrender ourselves in order to experience in Him the true law of our existence and our being.'[13] God mystique as direct identification with the infinite creative will of God is impossible. Because Paul contents himself with seeing the father relation with

God as fulfilled in communion with Christ, without trying to make this relationship a being in God, his mystique towers above the waves of eternity like a beacon based on the firm foundation of the historical phenomenon of Jesus Christ. 'Paul leads us out upon that path of true redemption, and hands us over, prisoners, to Christ.'[14]

Thus it is not merely that Schweitzer finds his theology confirmed in Paul: he is at one with him in the most profound communion, through the oneness in Christ.

V

ETHICS

Schweitzer the theologian, with whom we have been dealing thus far, is not interested in publicity. His Jesus and Paul investigations are primarily a matter of theology, however great the significance he may attach to them for the promulgation of the Christian Gospel. But, as we have already seen, he feels that theology should behave with proper restraint. It should leave mankind alone with the words of Jesus. In order to know and understand them man needs no learned leading strings—and this is the purpose of his own 'negative' theology. But if Schweitzer's theological-scholarly achievement is presented to a wider circle here, it is because the significance and the spiritual standpoint of the personality as a whole could not be shown in any other way, particularly as research and belief, scholarship and religious experience are indissolubly connected in him. He is present *in persona* in his scholarly writings to an extent which is regarded as positively improper in the scholarly world. His research bears the stamp of action, and therefore the translation to the active sphere appears as the practical realization of his New Testament studies, and by the same token as something quite natural. The same nature is at work here as there, and if one wishes to see it whole then one must also visit Schweitzer in his professorial workshop. On his part he has never made any effort to secure a wider popularity for his theological thought. The fact that he has avoided any discussion of his theses even in academic circles may perhaps be explained by his belief in the inherent life of the idea; more profoundly formulated by his belief in the spirit. Although he was always happy to stand in the pulpit he has never published any of his sermons, though at one time there was some idea of summarizing the gist of his sermons to the congregation of St Nicolai. Like a good many other things, this plan was never carried out. When he left Europe for the African jungle it was with the intention of remaining silent. The command of the Lord required no explanation; its execution no words.

But now something surprising happened: the elementary need to proclaim his ideas found its satisfaction outside theology. After confining himself for a number of years to teaching a small group of Negroes about the Gospel of Jesus, Schweitzer suddenly turned 'to all'. It was no longer a question of quietly influencing the individual soul (though the moral perfection of the individual is still the ultimate aim of human civilization) or of serving his neighbour in the silent obedience of unconditional discipleship. The man who was temporarily driven out of Africa by the First World War now entered the University forum at Uppsala (1920) and there announced an ethical teaching in words which were directed to all mankind. An audience of millions was not only desirable for this teaching; it necessarily presupposed it, because 'only what has been well turned over in the thought' of the many, and thus recognized as truth, possesses a natural power of conviction which will work on other minds, and will continue to be effective. Only where there is a constant appeal to the need of a reflective view of things are all man's spiritual capacities called into activity. . . . All real progress in the world is in the last analysis produced by rationalism.'[1] The aim here is nothing less that the destiny of man, who is to be guided towards it by 'constant appeal'. Its universality brooks no limitations imposed by a traditional doctrine. Free thought wishes to make Christianity available to 'modern' man, but Christian teaching is no longer the point. It is not the Christian who is appealed to, but the thinking man, or at least the man who must be made to think. The spirit speaks and what it says is 'intellectually necessary'. Its acceptance must therefore be expected of everyone who makes proper use of his capacity to think. It is unconditionally valid. The universality of this teaching is in accordance with its claim to absolute validity. The heritage of the Enlightenment, which, with reservations, determines Schweitzer's theology, becomes active in his belief in reasoning thought and in his missionary zeal. Here it is released from the inhibitions which the obligations of piety, the influence of the great teachers of Christianity, and his own religious experience impose on him in the sphere of theology. Here it can let itself go in sublime unconcern without becoming aware of the anachronism of the undertaking and the tension between religious and philosophical thought.

It was clear from the beginning that a tremendous amount of

combustible material was accumulated in this elemental personality, but at the same time it seemed likely that after being used up in so many different directions towards the end of his stay in Europe, the 'way of direct service to mankind' which the young man had planned, and which had led the mature man out of his profession and out of his normal world, would lead him into quiescence if not anonymity.

There is no doubt that when Schweitzer first went to Africa he had nothing else in mind than this: to alleviate pain anonymously in some out of the way place. And we shall see how modestly the work was begun. Contact between Europe and this outpost of humanity was maintained only to the extent the work itself required. Nothing was farther from his thought than to turn it into a symbol, or to set himself up as an example. No outward effect, either direct or indirect, was ever planned. But hardly had the prohibition of his work in the hospital led to enforced inactivity—at the outbreak of the First World War Schweitzer was treated as a prisoner and placed in the custody of coloured soldiers—than an outburst of pent-up spiritual energy took place. He wanted to return to his work on Paul, whose first draft had been completed in 1906. But then a part of his nature which had previously affected him only in quiet thought, took hold of him. He 'felt to the quick the fate of our time and the anxiety for humanity'.[2] The injunction to alleviate the sufferings of his 'neighbour' remained in force, but now 'humanity' appeared beside it and called for action.

It has been suggested that at this point there was a break in the continuity of Schweitzer's spiritual and mental tenor, and there is something in this suggestion. But in so far as the elements of his ethical-philosophical thought were always part of his nature there was certainly no break. His will never changed its direction; and 'the Lord' was never dethroned in his consciousness. However, the ethico-philosophical purpose and activity which now primarily occupied him did nevertheless involve a certain break—in fact to a greater extent than Schweitzer himself altogether realized. From this moment on the structure of a life determined solely by direct service as a follower of Jesus underwent a change. Under the pressure of tremendous contemporary suffering which beset him from within and without and brought his work of mercy to a temporary end, the jungle doctor now raised his voice and the whole world was compelled to listen. As a man himself hard hit by fate, he emerged from his solitude as a missionary of humaneness, to challenge the times, whose inhuman characteristics he had recognized even before the old order sank finally into ruins. From now on his mission was a double one. And for one who has once taken such a step there is no way back into solitude. Criticism of civilization; the apostolate of reverence for life; involvement in the apparatus of public activity; the burdensome demands of unsought fame; the Nobel peace prize; the struggle against atomic warfare—it was a progression inevitably set in motion in those days of August 1914 by that step out of the closed and protected circle of Samaritan activity: by Schweitzer's expulsion from the sphere of independent charity untouched by world events and subject to no worldly authority. The consequences were immeasurable. An existence based on spirituality believed it had cut itself off once and for all from a reality which was loathsome to it, to enter into the peace and freedom of unquestioning obedience, changing its name for that of the 'Lord', and renouncing all personal life and happiness. And now, suddenly, overnight, it was caught up in this same reality by an injunction which neither mind, nor heart nor conscience could withstand. The new burden was taken up without a moment's hesitation, but with it the whole background of life was changed. The heroic programme laid down by the twenty-one-year-old was certainly not abandoned, but it lost its exclusiveness. Schweitzer stepped on to the world stage. And when after the passing of a good few years it became possible to re-establish the work in the jungle, this too—how could it be otherwise?—was different in many respects. Aim and methods remained the same, but the growth of a philosophic superstructure destroyed its former seclusion. Something which had been an aim in itself now became a symbol. The verbal proclamation of a new ethic was followed by its practical application. The jungle seclusion, which had originally determined the form of humble service, now offered a possibility for demonstrating, if not actually realizing, the required ethical attitude in a borderline case of human existence. These unexpected results were brought about by a decision which at first looked like no more than an obvious re-disposition of a working programme. Schweitzer himself tells us about it unemotionally. There are moments when an inscrutable fate mixes the cards however much we may believe ourselves to be the masters of our fate.

The 'Problem of our civilization suddenly made urgent by the fact of war' pushed theology to one side. 'So on the second day of my internment, still quite amazed at being able to sit down at my writing table early in the morning as in the days before I took up medicine, I set to work on the philosophy of civilization.'[3] Thus the war, which began the decline of the west and exposed the brittleness of its cultural ideals, gave the direct impulse to the development of Schweitzer's philosophy of civilization. The poison produced the antidote. . . .

How did this man, whom friends, misunderstanding his motives, had accused of deserting human civilization, come to take such a decision? We turn once again to the biography and discover that the student who was passionately interested in the problems of theological research was at the same time no less passionately interested in the fate of human culture.

No sooner did independent thought begin than Schweitzer found himself anxiously participating in the condition of the world. Before long his participation was given an objective basis.

Schweitzer has always regarded his interest in public affairs as a heritage from his mother. When he was going to school in Mülhausen—he was living there with an uncle—he eagerly used the quarter of an hour before the evening meal (it was the only time available to him) to read the newspapers. To a reproach that he seemed interested only in shallow journalism he answered that in fact what he was really interested in was contemporary history. Whereupon his uncle questioned him concerning the princes at that time on the Balkan thrones, and their premiers. He had to give the composition of the last three French Cabinets, and finally the gist of the last speech of Eugen Richter in the Reichstag. The eleven-year-old boy passed the examination with flying colours. This inborn sense for contemporary affairs has remained with him throughout his life, although any discussion about politics has always been forbidden in the jungle hospital. At the end of his career—he was eighty-two years old at the time and staying in Günsbach—when his leisure for completing works he had actually started in his own field was limited enough, he took pleasure in the careful preparation of a never delivered speech on Pétain. Without this exceptionally lively interest in questions of public life, it would be difficult to understand why the youth should have been so moved at its decline. It is an interest rooted in the importance Schweitzer has always attached to human civilization, in the cultural enthusiasm of the Enlightenment, and in the general tradition, dominated by cultural ideals, of the German Protestant parsonage in which he grew up.

The landslide which was ultimately to shake the conscience of the world was let loose by a word. It was uttered at an evening meeting of scholars—Herman Grimm was also present—in the house of the widow of Ernst Curtius, Professor of Archaeology (*Altertumskunde*, which combined archaeology and the history of antiquity into one subject) in Berlin. 'We are all of us just nothing but epigones', someone said. 'We are just living on a great past!' This remark, probably made with no great seriousness, struck 'like a flash of lightning' into the heart of a young man who was sitting there quietly listening.

Schweitzer tells us[4] 'As early as my first years at the university I had begun to feel misgivings about the opinion that mankind is constantly developing in the direction of progress. My impression was that the fire of its ideals was already burning low without anyone noticing it, or troubling about it. On a number of occasions I had to acknowledge that public opinion did not reject with indignation inhumane ideas which were publicly disseminated, but accepted them, and that it approved of, as opportune, inhumane courses of action taken by governments and nations. Even for what was just and expedient as well there seemed to me to be only a luke-warm zeal available. From a number of signs I had to infer the growth of a peculiar intellectual and spiritual fatigue in this generation which is so proud of what it has accomplished. . . . When about the end of the century men began to take a retrospective view of every field of human activity in order to determine and fix the value of their achievements, this was done with an optimism which to me was incomprehensible. It seemed to me assumed everywhere not only that we had made progress in inventions and knowledge, but also that in the intellectual and ethical spheres we lived and moved at a height which we had never before reached, and from which we should never decline. My own impression was that in our mental and spiritual life we were not only below the level of past generations, but were in many respects only living on their achievements . . . and that not a little of this heritage was beginning to melt away in our hands.' A lively ethical consciousness reacted to the time, weighed it and found it wanting. Schweitzer was now impelled to examine this deeply disturbing state of affairs and bring it to the consciousness of the general public, so, soon after that evening in the house of Curtius, we find him engaged on a work which he entitled *Wir Epigonen* (*The Inheritors*). 'I often put before friends the thoughts contained in it, but they usually took them just as interesting paradoxes and manifestations of a *fin-de-siècle* pessimism. After that I kept my ideas strictly to myself, and only in my sermons allowed my doubts about our civilization and our spirituality to find expression.' But now the expected catastrophe had come about, and the need to become clear about its ultimate causes was peremptory. The first part of the *Philosophy of Civilization* was therefore given the title 'The Decay and the Restoration of Civilization'. For the first time

Schweitzer appears before the world as a philosopher, communicating very briefly his ideas on the significance of life and the destiny of man.

This introduction to the *Philosophy of Civilization* should have been sensational for those who had followed his development up to then—even though he had already accustomed them to surprises. It should have told them that with his first appearance as an independent thinker this exemplary follower of Jesus had abandoned the specifically Christian outlook on the world and on life—not by any rejection of dogmas but by freeing himself from the scale of values set up by a Christian interpretation of Creation. But no one noticed it; an omission which can be explained only by the fact, which the English critic John Middleton Murry was the first to point out, that people did not understand him. Murry protests indignantly at the 'unworthy and intolerable situation that we, while professing an immense admiration for the actual deeds of Schweitzer, should virtually ignore his thought which, to himself at least, is homogeneous with his acts'.[5]

This is hardly saying too much. Apart from one or two specialized investigations, the tension between Christian theology and ethical philosophy passes almost unnoticed. No one takes exception to it. Books about Schweitzer are accustomed to accepting both side by side, without bothering very much about this parallelism. But this can only happen because too little importance is paid to his thought.

Once a man has passed his fortieth year his ancestors seek to take control of him. This frequent observation is confirmed in Schweitzer. The Enlightenment spirit of grandfather Schillinger, of whom there is some talk in the early reminiscences, gets the upper hand. The idea that the important thing is the progress of mankind, and that this must be obtained by the triumph of what is conformable to reason, begins to take precedence.

The criticism of human civilization in the narrower sense, the enumeration of the 'anti-cultural circumstances in our economic and intellectual life' are to the point, and they have the vigour of all Schweitzer's utterances. He records the lack of independence, the lack of balance, the inability to concentrate, and the inhumanity of modern man. The prognosis is not favourable, provided there is no change. It was certainly worth while to bring these considerations to the notice of the contemporary world once again, but coming after the great critics of the age, Jakob Burckhardt, Nietzsche, Stefan George and others, it was neither new nor original—not that anything of the sort had been Schweitzer's aim. Every observant critic clearly recognized the sure signs of cultural decline, and an awareness of it necessarily arose wherever the idea of a humanity freely developing according to moral laws was still upheld. Here too Schweitzer certainly justified himself as a keen analyst, but to describe him, as has been done, as 'probably the most gifted genius of our age, as well as its most prophetic thinker'[6] is a misjudgement. His work is not prophetic and it is not intended to be. Dealing with the approaching disaster it conveys only an abstract idea of 'self-destroying civilization', whereas others have been more trenchant concerning the approaching age of world wars, the dominance of the '*terribles simplificateurs*' (Jacob Burckhardt), and the bureaucratization and admassing of social life (Alfred Weber, Ortega y Gasset).

But Schweitzer's world of ideas comes into its own when first the causes of the decline have to be determined, and then a way to the regeneration of human civilization has to be found. The mode of thought is that of the eighteenth century, and the anachronism is all the more obvious because the life and death of the modern world is at stake. The symptoms of the disease are sharply observed, but there is no real approach to the forces working under the surface and determining it both for good and evil, to its daemonism or to its future promise. The voice is never raised, and yet in its profound anxiety it is very moving, but it talks as though from the remote jungle to a time which is pregnant with great death and great birth, a time which cannot be approached with the formulas of the past which he uses without any feeling for their incongruity. The result is an oversimplified and wholly negative summary, which is then placed against the categorical imperative of ethical behaviour. From what sources of energy this is to feed it is not easy to say. Schweitzer's criticism of civilization amounts merely to a challenge of alternatives, and 'either, or', but it neither shows the profundity of the danger—surely something more than and different from the fate of human civilization is at stake?—nor finds contact with what is developing and emerging into the light from under the ruins.

Civilization is defined as 'progress', 'material and spiritual progress on the part of the individual as of the mass'. In other words, as 'the development of man to a state of higher organization and a higher moral standard'.[7] It presupposes the co-operation of two forms of progress: an increasing mastery over the forces of nature and a mastery of reason over human ideas in order to prevent the harnessing of natural forces from being used to intensify the struggle for existence. Now this struggle for existence must be abated in order to create 'the most favourable conditions of life', and this is to be achieved by correspondingly increasing 'the mastery of reason over nature and human nature to the utmost possible extent'. The objective here is 'the intellectual and moral perfection of the individual', which is the ultimate aim of human civilization. Reason as such is thus ethically determined. Its mastery of human ideas will express itself 'in the willingness of the individual and of society to allow their aims to be determined by the material and spiritual well-being of the many, that is to say, in their being ethical'.

With the Enlightenment movement the age of culture seemed 'definitely to have dawned'. Rationalism had set up ethical ideas based on reason, and they had begun to affect and change reality by influencing both philosophy and public opinion. At this point it should be remembered that all western social philosophy secularizes theological motives, and this is also true of those humanitarian ethical ideals which were adopted by the Enlightenment movement, and thus do not have their origin in reason. Towards the middle of the nineteenth century this battle of reasoned ethical ideas with reality began to lose momentum. 'Civilization abdicated silently and without a struggle.'

Whose fault was it? In that golden age of civilization philosophy 'produced a vigorous popular ideology which dominated public opinion and encouraged an enthusiasm for culture'. But in the long run this 'optimistic-ethical total ideology' or '*Weltanschauung*' could not stand up to the criticism of logical thought. Kant did his best to shore up the tottering edifice by reforming the ideology of rationalism to satisfy the requirements of a more profound theory of thought. By speculative means Fichte, Hegel, and other philosophers who upheld the reasoned ethical ideals of rationalism now sought to find a basis for a suitable optimistic-ethical total ideology. But the natural sciences, which had in the meantime grown stronger, revolted indignantly and destroyed the splendid edifices of philosophic idealism which fantasy had erected. 'Since then those reasoned ethical ideals on which culture is based, wander around the world homeless and poverty-stricken. . . .' And instead of this elementary wrestling with reality we have a well-meaning historical understanding of the given facts.

Here, therefore, is the position from which Schweitzer's philosophy of civilization sets out. This expression of a superbly confident and at the same time profoundly conscientious thought is impressive, though one is conscious of an ice-cold breath of spiritual isolation in those

6. On the way to visit the sick
(By permission of Erica Anderson, New York)

pages. How much of practical reality is there in his thought and how much of historical truth?

When the theologian Schweitzer rejected historicism he was more than merely right; he ended a period of New Testament research which had outlived its usefulness. But now that the historically based facts of civilization are at stake, the inability of the Enlightenment to think historically obscures the judgement. He remains caught up in the traditional outlook of liberal culture centred on the rational man from whose scientific mastery of nature, and from whose moral self-control, the creation of the good human society was expected. The 'moralistic' (Schweitzer's own word) conception of culture as a progressive realization of ethical ideas makes it impossible to think realistically about civilization and prevents any proper estimate of the practical civilizatory achievements of humanity. Thus those highly developed civilizations which were not interested in realizing reasoned ethical ideals and providing favourable living conditions for all—this is Schweitzer's conception of the ideal of Enlightenment philosophy: the greatest happiness for the greatest number—are not only unappreciated, but, like the whole Middle Ages, they are not taken into consideration. Thus whole periods of civilization which were far in advance of the eighteenth century not only in civilizatory activity, but also—which is not necessarily the same thing—in raising general standards of morality, are not recognized as creative in a civilizatory sense at all. And thus the question of whether an abatement of the struggle for existence really leads to an increase of those energies which create civilization is not felt as a problem. Similarly there is a failure to notice that the much praised 'age of civilization', which, according to Schweitzer, extends from approximately the first half of the eighteenth century to the middle of the nineteenth, saw, with the French Revolution and the Napoleonic Wars, outbreaks of irrational violence, and in consequence manifestations of inhumanity coupled with the destruction of cultural values, hardly paralleled in Western history since the early Middle Ages. The interesting thing about this period is that whilst it witnessed the maturing of ideas which had become due, the historical process itself was not in the least affected but continued to follow those impulses which have always determined it. Thus in the heyday of this enlightened popular philosophy, society was aware only of 'what could be comprehended and recorded in figures, patterns, rules and forms'.[8] And history was nothing but a museum of the plainly good and the plainly bad. This moralizing attitude towards public life proved just as incapable of understanding history as it was (with the exception of certain social reforms) of influencing it. Whenever matters important enough to affect history were concerned, amoral elemental forces tipped the scale. And they lay outside the scope of the Enlightenment movement. But where such things are ignored there is a danger that history, and therefore cultural history also, is interpreted by ideas and not by real happenings and their background.

According to the outlook of the Enlightenment movement, which Schweitzer adopts, a thinking ideology must be optimistic and adopt a positive attitude towards life in order to serve as a basis for cultural ideas and opinions. Now the attitude of the Middle Ages 'is fundamentally world and life negating because the interest of that stage of Christianity was concentrated on a super-sensible world'.[9] Thus the Middle Ages were hostile to human civilization except in so far as a positive attitude towards this world and towards life did nevertheless express itself. Where this was so it was due in part to the active ethics preached by Jesus, and in part to the creative forces of still vigorous peoples on whom Christianity imposed an outlook contrary to their true nature.

With the Renaissance arose a positive attitude to this world and to life, which was instinctively present in the peoples formed by the great migrations. It took on an ethical character by adopting the ethics of love preached by Jesus, which were thus joined to this positive attitude to the world and to life, and in this way the ideal of the realization of a spiritual-ethical world in the natural world developed. 'In modern times, under the influence of the Renaissance, the Reformation and the Age of Enlightenment, Christianity laid aside the world and life denial which clung to it as a survival from the primitive Christian expectation of the end of the world, and allowed room within itself for world- and life-affirmation. It thus changed into a religion which could work for a realization of civilization.'[10]

This interpretation of Western civilization, which regards the Middle Ages, for whose outlook 'Jesus is partly responsible', as bad and deplorable,[11] reflects the conflict between Christianity and enlightened thought. It is not resolved by the spiritual attitude Schweitzer adopts and the reconciliation is not even attempted. There are, in fact, no indications that it is even regarded as a problem at all. The obvious efforts to force the divergent elements of this ideology into a unified whole were subjectively successful. The idea of inner confusion, or doubt about convictions once arrived at, cannot be reconciled with Schweitzer's personality. To call them into question, though it might be helpful to others, would destroy Schweitzer. To lose the results of his thought would make him a Samson shorn of his locks; his strength would ebb away. He was spared this at least, because the spirit guides him with somnambulistic certainty, allowing him to skirt precipices. But objectively his submission to the 'follow thou me' of a Jesus who commands[12] cannot be reconciled with the idea of Jesus as seen by the dogmatism of enlightened historical interpretation, a Jesus who is also responsible for bad and deplorable things. The contradiction could be resolved even on the basis of cultural enthusiasm if the view of the facts were not barred by a preconceived judgement.

Mediaeval Catholicism developed a homogeneous ideology. On the basis of natural law this ideology produced a highly-developed social and political doctrine involving direct injunctions and impulses for political, social and cultural policy. They are the results of a Christian thought which in the consciousness of its mission to Christianize the world, embraces all spheres of life. Thus neither (in the negative sense) the conviction of the ultimate worthlessness of mortal and worldly things, not (in a positive sense) a 'nevertheless' effective influence of the 'active' ethics of Jesus, that is to say an influence directed towards world betterment, nor the effect of pagan influences favourable to life, were decisive for the civilization of this Christian aeon of Western history.

The civilization of the Western world which—remember the early history of the monasteries—tamed souls and caused cathedrals to rise up from the virgin soil, was a process of fructification. Something more profound and more embracing than the acceptance of an ethical teaching is involved. The process manifests itself as a creative one not merely by a change in behaviour, but by a change in being itself. This conquest of 'the still vigorous peoples' by the totality of a Christian spirit embracing all spheres of existence, and rebutting the objection of alienation by its own creative power, released a positively tumultuous development of human civilization such as has never been seen since. Its driving force was the firm belief that man was created by God for God and should therefore bear witness to God in his life and work. The civilizatory history of the Middle Ages shows that an acceptance of the nature of this earthly life as essentially provisional did not tone down its enthusiasm for the ennoblement of existence in this world; indeed, its relationship to God even heightened that enthusiasm.

Because he failed to recognize the cultural creative force of Christianity in its historical continuity, Schweitzer saw no reason to refer in any way to the existence of Jesus or of Christianity when discussing the decay and restoration of civilization.

How can the decay of civilization be arrested, and civilization be restored? By a thinking ideology, one world view. 'The Reconstruction of our age, then, can begin only with a reconstruction of the world view', and this is to be 'based on thought and only on thought'. 'It is true that the intellectual productions of the period which we designate historically as the Rationalistic are incomplete and unsatisfactory, but the principle, which was then established, of basing our views of the universe on thought and thought alone, is valid for all time. Even if the tree's earliest fruit did not ripen perfectly, the tree itself remains, nevertheless, the tree of life for the life of our spirit.' 'At that time, from the educated down to the uneducated, belief in truth and a respect for truthfulness prevailed.' 'For this reason alone that age stood higher than any age before it.' And again, only 'what is born of thought and which appeals to thought can become a spiritual power for the whole of humanity'.

Whoever has met Schweitzer and felt the indisputable impression not only of greatness but also of profundity, is at first helpless in the face of such formulas. Cut off from history, from theology, from contemporary philosophy (which in the very year of Schweitzer's *Decay and Restoration of Civilization* is shown by Berdyaev in his *New Middle Ages*[13] to be turning towards life), even from the empirical objectivity of life, such thinking seems to be shackled to the procrustean bed of eighteenth-century Enlightenment and condemned to complete isolation and impoverishment. But by two both astonishing and original steps he succeeds in finding a way out of the aridity of rationalism and making room for that for him vitally necessary minimum of spiritual freedom, and for the acceptance of the essential elements of Christian consciousness.

The first of these two unconscious moves, both inspired by the instinct of self-preservation, is an extension of the conception of 'reasoning thought'. What does Schweitzer mean by reason?

Reason is 'the totality of all the functions of our spirit in their living action and interaction. In it our intellect and our will hold that mysterious intercourse which determines the character of our spiritual being. The ideas about the world it produces contain all that we can feel or imagine about our destiny and that of mankind.'[14] With this Schweitzer cuts himself loose from 'outlived' rationalism. If it is to comprehend life, understanding must ultimately go over into 'thinking experience'. Only in this way can it arrive at a 'profound and elementarily based ideology or world view'. This thinking ideology must be thought out to its ultimate conclusion. But thought thought out to its ultimate conclusion leads 'somewhere and somehow' to a vital mystique that is an intellectual necessity for all men. In this context this statement must suffice. What Schweitzer means becomes clearer when we turn to his own world view. First of all we must realize that in this prelude to his philosophy of civilization Schweitzer immediately feels himself obliged to give this, for him fundamental, conception of reasoning thought an elasticity which allows it to accept every movement of the spirit as an act of thought. From this thought about man, his relation to all living things, and his own destiny, Schweitzer expects the salvation of the world and of the individual, just as even 'the entrance into the super-earthly and eternal . . . takes place through an act of thinking'.[15] But this way of escape is used only in dire need, primarily when an elemental religious experience overfloods the boundaries established by reasoning thought. The basic attitude remains rationalistic. The thinker is fundamentally entitled to bear witness only to 'the absolutely logical experience of thought'.[16]

The second reinsurance relates to the ideology. Schweitzer's cultural ideology is essentially optimistic and ethical. It derives from the optimistic-ethical total ideology of rationalism, except that, unlike this latter, it is 'unfinished'. We need not bother about Schweitzer's frequent terminological vacillations. A little later[17] the difference between a positive and a negative attitude to the world and to life is abandoned in favour of the difference between world and life affirmation, and world and life denial. It is essential for Schweitzer's cultural optimism and his 'active' ethics that one should adopt a positive attitude towards the world and towards life as things of value in themselves. But to produce a 'suitable outlook' for the betterment of the world and human society and 'the will to civilization as a universal will to progress' is not enough.[18] After all, in the last resort ideology—'only mysticism corresponds to the ideal of ideology'—is concerned with 'our spiritual oneness with the infinite being';[19] in other words the attainment of a standpoint which does not deny this world, but does denigrate it. 'It is only in as far as man is purified and liberated from the world by that which he experiences and endures, that he becomes capable of truly ethical action.'[20] One who has gone through the school of Jesus cannot be satisfied with an activist cultural optimism which would accord with Schweitzer's cultural philosophical thought pattern: 'In our own world- and life-affirming world view Christianity is in constant danger of being externalized. The Gospel of Jesus which speaks to us out of an expectation of the end of the world leads us off the highway of busy service for the Kingdom of God on to the foot-path of inwardness and urges us, in spiritual freedom from the world, to seek true strength for working in the spirit of the Kingdom of God.'[21]

Optimism and pessimism—or better, world acceptance and world rejection—are left, as Oskar Krauss has shrewdly noted, in an unresolved tension which reflects that tension which exists in Schweitzer's own soul between these two fundamental conceptions.[22] The clash between them leaves him no peace. On his return to Strassburg at the end of the First World War, when the manuscript of his philosophy of civilization was not available, his mind travelled far and wide in order to discover what the thought of mankind had to say on the point. He set out to discover what Judaism, Christianity, Islam, Zoroastrianism, Brahminism, Buddhism, Hinduism and the religiosity of the Chinese had to say about world affirmation and world rejection, and what their basic ethics were. The results of this study were made known in lectures delivered in the Friends' Meeting House at Selly Oak on Christianity and world religions in 1922, and in his book *Die Weltanschauung der indischen Denker* (*The Ideology of Indian Thinkers*) which appeared in 1935.

This latter publication made no claim to present the results of independent research and study. When Schweitzer left the Western world to go into the African jungle he definitely sacrificed all further possibility of scholarly research, a point which people are inclined to overlook. The *Mysticism of Paul the Apostle*, the only scholarly publication belonging to a later period, was already in draft in 1906. What now seemed important to Schweitzer—he tells us so clearly in his philosophy of civilization—is what is going on in the minds of the many. On this depends the salvation of human civilization, and therefore the salvation of the individual too. And thus with the logical determination which is characteristic of him Schweitzer becomes a popularizer. His book on the ideology of Indian thinkers sets out 'to make this generally understandable to the educated men of our day'. An examination of the religiosity of Chinese thinkers, which got as far as the final revision, and was of a similar nature, was never published.

These two excursions into the sphere of cultural philosophy were allowed to develop into independent books, whereas the promised work on the ideology of reverence for life never gets finished.

This explains two things which have given rise to a good deal of astonished misconception: his passivity towards a grossly indiscreet

Albert Schweitzer propaganda, and his grateful and pleased approval of every form of helpful publicity. In his old age Schweitzer contents himself with the thought that his ideas are now scratching around 'like hens in the barnyard of world thought'. And thus every 'fellow warrior' in spirit is welcome, if only he helps to spread these ideas. This attitude accords with his idea of the task of philosophy.

Intimate contact with the thought of the East deepened the rift in his own 'thinking experience'. In presenting 'the ideology of passivity' Schweitzer does not completely succeed in justifying his own affirmative attitude 'towards the world and towards life' as against this foreign mode of thought.[23] He grants it 'something full of nobility which retains its hold on us' but with which we shall never come to terms. For this ideology of world-rejection and life-rejection 'places the question of the spiritual perfection of man in the centre of all discussion and consideration. It is man's highest task to seek true self-communion, true inwardness, a true ethical outlook and true peace of soul.'[24] Despite all his 'active' ethics, surely this must appear to Schweitzer too as the true destiny of man? Is ethical voluntarism as the only motive of human behaviour in a position to attain 'the spiritual and moral perfection of the individual'? And this for Schweitzer is the ultimate aim of civilization. So he demands that our positive attitude towards the world and towards life should grapple with this negative attitude in order to clarify and intensify itself.[25] The true positive attitude towards life is that which has gone through its opposite, the rejection of life and the world. Ethics is 'a mysterious chord in which life-affirmation and world-affirmation are the key-note and the fifth, life-negation is the third'.[26]

Schweitzer has not made it easy for his readers to get at the background of either his reasoning thought or his optimistic ideology. He stresses the immediate, the passionately approved heritage of the eighteenth century, which he regards—despite all provisos—as his task to preserve and perpetuate, but at the same time he treats the 'real thing' with such embarrassed discretion that a superficial observer might be forgiven for overlooking it altogether. Indeed his absolute honesty and the splendidly naïve frankness of his character, make any concealment impossible. His frankness expresses itself with such spontaneity that now and again it quite alarmingly exposes unsuspected weaknesses, and it is not unduly perturbed at contradicting itself within the space of a few pages. However, the main ideas of an understanding which tends to schematism are expressed so forcibly and in such insistent repetition that the accompanying contrapuntal undertones of the soul can easily be missed. But unless one constantly remembers his own corrections of his thought such as we have just seen, there is a danger of completely misunderstanding a great spirit. But he still insists (this is the conclusion of his criticism of civilization), that 'The future of civilization depends, therefore, on whether it is possible for thought to reach a theory of the universe which will have a more secure and fundamental hold on optimism and the ethical impulse than its predecessors have had'.[27] This will be attained when it is possible to base optimism and ethics on thought; even more, when their intellectual necessity can be proved. This is what Schweitzer sets out to do in the second volume of his philosophy of civilization.

For the fourth time Schweitzer adopts his old method of first discussing a problem against the background of its own historical development; and then demonstrating the correctness, even the inevitability, of his own solution on the basis of a critical analysis of the previous attempts to arrive at one. He unrolls 'the tragic wrestling of European thought with the ideology of world and life acceptance' from Socrates to Haeckel, Bergson and Keyserling, but omitting the period from late Stoicism to the Renaissance. He shows that, despite innumerable attempts, Western philosophy has never yet been successful in solving this, its most important problem.

Even in this philosophical section his style is deliberately popular: 'My appeal is to thinking men and women whom I wish to provoke to elemental thought about the questions of existence which occur to the mind of every human being.'[28] It is not possible within the framework of this book to recapitulate this summary 'examination' of philosophy. It is also unnecessary because it would contribute nothing to an understanding of Schweitzer. But walking along the path of his predecessors proved helpful: 'In wrestling with the thought of others my own thought is clarified.' What was the result?

Whenever philosophy arrives at an ethical acceptance of the world and of life its conclusion is based on an interpretation of world happenings through which it seeks to make them understandable and purposeful and in some way directed towards an ultimate ethical purpose. It then sees men serving this ultimate purpose by their ethical behaviour. The last attempts of this kind were the great systems of speculative philosophy at the beginning of the nineteenth century. Educated men believed that these systems provided proof of the intellectual necessity of an ideology of ethical world- and life-acceptance. But in the middle of that century these 'logical castles in Spain' collapsed under the relentless pressure of scientific thought, and disillusionment set in. Thought is prepared to confine itself to grappling with reality as it is and extracting behaviour motives from it in the sense of ethical world- and life-acceptance—only to find that reality refuses to give what is expected of it. No world purpose can be described in which ethical behaviour on the part of man would make sense. The result is that the cultural ideals deriving from an ideology of world- and life-acceptance are no longer compelling.

Any future attempts by thought to arrive at an understanding of the world which would justify an ethical acceptance of life are similarly doomed to failure. We must be content to abandon all hope of interpreting world happenings as purposeful. Schweitzer believes himself to be 'the first among Western thinkers who has ventured to recognize this crushing result of knowledge, and the first to be absolutely sceptical about our knowledge of the world without at the same time renouncing belief in world- and life-affirmation'.[29] With this our attitude to life is made independent of our attitude to the world. As we cannot bring the one into line with the other we must put the former above the latter. It is able to stand on its own, because it is rooted in our will to life. What is given to us in this will to life goes beyond our knowledge of the world. 'What is decisive for our life view is not our knowledge of the world but the certainty of the volition which is given in our will-to-live. The eternal spirit meets us in nature as mysterious creative power. In our will-to-live we experience it within us as volition which is both world- and life-affirming and ethical. Our relation to the world as it is given in the positive certainty of our will-to-live, when this seeks to comprehend itself in thought: that is our world-view. World-view is a product of life-view, not vice-versa.'[30]

But how are we to understand the identity of world- and life-acceptance with ethics as an intellectual necessity as laid down in 'civilized ideology', whereby on the one hand it receives its justification before the highest court of knowledge, and on the other hand an absolute validity, so that all that is then necessary is to persuade men to think in order that they should accept this world ideology? As we can see, Schweitzer's unprejudiced reasoning thought, once arrived at this decisive stage, turns towards dogmatism. It is not content with demonstrating knowledge which it believes it has obtained; it canonizes it. Every world-view which fails to start from resignation in regard to knowledge is 'artificial and a mere fabrication' and rests upon 'an inadmissible interpretation of the universe'.[31] The claim advanced here is the result of thought which is convinced that by using reason without illusions and with the courage to accept the consequences it must necessarily arrive at truth.

What is this elemental, universal, and intellectually necessary conception of the ethical which we have to find? It would be unlike Schweitzer if this adventure in thought did not develop dramatically. As formerly with the wrestling to reveal the 'secret' of the life of Jesus, so now too he has to find an 'Open Sesame!' 'Faced with this task I felt like a man who has to build a new boat to take the place of the ramshackle old tub in which he can no longer put to sea, but doesn't know how to start.'

The 'central province of philosophy' into which Schweitzer is carried by his thought on cultural and world ideology appears to him as 'unexplored territory'. 'For months on end I lived in a continual state of mental excitement. Without arriving at the least success I concentrated all my thoughts, even all through my daily work at the hospital, on the real nature of life and world affirmation, and on the question of what they necessarily have in common. I was wandering about in a thicket in which no path was to be found. I was leaning with all my might against an iron door which would not yield to my importunities.

'While in this mental condition I had to undertake a longish journey on the river. I was staying with my wife on the coast of Lopez for the sake of her health—it was in September 1915—when I was summoned to visit Madame Pelot, the ailing wife of a missionary at N'Gômô about 160 miles upstream. The only means of conveyance I could find was a small steamer towing an overladen barge, which was on the point of starting. Except myself there were only natives on board. . . . Slowly we crept upstream, laboriously feeling—it was the dry season—for the channels between the sandbanks. Lost in thought I sat on the deck of the barge struggling to find the elementary and universal conception of the ethical which I had not discovered in any philosophy. Sheet after sheet I covered with disconnected sentences, merely to keep myself concentrated on the problem. Late on the third day, at the very moment when, at sunset, we were making our way through a herd of hippopotamuses, there flashed upon my mind, unforeseen, and unsought, the phrase "Reverence for Life".

'The iron door had yielded. The path in the thicket had become visible. Now I had found my way to the idea in which world- and life-affirmation and ethics are contained side by side! Now I knew that the world-view of ethical world- and life-affirmation, together with its ideals of civilization, is founded on thought.'[32]

Let us allow this now famous description of Schweitzer's stroke of inspiration to sink in as it deserves. That evening hour, 'on the edge of the primeval forest', saw the birth of that conception to which Schweitzer's ethical teaching owes its popularity; and he was not mistaken when he felt that something of real importance had happened. Before we go on to consider its importance let us first ask ourselves just what Schweitzer's 'discovery' really means.

At first glance the exhortation that men should regard life with reverence sounds like a commonplace; the sort of thing which is already a matter of course for any civilized man—no matter how often he may offend against it. Our civilization already forbids and punishes any attack on human life. The state regards the maintenance of public health and hygiene as one of its most important tasks. In most civilized countries every sick person, whether rich or poor, is entitled to medical attention. And one of the many tasks of the police is to prevent people from taking their own lives. Cruelty towards both man and beast is forbidden by law. Even the death sentence itself is falling into disrepute. Thus the injunction to respect life seems to be simply an appeal for ordinary, matter-of-course, humanitarian behaviour, an appeal for a 'humane' attitude to man and beast. One feels almost that it is really putting the matter too high to describe such ordinary, seemly conduct as the fulfilment of an ethical law. I am not conscious of any particularly ethical behaviour when I do my best to avoid knocking down a pedestrian with my car, or even when I scatter a few crumbs for the birds in winter. No matter how often they may be threatened, there are still moral standards that are, at least in normal times, part and parcel of man's ordinary behaviour—so much so that any falling away from them is generally regarded as scandalous. All the same, the temptation to violate them is never far away, and the accepted humanitarian moral code is constantly being broken. A further exhortation to maintain it is therefore not altogether out of place—but not as the promulgation of a new moral law, because the law is already familiar and generally recognized, merely as a further exhortation. And when this is reinforced by a very impressive fulfilment in practice then there is truly some cause for enthusiasm. Generally speaking, this is how people really see Schweitzer—particularly in the Anglo-Saxon and Scandinavian countries, whose humanitarian idealism finds itself confirmed in the behaviour of this 'philanthropist'. His teaching is so obviously and immediately compelling to all men of good will, and in particular to 'his friends [who] are mild, gentle, freedom-loving liberals' who surround him and to whom he feels himself attached by bonds of friendship,[33] that they feel themselves under no obligation to go into the matter more carefully. After all, it seems to express just what they themselves regard as the ideal of human behaviour, though perhaps with him it shines forth with greater purity and intensity. They therefore feel that his teaching offers encouragement whilst at the same time giving no cause for misgiving; in fact there is, they feel, confident, nothing problematical about it at all. Be kind to man and beast! What sensitive spirit would not feel moved by such an exhortation? What good man would, or indeed could, harden his heart? Surely to attempt to find a basis in thought for an injunction whose validity is so immediately obvious is a waste of time? And any attempt to give it a philosophic foundation need not be taken too seriously?

Now Schweitzer's ethic of reverence for life certainly does include such humanitarian behaviour as we have described, but it is by no means identical with it. In fact its character is quite different. It differs by an incomparable greater intensity of the life feeling as well as by an extreme intensification of suffering at the harsh reality of life.

Schweitzer's description of how he lighted on this 'elementary and universal ethical conception' leaves one with an impression that the jungle itself had spoken to him. In fact down to this day the 'idea' on which his ethical philosophy is based is connected with the three 'islands of reverence for life' near the village of Igandja in the Ogowe area. 'They are covered by the jungle, and human beings hardly ever set foot on them.' It was there that the expression 'reverence for life' occurred to him. Occurred? It was like a flash of lightning. It is reminiscent of that mystical devotion to the life force, the cult of life, which is to be met with amongst Negroes, to whom sickness, pain and early death appear as acts of fate, as a curse laid upon them by magical powers—unlike the Christian who understands them. The background of their attitude is a world in which life has to struggle to survive at all against constant and acute threat, and is therefore constantly made aware of itself.

This absolute appreciation of life as the highest value is just as foreign to Christianity, though in a different sense, as it is to any civilized community which pays for its security with a diminished feeling for life. But here it appears as the second component of Schweitzer's ethical philosophy, and takes its place beside his absorption with the 'cruel' spectacle of the self-destruction of life.

In the *Sorrows of Werther* Goethe similarly combined a hymn, if not to life then to the 'Universe' which eternally produces life, with regret for the complementary tragedy of the 'destructive force which lies hidden in universal nature.

'Must those things that make a man happy necessarily become the source of his misery?

'The full and ardent sympathy of my heart for that living nature that fills me with so much joy, that turns the world around me into a paradise, has now become an intolerable torment, an agonizing spirit which follows me wherever I go. . . . It is as though a curtain had been drawn back from before my soul, and the scene of infinite life transforms itself before my eyes into the yawning grave. There is not one single moment when man is not a destroyer, when he is freed from the compulsion to destroy. The most innocent stroll costs a thousand small, harmless creatures their lives; a kick destroys the patient work of the ant and turns a small world into ruin. It is not the great and rare disasters of the world which move me, not the floods and the earthquakes which swallow up our towns! What anguishes my heart is the destructive force which lies hidden in universal Nature, the force which has never formed any single thing that has not at the same time destroyed both its neighbour and itself. And so, surrounded by the interlocking powers of heaven and earth, I stagger on in fear and apprehension. And on all sides I see nothing but an endlessly devouring monster endlessly chewing the cud.'

In his enumeration of the affinities he encountered in Goethe, Schweitzer does not mention this one. And yet Werther's classic outburst of despair expresses one of the compelling motives of Schweitzer's own being—with the difference that in Werther's case, because of his passivity, the tragic undertone led ultimately to self-destruction, whereas Schweitzer's activism draws its main strength from this same source.

The parallel is significant. In Werner Goethe gives expression to his own melancholia, or '*Weltschmerz*'. Something of the sort may well be seen in Schweitzer's answer to the call of the jungle. The effervescent feeling for life which finds expression, for example, in tribal dancing in the jungle gloom is foreign to him despite his own great vitality. His glorification of life cannot be traced back to his own temperament. Indeed, it sounds incongruous on his lips, and it remains incomprehensible unless it is traced back to its real source. Suffering from the contradictory secret of life is inborn in a man who acknowledges that 'only at quite rare moments have I felt really glad to be alive'.[34]

His attitude of reverence for life comes from the clash of these two attitudes, both highly charged. Its origin tells us that its spiritual climate is different from that of humanitarian idealism. Far from confirming the latter, it condemns its inadequacy. It is not even satisfied with the ethics of love as pronounced by Jesus. Its own 'absolute' ethic develops from a heroic-tragic ideology. Its uncompromising ruthlessness is reminiscent in its vehemence of certain ethical exhortations of Jesus. Let us first seek to understand the thought pattern of his outlook on life and the world, and then to understand the significance of the ethical teaching based on it.

According to Schweitzer the most direct fact of human consciousness is summed up in the words: 'I am life which wills to live, in the midst of life which wills to live.' As will to life in the midst of will to life man is conscious of himself every time he thinks about himself and the world around him. But in comprehending himself as the will to life he also discovers the self-alienation of the will to life. 'It remains a painful enigma for me that I must live with reverence for life in a world which is dominated by creative will which is also destructive will, and destructive will which is also creative.'[35] This self-alienation of the will to life gives rise to suffering. 'All life is suffering.'[36] This casts doubt on the will to life. And man is faced with the problem of what attitude he should take towards it. If man affirms his will to life then he acts paradoxically, but nevertheless, according to Schweitzer, 'he acts naturally and honestly. He confirms an act which has already been accomplished in his instinctive thought by repeating it in his conscious thought.'[37]

But now something tremendous and incomprehensible happens. Where this will to life in creation becomes conscious of itself, where it becomes 'thought' in man, then man within the sphere of his own activity feels the urge to negate this self-alienation of life, and to remedy creation, which is itself disunited. The universal will to life expresses itself within him as something ethical. Man, having become thinking man, experiences a compelling urge to treat every form of the will to life with the same respect he pays to his own. He experiences that other life in his own. For him now it is good: to preserve life, to encourage life, to bring life capable of development to its highest value. Conversely it is bad: to destroy life, to damage life, to hamper and hold back life capable of development. 'This is the absolute, fundamental principle of the moral, and it is a necessity of thought.'[38]

This basic moral principle is unrestricted in two respects. It is no longer satisfied merely with respect for the life of fellow human beings, and, in an extended sense, respect for their existence—not even when this respect for other life expresses itself in combating sickness and death. No! Respect now applies to the will to life as such. Two things follow from this.

'The essential nature of the will-to-live is determination to live itself to the full. It carries within it the impulse to realize itself in the highest possible perfection. . . . In everything that exists there is at work an imaginative force, which is determined by ideals. In us beings who can move about freely and are capable of pre-considered purposive activity, the craving for perfection is given in such a way that we aim at raising to their highest material and spiritual value both ourselves and every existing thing which is open to our influence. How this striving originated within us, and how it has developed, we do not know, but it is given with our existence. We must act upon it, if we would not be unfaithful to the mysterious will-to-live which is within us.'[39] Thus for Schweitzer the will-to-life is at the same time the will to perfection. To behave ethically means to enter into the service of progress, a progress which is directed by the need of the individual vessel of the will to life to 'live itself out' to the degree of perfection within its reach. 'True ethics are always subjective.'[40] The breath of its life is irrational enthusiasm.

If all this seems to mean is that the will to life is given a moral *carte blanche* with the rejection of any objective normative ethics, this ethical passe-partout is soon hedged about as far as human beings are concerned. The freedom for self-realization in which the individual being is to be brought to the highest material and spiritual level of perfection, thereby creating civilization, soon finds itself subject to radical limitation. The ethics of the ethical personality are seen to consist of two elements: an ethic of resignation is 'the ethic of passive self-perfection in inward self-liberation from the world (resignation)'. The ethic of duty, or obligation, is 'the ethic of active self-perfecting, effected by means of the mutual relations between man to man'.[41] And this expresses itself in service to the life will outside itself. Man as an ethical being is under an obligation to be the protector and encourager of 'the urge to perfection' in every form. This presupposes the sympathetic experiencing of the will to life in all states and aspirations, including its urge and its longing to live itself out.

This inner infinite extension of the moral injunction accords with its extension to embrace all creatures. The ethic of reverence for life makes no distinction between higher and lower, valuable and less valuable, since: 'Who among us knows what significance any other kind of life has itself, and as a part of the universe?'[42] It consists in the compulsion to pay the same respect to all forms of the life will as to one's own—'no knowledge can tell us what life is'. Even to walk over a meadow or to break a crystal is a guilty act.

The contradiction between the merging of man into nature as the object of ethical behaviour, and the rise of the individual, whose perfection Schweitzer regards as 'the progress of all progress', is not felt as such because it is provided for in the ideology which lies at the basis of his philosophy of civilization, which is itself dominated by the three aspects: nature, personality and culture as the phenomenological forms in which the modern consciousness of being is perceived (Guardini). It shines in the zenith of Goethe's heaven, but since the beginning of our own century it has been constantly declining. In this constellation the autonomous personality is no longer the centre of creation, but merely a part of the world. As such it is not able to prevail in its own right, but becomes a part of nature which is not fundamentally different from plant or animal. The 'responsibility without limit towards all that lives'[43] is neither an arbitrary demand of some ethical rigorism nor 'the intellectually necessary absolute basic principle of morality'. Schweitzer's 'universal ethic' is the consequence of the application of logical ethical thought to the modern conception of the world.

This responsibility—and with it the ethic of reverence for life—is described by Schweitzer himself as 'terrifying'.[44] It follows from the 'horrible necessity' in which man finds himself as a result of the self-alienation of the will to life of reconciling this with itself.[45] The will to life, which is identical with the existence of man ('I am life which wills to live') experiences, in so far as he is an ethical personality—and only as such is he a true man—an irrational transformation in him. It makes its presence felt as an absolute *veneratio vitae*, and thus stands in opposition to the antimony which arises from the very beginning in the will to life. Life can exist only at the cost of other life. Higher forms of life prevail at the cost of lower forms. In this chaotic struggle for existence, which determines all life, the will to life which has awakened to thought about itself, thereby becoming ethical, finds itself saddled with the absolutely obligatory task, which is indeed what justifies the existence of the human being, of making peace.

So understood, the situation of the ethical personality is a tragic one. Not only is its titanic task of correcting Creation impossible to fulfil even approximately, but, because it is subject to the law of this Creation, it is itself constantly compelled—not from any inadequacy, but of necessity—consciously to damage life, i.e. to act unethically.

7. Schweitzer the veterinary surgeon
(By permission of Erica Anderson, New York)

This ethic, which is based on the fact that 'nature as such comes into contradiction with itself in man'[46] imposes the permanent existence of bad conscience—'the good conscience is an invention of the devil'.[47] It creates constant disturbances 'such as the world does not know'. The bringer of peace is driven without surcease by the ethical will in which his existence is summarized. And, nevertheless, the only path to the oasis of peace, by granting him moments of the greatest joy, preserves him from 'languishing in the desert of life', runs through the gauntlet of self-destruction, and self-scourging life. 'If I save an insect from a puddle, life has devoted itself to life and the division of life against itself is ended. Whenever my life devotes itself in any way to life, my finite will-to-live experiences union with the infinite will in which all life is one.'[48]

'The land of humanity's future', as one of Schweitzer's biographers has described his ethical province, truly lies worlds away from that edifying imaginary world which has been built up around the jungle doctor as the, so to speak, Fransciscan friend of man and beast.

Whoever accepts the ethic of reverence for life can certainly go with Schweitzer part of the way along the road without realizing the dangerous adventure into which he has let himself. The way passes first through pleasant places warmed by the rays of human love and gay with the blossoms of good works. 'There is, however, a wide field of which our ethics can take possession without any collision with the troops of egoism. Man can accomplish much that is good, without having to require of himself any sacrifice. And if there really goes with it a bit of his life it is so insignificant that he feels it no more than if he were losing a hair or a flake of dead skin.'[49] But that is relative, applied ethics, and readiness to compromise. It believes that it can determine how much of life and happiness may be sacrificed, and how much may be retained—at the cost of the existence and happiness of some other life. It puts forward as ethical what is in reality not ethical at all. Thus to dawdle in this inviting fore garden of true ethical behaviour is not enough; indeed it stands condemned as unethical before the court of the ethic of reverence for life, since it creates confusion and obscures the conception of the truly ethical. The epic of reverence for life knows no relative ethics. And yet its own fulfilment will hardly ever be more than figurative—like the rescuing of the one insect from the puddle when millions of other insects must inevitably perish nearby. The task is to clear a jungle, and the force available suffices for felling one tree. He who has saved the insect from the puddle finds himself compelled to destroy life a thousandfold in order to exist himself. And thus he becomes guilty. And if he were a saint, if he were love personified, he would, because he too is a creature, find himself compelled to destroy and damage life, and thus be driven into guilt.

But this ethic does not content itself with burdening man with an inevitable weight of guilt, it also takes him in the cross-fire of contradictory demands. The reverence for life on which it is based extends with logical necessity to his own experience. But this ethic gives him no indication of the length to which he may go in permissible and indeed obligatory self-preservation. Schweitzer's philosophy of civilization has postulated the affirmation of life (=optimism). 'All imaginable ideas and convictions of that character spring from optimism and the ethical impulse.'[50] But Schweitzer's ethic is unable to maintain this position: 'Life-affirmation and life-negation are both for a certain distance ethical; pursued to a conclusion they become unethical.'[51] But here again, it is impossible to discover where the ethical attitude changes into its contrary. The ethical attitude consists neither in the affirmation nor the rejection of life, but in a mysterious combination of both. This relationship defies analysis. All that can be said is that the acceptance of life according to the definition of human existence enjoys the primacy. The rejection of life is the paradoxical consequence of life-affirming ethics. 'Subjective responsibility for all life which comes within his reach, responsibility which widens out extensively and intensively to the limitless, and which the man who has become inwardly free from the world experiences and tries to make a reality, that is ethics. It originates in world- and life-affirmation. It becomes a reality in life-negation.'[52] The rejection of life comes about when, precisely because of reverence for life, a man sacrifices his own life. It is demanded of the affirmation of life by the given circumstances. Spontaneous and independent self-denial (as referred to in Mark viii. 34) has no more place in this ethic than asceticism and sacrifice as such as the price of spirituality. But by regarding the self-denial demanded by reverence for life as a way of self-perfection, Schweitzer approached within a hair's breadth of the knowledge by experience of Christian spiritual life.

The behaviour of the ethical personality must therefore steer a middle course between the affirmation and the rejection of life. Obedient to the ethic of the reverence for life, it must constantly come to terms with the absolute ethic of self-denial. 'I have to decide in accordance with the responsibility of which I am conscious, how much of my life, my possessions, my rights, my happiness, my time and my rest, I must devote to others, and how much I may keep myself.'[53]

Schweitzer is under no illusions about the tyrannical character of the ethic of reverence for life. He knows it in his own experience and he has described it in his own graphic fashion.

The ethic of reverence for life is 'an inexorable creditor'. It is 'hard-hearted'. 'If it finds that a human being has no more than a little time and a little leisure, then it will take them both.' 'Nor will reverence for life grant me my happiness as my own. At the moments when I should like to enjoy myself without restraint it wakes in me reflection about misery that I see or suspect, and it does not allow me to drive away the uneasiness I feel. . . . It is an uncomfortable doctrine which the true ethics whispers into my ear. You are happy, they say; therefore you are called upon to give much. . . . To the happy the voice of the true ethics is dangerous, if they venture to listen to it. When it calls to them, it never damps down the irrational which glows within it. It assails them to see whether it can get them off their smooth track and turn them into adventurers of self-devotion.'[54]

And so whoever accepts the ethic of reverence for life lives in constant inner conflict with himself, a conflict he must seek to resolve as the case arises on his own personal responsibility. His situation is certainly not a simple or easy one. Yet should he now suppose that he has been given enough to bear he will soon discover that he is not to be let off so lightly. It is not only as an individual that he bears responsibility towards his fellow men and fellow creatures, but at the same time, as a member of human society, he is the bearer of a more than personal responsibility. But this cannot be reconciled with the absolute ethic of the ethical personality. ' . . . it is impossible to succeed in developing the ethic of the ethical personality into a serviceable ethic of society.'[55] Right social ethics do not result from right individual ethics. We must realize that the two stand in conflict with each other, a conflict which must not be mitigated. It finds expression in the ethical philosophy of Schweitzer as 'the suffering of the pathetic man in a rational purposefully-ordered society',[56] a truly Goethe-like experience.

The ethic set up from the standpoint of society is 'not ethics in the proper sense of the word'. 'The essence of ethical progress is to regard the ethic of society pessimistically.' This is subject to a relativism of expediency. However, 'Only the most universal and absolute purposiveness in the maintenance and furtherance of life, which is the objective aimed at by reverence for life, is ethical. All other necessity or expediency is not ethical, but only a more or less necessary necessity, or a more or less expedient expediency. . . . If, under the pressure of the supra-personal responsibility, I yield to the expedient, I become guilty in some way or other through failure in reverence for life'.[57] All the same, I may not evade the guilt of inhumanity which derives from the operation of this supra-personal responsibility, by withdrawing into myself. That would be a surreptitious evasion of guilt. 'Since ethics arise in the form of life and world acceptance it does not allow us to escape into world-denial. It forbids us to follow the example of the housewife who leaves it to the cook to boil the lobster.'

The ethic of reverence for life places a human being in a permanent condition of guilt from which there is no escape and for which there is no absolution. Even acts of charity lead only deeper into the morass. To save his patient the doctor destroys bacteria—and is thereby guilty of an offence against life. On one occasion Schweitzer bought a young osprey from natives in order to save it from cruelty at their hands. But having done so he found himself in the dilemma of letting the osprey starve to death or seeing it kill fish in order to live. 'I decided on the latter course, but every day I feel it hard that this life must be sacrificed for the other on my responsibility.'[58]

The independent moral self-responsibility with which the ethic saddles the individual far exceeds anything with which Protestantism has burdened the Christian by insisting on his personal responsibility. Unconditional freedom represents a very great burden. A motive of theological thought is carried through to its ultimate conclusion here. Together with this—and not only at this point in Schweitzer's thought—we observe a surprising recurrence, though in a different form, of a routine piece of orthodox theology rejected by liberal thought: the belief that a state of guilt hangs over the human being as an *a priori*, and irrespective of his moral behaviour, that man is born into this state, either as a result of original sin or of the self-alienation of the will to life. The accent lies in the one case, of course, on the state of the soul, and in the other on the unethical act.

As a vessel of the will to life man from his very birth appears as an enemy of the will to life outside himself. This hostility to other life is guilt, even when it takes place without a feeling of guilt; even, in fact, when it is unavoidable, or even when it is actually enjoined by the ethic of reverence for life itself. This guilt grows like a landslide throughout life. There is no mercy for the guilty. He is responsible solely to his own conscience, that is to say, to a court which has power to judge but not to acquit.

It is the task of ethics to bring this guilt to man's consciousness, and in this way to persuade him, as will to life drawn into the self-alienation of life, to set up a historically defiant banner of peace in the midst of the all-embracing battlefield of creation.

'The system of ethics hitherto current has hindered us from becom-as earnest as we ought to be by the fact that it has utterly deceived us as to the many ways in which each one of us, whether through self-assertion, or by actions justified by supra-personal responsibility, becomes guilty again and again. True knowledge consists in being gripped by the secret that everything around us is will-to-live and in seeing clearly how again and again we incur guilt against life.'[59]

So far Schweitzer has not finished his philosophy of civilization. A third volume was to deal in detail with the ideology of reverence for life, and a fourth with the cultural State. Seaver[60] tells us that this latter volume was to contain a history of European social and political movements from Charlemagne down to the present day. It would, presumably, have analysed the life of society from the standpoint of Schweitzer's ethical principles, just as *Kultur und Ethik* (*Culture and Ethics*) analysed Western thought.

Schweitzer regards what he has given us so far in the ethic of reverence for life, as a sketch; but it clearly outlines the edifice as a whole, and it is hardly likely that its extension would alter the picture in any fundamental aspect.[61] As far as the existing torso of the philosophy of civilization allows us to judge, we feel that the impulsive, graphic, formally-developed manner of the draft, renouncing terminological precision and systematic balance, is the appropriate form for presenting Schweitzer's fundamentally unfinished ideology and ethics.

In forty years the philosophy of civilization based on reverence for life has not gone beyond the stage of splendid improvisation. There are more important reasons for this than mere outward hindrances. Schweitzer's 'aim is to arrive at a conviction concerning the value and essence of the world, but not at a scientific method that leads to it'.[62] The 'elementary' and 'naïve' thought which he favours does not need this. His philosophy is 'thinking experience'. It replaces a theology which lacks a theologically consolidated doctrinal content and thus sooner or later becomes, in the literal sense of the word, pointless. The result: religion is ethics. Ethics is the theme of any serious consideration of the essence and significance of life. In consequence 'All serious thinking is religion'.[63] Thinking experience can be expressed only in the form of avowal. 'Any profound discussion of ethics becomes a sermon, becomes an avowal of what has been experienced as true.'[64] The ethic of reverence for life is this and nothing else.

One could leave the matter there if Schweitzer confined himself to the exposition of the experience in thought and left its operation with confidence to its inherent force of conviction. But two things prevented this. The first is the claim of this experience in thought to objective intellectual necessity. The second is the lack of harmony with Schweitzer's subjective experience. Both the one and the other require an explanation.

The merging of 'negative' theology into natural philosophy has the logic of an independent movement of thought. In taking this path Schweitzer's thought remains logical. His urge to arrive at knowledge which will satisfy reason is so vehement that to stop halfway would be impossible for him. His philosophy is not, as might appear from the development of his philosophy of culture and his own description of it, impelled solely by a desire to come to the assistance of culture—which, of course, would, in any case, not be a philosophical impulse. It accords with a necessity arising from the premises of his thought.

But the intellectual necessity which Schweitzer claims for the results of his philosophy involves something quite different. He identifies it with reasoning thought. He is convinced that he has discovered the relationship of man to the universe, the essence of human nature and the unshakable foundation of ethics. If man, having become thinking man, 'perseveres with thinking he can come to no other result than reverence for life'.[65]

The need to base the highest content of knowledge on intellectual necessity is inborn for Schweitzer. 'From my youth I have held the conviction that all religious truth must in the end be capable of being grasped as something that stands to reason.'[66] He is similarly convinced that he has remained religious and Christian through thought.[67] 'Living truth is that alone which has its origin in thinking'.[68] He sees himself living and acting in the world 'as one who aims at making men less shallow and morally better by making them think'.[69] If the truth arising in thought is intellectually necessary, then all one need do is to persuade men to think, and this, without anything else, will guide them infallibly to the same truth. They will then not regard it as authoritarian truth but as one which they have independently achieved, and with this a perfect synthesis of authority and liberty is brought about.

Schweitzer has not succeeded in demonstrating the intellectual necessity of his ethic. Reverence for life is such a self-evident *a priori* for him that he does not bother himself much to prove its intellectual necessity. Indeed it isn't easy even to discover just what we are to understand by this.

Schweitzer has defined thinking as 'the argument between willing and knowing which goes on within me'.[70] The 'new' rationalism Schweitzer leaves to reason, 'the attaining to clarity about the will-to-live which is within us',[71] without at the same time explaining the world. Unprejudiced reasoning thought is thus sent out on a previously arranged route. It must proceed from the postulate that the will to life is the only relevant subject for thought. But it is not at the same time authorized to examine its essence and conditions. Its authority is limited to thinking out the consequences of the will to life. Information about this will is provided by another source: 'The knowledge derived from my will-to-live is direct, and takes me back to the mysterious movements of life as it is in itself. The highest knowledge, then, is to know that I must be true to the will-to-live.'[72] It is thus, like all valuable knowledge, irrational; the result of this reasoning thought is also laid down in advance. If it is 'truthful', then it merges into ethics. And 'to become ethical means to begin to think sincerely'. This ethical thinking receives proper guidance from the beginning. If it proceeds in the right direction and does not lapse into abstract thinking then it will ultimately arrive at 'self-devotion of human life to every form of living being with which it can come into relation'.[73]

Schweitzer does insist that his principle is 'not to say anything more in philosophy than what is absolutely logical experience of thought'.[74] But this principle contains an inner contradiction. There is no such thing as an 'absolutely logical experience', because all experience is subjective, whilst logic is the sheerly objective form of thought. The *tour de force* which seeks to save rationalism whilst at the same time seeing itself compelled to abandon it does not achieve its objective. Seaver, who, as an apologist for Schweitzer, upholds the 'intellectual necessity' of his ethics, is quite right when he says that the optimist-ethical outlook on life cannot be based on any formal-logical thought process. But, he goes on to say: 'It can be experienced—as no metaphysical world-view can—as an inner necessity for thought.'[75] However, as is the case with Schweitzer, this is a mere assertion. We know today that the structure of being is not in accordance with the structure of logic. Going against the methods of thought to which he is traditionally attached Schweitzer evades the latter, and, thereby, proves, although he does not see through the philosophical significance of this step, the profundity of his 'elementary thought'. But the abandonment of the formal laws of logic means an abandonment of objectivity; it means an abandonment of the compulsive general validity of the results of thought.

The subjective and therefore disputable nature of this 'intellectually necessary absolute fundamental principle of morality' becomes fully clear when we examine its content.

Even its premises are not compelling. The will to life supports life. It secures its perpetuation. Like the engine hidden in the hull of the ship, rarely seen by the passenger on board, it provides the blind motive force. Without it the ship could not move. But the will which guides the ship and which is able to stop the engine is of a different and superior nature. It belongs to the category of the spiritual. The progress of the ship may be a necessity for the man on the bridge, but his mind is not concentrated on keeping the engine going.

And in the same way a human being is not primarily conscious of himself as a will to life, but as a personality. The proud and ecstatic realization: I am—either because this ego has unexplainably entered into being, or because God has called it by his name—is nullified by the rider 'will to life'. The ego which has just been lifted out of darkness into light sinks back into the sea of universality which robs it of every ego sense. In truth, although this ego is impelled by the will to life it is not completely subject to it either as a slave of its own will to life, or in the merciless subordination to a responsibility for the preservation and furtherance of everything 'which wills to live'. It plays a dangerous game with life, both risking and wasting it. In the personification of the ego life becomes not only conscious of itself but also able to dispose of itself. When it is raised aloft on the wings of passion it is carried high above itself. It 'stakes itself' without needing any ethical expenditure for the purpose. Significance and value do not derive from the mere fact of being alive, but from the use made of life. The life which the breath of the spirit has awakened to the ego does not take itself so seriously as vitalism supposes. To say that it is not the highest treasure is not a pathetic declamation but a realistic experience.

But if I set out to raise the anonymous life which is in me to consciousness, if I act in accordance with Schweitzer's injunction and make it the subject of 'thinking experience', then two things happen, neither of which increases my readiness to regard myself as life that wills to live.

This life which is constantly thinking of its own preservation and perpetuation, whilst at the same time being self-alienated and constantly self-destructive, this paradox of a suicidal will to life, is—as Schweitzer in his own fashion has expressly stated—a phenomenon which is as mysterious as it is senseless, and the self-knowledge, even the instinct of self-preservation of the human ego, hesitates to identify itself with it. The rise from a condition of mere existence into a condition of conscious existence is not without its dangers. If the now thinking ego can find no purpose in its existence it falls victim to nihilism. In this situation, an ethic which sees the purpose of man's existence in finding a remedy for the self-alienation of life does not offer us any very firm foothold. Compared with the fundamental fact of personal being, all ethics are secondary. They cannot explain it, and the manifold urges and expressions of life cannot be reduced to ethics. Schweitzer did succeed in this respect but that was due to a heroic act of self-abnegation. The exceptional case makes it clear that the destiny of man is not defined here.

The now thinking life discovers a second factor which contradicts the premises of the ethic of reverence for life. Vitalistic thought, for which life is a magnitude constantly equal to itself, leaves out the time factor. This accords well enough with the emancipation of Schweitzer's theology from history, but in its individuation life is a passage of time ending in death. It may be regarded as a gradual 'filling up with death'[76] —the exact proof has been provided by Rudolf Ehrenberg's profound metabiological investigations. In the consciousness of being inserted between birth and death, life becomes a human existence. For Hofmannsthal death is the interpreter of life. 'Thus we are all living towards this hour of death, and whilst doing so justify ourselves.'[77] Ahasverus, who is unable to die, lives under a curse. Schweitzer's view of life takes no account either of the biological or the metaphysical significance of death.[78]

The moral injunction 'to accept, preserve and treat life with reverence' (Karl Barth) retains its validity even when this injunction is not regarded as the supreme law of life. To regard reverence for life as an absolute thus becomes untenable; it is no longer the highest criterion of virtue. Nevertheless, it remains the only proper, the only ethical attitude towards life.

But an appeal to it will find an echo only where the organ of reverence is present and where it reacts to the phenomenon 'life'. 'From an inner compulsion to be true to itself', says Schweitzer, 'our will-to-live enters into relations with our own individual being, and with all manifestations of the will-to-live which surround it, that are determined by the sentiment of reverence for life.'[79] The subjective factor unmistakably reveals itself in this formulation. There is no outlook which is common to all (thinking) men as a result of inner compulsion.

A further objection threatens the very substance of this 'fundamental principle of morality'. If life is not an absolute value then 'the infinitely extended responsibility for everything which lives' ceases to be valid. Though we may observe the spectacle of life around us with awe, as life develops in a struggle against life, this does not involve any obligation to take part in it. It may well be reverence for life which prevents us from freeing the fly from the spider's web. The tiger attacks the deer, but both are entitled to the same consideration. Reverence for life cannot exclude that aspect in which the will to life appears as an enemy of life. This is the form in which it presents itself to us. Even the human organism itself, right into its most secret recesses, is the arena of a constant struggle for existence. Every intensification of the urge to live results in a corresponding destruction of life, both as a preliminary and as a consequence. The jungle is evidence of this. Birth and death are two aspects of the same process. The reverence, or awe, which this process deserves also has an element of fear, even horror, a shudder at something which goes beyond our own standards. We incline ourselves in awe before the impenetrable, mysterious secret of creation; within the orderly world of human beings, man is certainly called upon to preserve life, whether it be human life or the lives of those creatures it includes. Whether as law giver, active doer or witness—man owes solidarity to that life which has been entrusted to him, and this includes sacrificing it at need.

The thinking experience of Schweitzer tends to extremes. As we have already seen, the unlimited moral responsibility which recognizes no difference between the scope of man's authority and the blind operation of the life force in free nature, is paralleled in the rejection of any generally valid differences between higher and lower, between valuable and less valuable life. This attitude is justified by saying that to make any such differentiation could lead to the idea that there could be life without value, life which could therefore be destroyed with impunity. 'Then in the category of worthless life we come to include, according to circumstances, different kinds of insects, or primitive peoples.'[80]

Both the conception of reverence for life, and the conception of life itself as defined by Schweitzer's vitalistic ethic raise questions which they do not answer. Let us confine ourselves to three of them.

The aim of the ethic of reverence for life 'is to create values and to realize progress.'[81] But at the same time it rejects the setting up of differential values. However, to create and increase values presupposes, as Oskar Kraus points out in his criticism of Schweitzer's ethic,[82] a hierarchy of values and preferences. Without an evaluation of values the task of raising human life to its highest value cannot be fulfilled. The fear that an ethical doctrine may be abused is no reply to this.

To regard life as an absolute value does not remove the necessity *in praxi* of establishing differential values, because, standing in the full stream of life, man is constantly compelled to sacrifice life in order to preserve life. The ethic of reverence for life does not help him when he is faced with this necessity. ' . . . he is conscious of acting on subjective grounds and arbitrarily, and knows that he bears the responsibility for the life which is sacrificed.'[83] This places too great a burden on him, and the lack of guidance in this respect conjures up much greater dangers than those which led to the abandonment of all differentiation between higher and lower forms of life.

The third objection is that because the ethic of reverence for life proposes that all life, life as such, should enjoy the highest measure of protection, human life is deprived of its special taboo; it subjects all life to the arbitrariness of personal judgement.

Seaver identifies himself with Schweitzer's philosophy in this matter, and in so doing he shows us clearly where it can lead. It is a matter of course for Seaver that we should save the bird from the cat, but at the same time it strikes him as advisable to leave open the question of why we act in this way—human instinct or rational ethic. But when a rat, and not a bird, is involved he is 'not so sure', because 'rats are nasty, dangerous creatures'.[84] In other words, rats are proscribed because we don't like them and because we regard them as dangerous. So once the ethic of reverence for life has deprived human life of the special sanctity which previously protected it, there is no reason why this argument should not be applied to unloved races and peoples; since, despite its radical nature, this ethic cannot provide absolute protection for life, only a protection qualified by human judgement. This, of course, does not apply where Schweitzer himself is concerned. Whenever he looks through the microscope at the bacteria which cause sleeping-sickness he experiences misgiving at the thought that he must destroy life in order to preserve it. But we see that in one of his disciples, a man who as Schweitzer's biographer exercises an important literary influence, the ethic of reverence for life, whose significance for every thinking person is supposed to reside in its obligatory universal validity, is thrown overboard the moment it conflicts with sentiment. It follows therefore that in order to behave ethically a man faced with the 'subjective and arbitrary decisions' he is compelled to make from time to time, must exclude his feelings because, as a result of his cosmic mission, they would in all probability influence his decision or sentimental grounds. But once again this cannot be reconciled with the *chaud-froid* of an ethic in which the spheres of abstract thought and of warm human feelings merge in a quite extraordinary fashion.

The more deeply you examine Schweitzer's ethical teaching the more you are forced to the conclusion that it cannot be squared with his personality. He certainly lives according to his teachings, and the uncompromising fashion in which he puts his own thought into practice is beyond reproach, but the more vitally we see the man Schweitzer before our eyes the greater misgiving we feel at this discrepancy. It is as though the thought process had shifted its focus, and that the picture which appears on the screen of the thought apparatus is not a projection of the original content of its consciousness. Middleton Murry, who knew the man only from a distance, but with the shrewd feeling of the literary critic for the degree of concordance between opinion and statement, found himself in similar difficulties, and he writes: 'In the struggling to understand his thought one is haunted by the sense that his real meaning is not contained in the actual words he uses, and that he is forcing an authentic liberating vision of some kind—indeed a mystical experience—into a purely rational language which will not contain or communicate it.'[85] Middleton Murry also complains of the, to him, terrible nakedness of *Civilization and Ethics*, and, in fact, Schweitzer himself confirms the justification of this when he confesses that the definition of his ethic 'does not make a very moving impression'.[86] As against this, however, he contends that is 'the only complete one'.

Here we have it: the titanic urge of the born ethicist to put ethics as 'the highest and the only vital spirituality'[87] in the place of religion, and then to elevate the requirements of this 'cosmic ethic' (Martin Werner) above human standards and capacities into the absolute, has driven Schweitzer's ethical thought from the human, down-to-earth warmth which is natural to him, up to the cold, bare peaks of philosophic abstraction.

Sympathy and love were, and are, the elementary driving forces of his nature. Their personal accent can be seen in his declaration of war on pain. 'Pain is a worse master even than death.' But his definition of ethics is not satisfied with this alone. 'Sympathy is too narrow to serve as a conception of ethics. It describes only fellow feeling with the suffering will to life. But ethics include the experiencing of all the conditions and all the aspirations of the will to life'—that is to say not only an ethically unfruitful, all-embracing understanding, but its inner co-fulfilment, for which Schweitzer himself is neither prepared nor capable of. Suffering is no longer in the foreground of this teaching. It finds its place in the middle of innumerable other expressions of life. Indeed, it is questionable whether pain, the alarm signal of threatened life, can be described as a diminishment of life at all, and whether the duty to struggle against it can be derived from reverence for the former. Indeed, at a certain stage of spiritual development the unconditional rejection of pain is replaced by a preparedness to accept the inevitable, the unfathomable. Once accepted its indications change: from an enemy it can become an ally on the way to a higher life. Catherine Mansfield, who herself suffered a great deal, bears witness to this in a letter to John Middleton Murry written in October 1920: 'Bodily suffering such as I've known for three years has changed forever everything—thus the appearance of the world is not the same—there is something added. Everything has its shadow. Is it right to resist such suffering? Do you know I feel it has been an immense privilege. Yes, in spite of it all. I don't mean a thorn in the flesh it's a million times more mysterious.'

And love? According to Schweitzer it represents ethics only symbolically. 'It makes the solidarity produced by ethics analogous to that which nature calls forth on the physical side between two beings which complement each other sexually, or between them and their offspring.'[88] The alienation of thinking and being is unmistakable.

For Schweitzer there is no breach between his theological thought and his ethical philosophy; indeed, the latter fulfils the former. He is obviously very anxious to convince himself and others of the unity of the two. The religion of Paul is 'Will-to-Live' in a large, elemental sense.[89] The ethic of reverence for life is 'the ethic of Jesus, now recognized as a necessity of thought'.[90] This is a tragic self-deception. In passing via unconditional reasoning thought the love ethic of Jesus has suffered a fundamental change. The universal extension was obtained at the price of surrendering the spontaneity of the personal love relationship. In place of the 'neighbour' comes an anonymous vessel of the will to life; in place of the elementary movement of the heart comes an ethical principle. A human being is just not capable of a spontaneous feeling like love for a disease germ or a bird-catching spider. When Schweitzer conceived the idea and the formula 'reverence for life' he was not thinking of Jesus but Buddha.[91] Jesus was not remotely interested in raising life to a dominant principle, nor would any Christian theology be prepared to recognize it.

The love ethic of Jesus is rooted in love for God the Father. Love for one's fellow man and for all creatures is rooted in this. If the premises cannot be fulfilled then the injunction to love, directed to hearts overflowing with filial love, withers away to an ethical obligation. If Schweitzer had not proceeded from the assumption that the idea of moral world perfection were inborn and derived from the moral will presupposed as an attribute of human kind, he would hardly have supposed that man would subject himself to this under the compulsion of intellectual necessity.[92] Such an asumption contradicts all experience.

These considerations would appear to end in a contradiction. They lead to the conclusion that Schweitzer's ethical teaching is neither theologically nor philosophically satisfactory. Indeed a doubt arises as to whether there is even one single person, either amongst his followers or amongst his immediate collaborators, who unconditionally accepts the inflexibility and exclusiveness of an ethical idea that permits no other form of spirituality. Nevertheless we know that the influence of this ethical doctrine is immeasurable.

But this admission does not dispose of the objections to it, because in the last resort it was their purpose to underline this contradiction as probably the most astonishing phenomenon in Schweitzer's whole career, which has certainly never lacked surprises. But we are still left wondering as to the nature of an ethical teaching which is rejected by theology[93] and hardly noticed by philosophy, but which has nevertheless affected ethical thought and feeling more deeply than any other ethical teaching of our time.

Karl Barth has very accurately described the essence of the ethic of reverence for life: it is—under a philosophic cloak—'an outcry'.[94] The significance of that experience on the Ogowe lies in the fact that a soul anguished by the suffering of the world, a soul which had passed through the school of the love ethic of Jesus, at last found the articulate expression for its feeling. And it was of such passionate intensity that it could understand itself only as something necessary to every man come to self-knowledge, i.e. become thinking man.

With this it becomes not only communicable but reaches a high stage of reality. 'Nothing is where there is no word to express it.' The exceptionally ethical will that struggled for this word and formed it, also lent it wings. The act in which it realized itself gave it credibility. It was a revelation at a moment when men were seized with horror at the tangible results of the failure of humanness. It was the word of a prophet in a historical moment of appalling danger.

The impressiveness of the event is not diminished, but rather increased, by the fact that the compelling power of this appeal is independent of the ideological scaffolding Schweitzer provides for his ethic. In view of the harvest it has produced, theological and philosophical objections have no decisive weight, though they have to be considered not only in order to clarify the facts but also as a matter of proper obligation. However, such criticism is powerless to affect the influence which is at work here, since it is on a higher level than any reason.

Schweitzer ascribes the force of the ethic of reverence for life to its intellectual necessity. But when he then attaches so little importance to its systematic development this may well be because he senses that this is in any case no longer so important today. The ethical will which it embodies works directly from will to will. Having staked everything on the card of thought, yet acting with blind obedience at the critical moment, Schweitzer was granted a fulfilment both independent of and unassailable by thought, such as has been given to few mortals. He was allowed to light a beacon on earth.

VI

THE KINGDOM OF GOD

What has become of the theologian Schweitzer as a result of his ethical philosophy? The question cannot be ignored.

He has not merely remained a theologian, but the theological element in his thought proves itself the decisive one. Theology rounds off the philosophy of culture without coming into conflict with it. The encounter is a culmination for both, and nevertheless it takes place without a clash. Schweitzer's thought is immune from inner conflict.

Although the teachings of Jesus were the subject both of investigation and of his preaching during the decisive years of his spiritual development, his cultural-ethical ideology is nevertheless independent of Christian teachings.[1] But as he has no desire to separate himself from Christian thought, or would, since he is so deeply rooted in it, be able to, he is compelled to seek a synthesis between the two. At first the prospect seems favourable.

Although Schweitzer's philosophy of civilization does not expressly acknowledge any such origin it is the logical result of his investigations into the life of Jesus. The uncompromising rejection of the world and of this life by Christianity stems from the solution adopted by logical eschatology; in other words, from the exclusive interpretation of the teachings and the acts of Jesus as being based on the expectation of the imminent coming of the Kingdom of God. This is quite in order for early Christianity, but it arouses misgivings when the coming of the Kingdom of God is seen to move farther and farther into the future.

'Christianity's rejection of this world takes on a very different complexion when this event is expected in the far distant future instead of, as it was in the beginning, as a matter of the immediate

8. Portrait
(By permission of Erica Anderson, New York)

future. In the latter case it made no great matter since the Kingdom of God, in whose favour this world was rejected, was already at hand. But when the hoped-for event recedes into the indefinite future, man finds himself called upon to reject this world throughout the whole of his life whilst not being entitled to hope that he may experience the coming of the Kingdom in it. There is nothing more he can hope for either for the world or for mankind. Despair of the present exists side by side for him with a belief in the coming of the Kingdom of God at the end of time.

'The fact that the Kingdom of God was now entirely a matter of future expectations produced an unfortunate effect in itself: when the Kingdom of God was regarded as immediately imminent it did not matter that its coming was considered to be automatic, but when its coming receded into the distant future and it therefore became a matter of persisting in sheer expectation, it is obvious that the attitude imposed on believers by the idea that the coming of the Kingdom is automatic is unnatural. Both their rejection of this world and the idea that the Kingdom of God will come of its own accord condemn them to do nothing to improve the present.'[2]

But Schweitzer does attach importance to the betterment of this world, and for him this involves working for a higher development of human civilization. The ultimate aim of ethics is to secure a 'civilized mankind.'[3] But human civilization 'is the product of an optimistic-ethical conception of the world. Only in proportion as the prevalent philosophy is world- and life-affirmation and at the same time ethical, do we find ideals of civilization put forward and kept influential in the habits of thought of individuals and of society.[4]

Thus, to put it mildly, Christianity as a civilizing factor is a doubtful quantity. Not for nothing have the Middle Ages been called 'Dark'. Both the beginning and the development of modern civilization proceeded largely apart from, and even in opposition to, the Christian Church.[5]

'What then is civilization? It is the sum total of all progress made by men in every sphere of action and from every point of view, in so far as this progress helps towards the spiritual perfecting of individuals as the progress of all progress.'[6] But 'all real progress in the world is in the last analysis produced by rationalism',[7] the result of an enthusiasm that comes from thought. It pre-supposes a 'thinking ideology'. This is the source of the obligation to work personally to establish an ideology based on inward and outward thinking experience.

This is the path Schweitzer travelled. Following an examination of all the possibilities present in human history for a civilized ideology based on thought, the ethic of reverence for life derives from its alleged intellectual necessity and not from Christian teachings.

This independence cannot be maintained. Has it, Schweitzer inquires, led away from the path laid down by Jesus? And is not the world-view of reverence for life 'essentially related to that of Christianity?'[8] Even this is not enough. Because Schweitzer has never ceased 'to regard Jesus as the highest spiritual and religious authority',[9] he is forced to come to the conclusion that this ethic, for which the conception of love alone has proved inadequate,[10] is nothing but 'the ethic of Jesus now recognized as a necessity of thought'.[11] He then finds his own views confirmed in Paul's spiritual teaching—'Our thought finds itself at home with it as completely as if it had been a modern synthesis'.[12]

But this is not sufficient to complete the theological rehabilitation of his civilizatory ideology. The teachings of Jesus are more than, and different from, the proclamation of an ethic of love. They are dominated by the idea of the coming Kingdom of God. 'The one important thing is that we should be as thoroughly dominated by the idea of the Kingdom, as Jesus required His followers to be.'[13]

The structure of Schweitzer's civilizatory philosophy is also determined by a double theme: reverence for life and civilizatory will. What is more natural, therefore, than to place the latter in relation with the eschatological teaching of Jesus, just as the former was interpreted as a variant of the ethic of love? Schweitzer's argument goes as follows:

As the imminent expectation of the Kingdom of God recedes into a far distant expectation, so eschatological belief experiences a transformation into the uneschatological. Instead of expecting world perfection from the supernatural intervention of God man sees himself compelled to bring it about by his own activity. This presupposes a fundamental change in his attitude towards the world and towards life. This became possible only at the Reformation, and even then only gradually. But the process was facilitated by the fact that the ethics of Jesus, in so far as they embrace the ideal of activity, have an affinity to the acceptance of the world and of life. 'The ethic of love preached by Jesus and the ethic of humanness taken over from neo-stoicism by the acceptance of the world and of life are reconcilable.'[14] Thus eschatological belief becomes cultural will, and its aim, the 'ultimate moral perfection of the whole of mankind', can be 'defined in relationship with the teachings of Jesus as the Kingdom of God'.[15]

The equation seems to work out. Not only can the philosopher of civilization console himself with the thought that his results are in accordance with the teachings of Jesus, but thought operating independently provides proof of the absolute and universal validity of those teachings in their extended form freed from the dross of a contemporary ideology. The truth of Christianity is no longer 'based on one of its untenable historical aspects, but solely on profound self-knowledge and world experience through thought'.[16] The circle has now closed. Christianity has justified itself to reasoning thought. 'Christianity as the most profound religion, is to me at the same time the most profound philosophy.'[17]

But has the equation worked out? Has Schweitzer really succeeded in combining the results of his philosophy of civilization with his investigation of Christianity 'into a unified Christian-ethical ideology pointing the way to a Christian civilizatory ideology' with 'the normative interpretation of the early Christian teaching from the standpoint of his philosophy of civilization'?[18]

We have already pointed out that the ethic of reverence for life cannot be reconciled with the ethical teaching of Jesus. This discrepancy may be hidden behind the 'affinity' between the New Testament exhortation to love and Schweitzer's own loving attitude towards all creatures, but the arbitrarily erected edifice can certainly not withstand the explosive force of the idea of the Kingdom of God.

Eschatological belief has grown feeble, even where it is still part of Christian teaching. It hardly gives off any further ethical energy since Western theology concerns itself primarily with the doctrine of the forgiveness of sins. However, Schweitzer pushes the idea of the Kingdom of God into the foreground again. The significance of this action by his theological thought is not affected either by a criticism of the logical eschatological solution, or by Schweitzer's own teaching of the transformation of eschatological into uneschatological belief. As a prisoner of Jesus he knows that 'the Kingdom of God must recover for us the importance it had for Jesus and the early Christians'. This is essential 'if the real essence of Christianity is to remain what it was in its beginnings: a religion dominated by the idea of the Kingdom of God. The role which the Kingdom of God plays in belief determines the essence of that belief. The conception of the Kingdom and its realization are of secondary importance.'[19] 'All that matters is that we should think the idea of the . . . Kingdom with the same vehemence with which Jesus believed in the Kingdom which was to come in consequence of God's intervention, and know one and all that we must be prepared to sacrifice everything for it.'[20]

In saying this Schweitzer still believes that ethical reasoning belief and Christian teaching go hand in hand. But the connexion he uses to join the two together proves inadequate. The identity of the sermon on the Kingdom of God and the civilizatory ethic is an illusion. No process of 'spiritualization' can turn the Kingdom of God into a paradise of civilization.

As master of the organ, Schweitzer will hardly fail to admit the importance of the difference of register when he speaks of the one or the other.

'From the ethical comes ability to develop the purposive state of mind necessary to produce action on the world and society and to cause the co-operation of all our achievements to secure the spiritual and moral perfection of the individual, which is the final end of civilization.'[21]

'Our belief in the Kingdom of God must remain Primitive Christian, in the sense that we expect its realization not from deliberate organized measures, but from a growing power of the spirit of God. For we also know that the manifestation, arising out of an inner necessity, of the spirit of the Kingdom of God, of which we become partakers in the dying and rising again with Christ, is the true way of working for the Kingdom of God, without which all others are in vain.'[22]

Unquestionably these two utterances refer to very different things.

To be 'possessed and dominated by a hope of the Kingdom of God, and a will to work for it, which bids defiance to external reality' is belief 'in that as a miracle'[23] even when this is not conceived of, as did the early Christians, as the elevation of the world into a supernatural condition. Schweitzer is strengthened in this conviction by historical experience, and, last but not least, by the nuclear threat. 'The time in which we live summons us to new faith in the Kingdom of God.' But the 'illusion' that 'the appeal to reason' (thought) would suffice can 'no longer be maintained'. 'The concluding words of the "Our Father" are true for us once more in their original sense of a delivery from the dominance of evil world powers'[24]—even though we no longer see them embodied in anti-God angel-like beings.

Confidence in independent thought is shattered on the rock of belief in the Kingdom of God.

'To believe in the teaching of Jesus means to make the belief in the Kingdom of God proclaimed by Him live in us in our belief in

Him and in the salvation we experience through Him. Paul in His Christ mysticism was the first to fulfil this. Must we ignore his achievement and attempt the same from our own strength and in our own thought?

'However much confidence we rightly or wrongly feel in ourselves, if we have any real appreciation of unique greatness we cannot fail to come under the attraction of the powerful thinking and deep personal religion, in which Jesus' Gospel of the Kingdom of God first became the religion of belief in him and in the Kingdom of God. No other road is available to us than that which Paul opened up.'[25]

Schweitzer, whose Jesus investigation revolves around the belief in the coming Kingdom of God, is under its spell. However poor in faith his theology may seem, this article of belief is unshakeable. Indeed, Schweitzer regards it as 'the greatest and the most important which is asked from Christian faith'.[26] That this belief is held seems more important at this juncture than whether the form of belief can survive in the light of reasoning thought.

Belief finds its way into Schweitzer's theological thought through the door of eschatology, even if disguised and without any official legitimation. In the last resort this belief rises above all anxieties concerning the fate of culture and above all the results of thought. The words 'If only I have Thee, I care nothing for Heaven and Earth', and 'All things work together for good to them that love God'—appear to Schweitzer as the peaks of Arrarat appeared—'a place where men might take refuge when the flood of the inexplicable overwhelms all around.'[27] In the words of the Sermon on the Mount, because he sought first the Kingdom of God, and his righteousness, all these things were added unto him.

VII

LAMBARÉNÉ

Schweitzer's career began in the heart of the Western world on age-long cultivated soil where nature had been tamed by the hand of man for thousands of years; a soil impregnated with history, a nature whose *juste mesure* accorded with man's disposition; a nature, which, as it were, offered to its children with a gentle hand all they needed for soul and body. But then it went on into the immeasurable wastes of a formless jungle landscape. Something unforeseeable and unimaginable had come about: seemingly held fast by the innumerable strands of a closely-knit web of civilization, Schweitzer suddenly broke away and found himself as though by magic in a world which was more in accordance with the longing of his soul for the elemental and with the independence of his thought.

Just read his description of the entry into this new world in his book *On the Edge of the Primeval Forest*:

'We seemed to be dreaming! Pictures of antediluvian scenery which elsewhere had seemed to be merely the creation of fancy, are now seen in real life. It is impossible to say where the river ends and the land begins, for a mighty network of roots, clothed with bright-flowering creepers, projects right into the water. Clumps of palms and palm trees, ordinary trees spreading out widely with green boughs and huge leaves, single trees of the pine family shooting up to a towering height in between them, wide fields of papyrus clumps as tall as a man, with big fan-like leaves, and amid all this luxuriant greenery the rotting stems of dead giants shooting up to heaven. . . . In every gap in the forest a water mirror meets the eye; at every bend in the river a new tributary shows itself. A heron flies heavily up and then settles on a dead tree trunk; white birds and blue birds skim over the water, and high in air a pair of ospreys circle. Then—yes, there can be no doubt about it!—from the branch of a palm there hang and swing—two monkey tails! Now the owners of the tails are visible. We are really in Africa!

'So it goes on hour by hour. Each new corner, each new bend is like the last. Always the same forest and the same yellow water. The impression which nature makes on us is immeasurably deepened by the constant and monotonous repetition.'[1]

The affinity between this environment and his own personality, which appreciates only the grandly simple and direct, is obvious. It is so striking, that looking back after the event we can see clearly enough that what appeared to all his friends as an incomprehensible eccentricity when he told them of his decision now appears as an extraordinarily reasonable, even 'symbolic' choice.[2] What seems more natural than that a man who a few years later was to proclaim the decline of our civilization, should turn his back on 'the over-historicized, over-refined, senile atmosphere of Europe' (A. Albers) and, with that uncompromising forthrightness he has accustomed us to, take refuge in its radical opposite, the jungle?

Such an interpretation of his motives is not irreconcilable with the ethical impulses which imposed an obligation from youth on to live his life in the service of his suffering fellow men. But all the same it fails to grasp the essence of what happened. Apart from his desire for some absolutely personal and independent activity Schweitzer's decision to migrate to the jungle contains no trace of any individualistic motive. It was not the result of a choice in accordance with personal needs; it was, in fact, not the result of reasoning considerations at all. Schweitzer did not go into the jungle in order to escape conditions which did not suit him; he went into the jungle in order, as he wrote to his sister, 'to man one of the outposts of the Kingdom of God'.

The decade which, as a twenty-one-year-old, Schweitzer had allowed himself for free activity was drawing to an end, and as yet he had not made up his mind as to what form his 'direct service to humanity' should take. His work on behalf of vagabonds and released prisoners did not entirely satisfy him. Then one day—he was on a train journey to friends, and attending to his correspondence, as he usually did in such circumstances—the veil over the future parted for a matter of seconds. 'Like a flash of lightning' he realized: you must make a clean break! And then the veil closed again.

He has described in detail the moment, which came a little later, when he was given clear instructions: 'One morning, in the autumn of 1904, I found on my writing table in the College [whose director he was at the time] one of the green-covered magazines in which the Paris Missionary Society reported every month on its activities. A certain Miss Scherdlin used to put them there knowing that I was specially interested in this Society on account of the impression made on me by the letters of one of its earliest missionaries, Casalis by name, when my father read them aloud at his missionary services during my childhood. That evening, in the very act of putting it aside that I might go on with my work, I mechanically opened this magazine, which had been laid on my table during my absence. As I did so, my eye caught the title of an article: '*Les besoins de la Mission du Congo.*'

'It was by Alfred Boegner, the President of the Paris Missionary Society, an Alsatian, and contained a complaint that the Mission had not enough workers to carry on its work in the Gaboon, the northern province of the Congo Colony. The writer expressed his hope that his appeal would bring some of those "on whom the Master's eyes already rested" to a decision to offer themselves for this urgent work. The conclusion ran: "Men and women who can reply simply to the Master's call, 'Lord, I am coming', those are the people the Church needs." The article finished, I quietly turned to my work. My search was over.'[3]

No psychological or secularizing interpretation touches the core of this happening. The simple facts speak for themselves. Nevertheless there is still no general agreement concerning the significance of a step whose motives are foreign to present-day thought, whose unreasoning spontaneity appears to short-circuit with sublime contempt, the necessary consideration of pros and cons and whose adventurous and picturesque aspects do not make it any the more understandable. But one thing we do begin to notice on closer examination: an instinctive attempt on the part of others to gloss over and explain away this call, which is as awkward for Schweitzer's free-thinking followers as it is for non-Christians, and which even the orthodox—after all, they have an agnostic to deal with—find somewhat embarrassing. It has even been suggested that the radical-critical theologian lost his faith, and 'in despair' decided to fulfil at least his human obligations by devoting himself to the well-being of Negroes.[4] It has also been explained as the result of his cultural critical views. It has been neutralized by popularizing it for the man in the street as the expression of a warm-hearted humanity. The 'man of Lambaréné' in whom allegedly only 'problems of spiritual comprehension' are able to produce 'high spiritual tension', has been removed from the category of great religious personalities and approximated to Goethe.[5] This over-zealous juggling with the plain facts of the matter naturally makes people wonder why a simple jungle doctor should merit any particular attention at all.

Schweitzer himself is to some extent responsible for these misunderstandings. The philosophical explanation of his behaviour as the result of the ethic of reverence for life has caused wide circles of people to overlook the real origin of his work of charity as an unconditional act of obedience to 'a gesture of the Master', and therefore needing neither discussion nor explanation. But apart from this translation of a religious happening into the sphere of philosophical ethics, spiritual modesty and inclination to sober objectivity have usually persuaded him to cloak what happened to him. And, above all it was probably in order that the spiritual message of his undertaking should be understood even in the absence of religious ideas.

On the Edge of the Primeval Forest, the book of African memories to which we have already referred, was written in 1920. It begins with a chapter entitled 'How I came to be a doctor in the forest'. But whoever reads it in the hope of finding an explanation for the irrationality of his abrupt break with a form of existence which accorded so well with his tremendous intellectual vigour will be disappointed. The objections made when he announced his decision were not convincingly answered: 'Talent carries its own obligation; the cultural world needs abilities such as yours; your own country offers ample opportunity for charitable works; what can one penniless man do in the jungle—even with a wife who's a trained nurse—against the misery of a whole continent, when with a stroke of the pen one government official can do more harm than a whole lifetime devoted to charitable works can repair?' The rational objectivity, and the stressed practicality of the explanations given by Schweitzer for a decision whose enthusiastic character impressed those nearest to him as an unforgettable experience which thereafter continued to affect their own lives like the warning ticking of a clock, is positively oppressive: 'Thanks to the progress of medical science, the European has great resources against sickness and pain; he is the rich man compared with poor Lazurus, the coloured peoples. The few hundred European governmental doctors can shoulder only a very small part of this burden, and therefore volunteer medical men must go out, in numbers corresponding to the need', and work amongst the natives. Schweitzer was told by the Paris Evangelical Missionary Society that a doctor was badly needed in the Ogowe territory, particularly on account of the spread of sleeping-sickness, a disease treated since 1928 in special sleeping-sickness camps set up by the authorities. He therefore decided to volunteer. This version is briefly repeated in *Das Spital im Urwald* (*The Jungle Hospital*), a short introduction to a series of pictures.[6]

But in his book of African memories Schweitzer records almost casually how a Negro recovering from the anaesthetic after an operation to relieve him from pain seized Schweitzer's hand gratefully and would not let it go, whereupon Schweitzer told him quietly 'that it was Jesus who had sent the Doctor and his wife to the Ogowe'. It was to this Negro who had been saved by his scalpel, that in the simplest and most convincing words, Schweitzer revealed the secret of his decision and the spirit in which his task was being performed.

But why did the theologian Schweitzer go to Africa as a doctor and not as a missionary? To puzzled friends this seemed the most unreasonable aspect of his whole decision, particularly as it involved seven years of preparatory medical studies (1905–12), tremendously arduous because they had to be shouldered in addition to his other activities: sermons, theological lectures, scientific work and concert performances. But the motive was simple and compelling. If this were all we knew about Schweitzer we should still hold the key to his character.

The 'senseless' project developed from a double root.

The impelling motive of Schweitzer's consciousness from early youth on, was, as he tells us in *Jugenderinnerungen* (*My Childhood and Youth*), p. 75, 'my deep sympathy with the pain which prevails in the world around us. . . . We must all carry our share of the misery which lies upon the world. Darkly this thought worked in me, and sometimes it left me, so that I breathed freely and fancied once more that I was to become completely the lord of my own life. But the little cloud had arisen above the horizon. I could, indeed, sometimes look away and lose sight of it,—but it was growing nevertheless, slowly but increasingly it grew, and at last it hid the whole sky.'

When the moment came to draw the inevitable and saving conclusion from this temperamental disposition the need for wordless activity had become very powerful. 'For years I had been giving myself out in words, and it was with joy that I had followed the calling of theological teacher and of preacher. But this new form of activity I could not represent to myself as being talking about the religion of love, but only as an actual putting it into practice.'[7]

The 'way of service' developed from the encounter of profound personal experience and religious necessity.

The fact that the call to medicine became clear to Schweitzer only at the last moment, although as a boy the need to struggle against pain was already adumbrated in his soul, merely confirms the irrationality of the whole affair.

'As one who demands that idealism shall be sober' he felt himself compelled, 'like the man in the parable who "desiring to build a tower, first counts the cost whether he have wherewithal to complete it" '. His thirtieth birthday was occupied with such considerations. In the upshot he decided that his health was good enough, and his nerves strong enough, and that he had the required practical sense, sufficient energy and persistence, circumspection and frugality, 'and whatever else might be necessary to carry the idea into execution'. In addition he felt that his temperament would allow him to bear the possible failure of his project. Only after he had decided all this did the letters go out informing his friends and relatives of his decision.

How did Schweitzer start? He had already won a name for himself, so did he first secure financial backers? Did he gather helpers around him? Did he draw up plans for his hospital? Nothing of the sort, and it was not until 1920 that his appeal to 'the Fellowship of those who bear the Mark of Pain' was issued, when the work which had been destroyed by the First World War had to be started all over again. His original estimate of the cost of his undertaking was 15,000 francs (about £600 at the time) a year, a very modest figure but one far beyond his own means. Most of the money for the first two years came from the royalties on his Johann Sebastian Bach book, which appeared in French, German and English. Even then, the biblical tithe was deducted for distribution in the form of gift parcels for the poor.[8] The rest was raised by organ concerts. And on Good Friday of the year 1913, he set off to Africa with his wife.

Since then 'the jungle hospital' has become an institution, and there is no lack of edifying and heart-warming descriptions of its work of human charity. The rugged and powerful figure of its creator; the Negroes suffering from tropical diseases; the frugal lives of the doctors and their assistants; the animals, chimpanzee and antelope, the friends of this friend of dumb creatures; and the exotic beauty of the natural surroundings—thanks to photograph and film, they all play a role in our picture of Lambaréné. But an excess of illustration can even dull the fantasy, and we shall need a good deal of imagination to get any real idea of the herculean labours which were necessary to hew this work out of the surrounding jungle. It required the ingenuity of a Robinson Crusoe, the daring of a Davy Crockett, the organizational capacity of a staff officer, and the never-ceasing alertness of a polar explorer making his way ahead to an objective lost in infinity; and in addition to this improbable combination of talents in a preacher, a theologian and an organist comes an all-embracing human sympathy. The wave of suffering he had set out to fight broke over him almost as soon as he set foot on shore, and before even the simplest measure had been taken to safeguard his own existence in the jungle.

As a preliminary shelter the Mission placed a long-disused hut at his disposal, and there the life devoted to reverence for life had to begin with a mass slaughter of huge spiders and beetles even before it was possible to lie down and rest.

The arrival of the doctor was expected, so patients began to stream in at once, and treatment began even before the cases of medicaments and instruments had arrived. It was planned to build a corrugated iron shed to serve as hospital, but not even the timber framework had been erected when Schweitzer arrived. The Missionary Station had found it impossible to get labour. And therefore, because in order to avoid the danger of infection patients were not allowed to enter the staff quarters of the Whites, medical activity had to start in the open air, that is to say, in the burning tropical sun. When he succeeded in turning a windowless old fowlhouse into a hospital by knocking holes in the walls, whitewashing over the worst dirt and installing an old camp bed, Schweitzer was delighted. And so the work in the jungle began. At first the doubts of those who could see no sense in the whole undertaking seemed confirmed. But 'only in so far as we all become less reasonable in the ordinary sense, does ethical feeling begin to operate amongst us and allow problems to be solved which previously looked insoluble'.

In the meantime, thanks to the unflagging will of this one man, that old fowlhouse has blossomed out into an extensive hospital settlement in which up to six hundred persons must be fed every day.

This book must confine itself to essentials, and therefore we cannot go out of our way to erect a monument, however deserved, to those helpers of both sexes who devoted years of their lives to the building up of this work and without whose help it would indeed have been impossible. There were many of them, and they acted anonymously; it was, and still is, a fulfilment for them to work with Schweitzer in the name of practical charity. So let me mention only the names of Emma Hausknecht and Mathilde Kottmann, and that of Frau Emmy Martin, the widow of an Alsatian parson, who stayed behind in Günsbach to maintain the necessary contact between the jungle hospital and the outside world. A special word of appreciation is also due to 'the loyal comrade', as Schweitzer called her in his dedication of *Kultur and Ethik* (*Civilization and Ethics*), the woman who accompanied him selflessly into the jungle and without whom he would surely never have succeeded in laying the basis for his work so successfully.

Helene Bresslau was the daughter of a Strassburg historian, and she was Schweitzer's friend and helper from the year 1902 on. They married in 1912. She understood his decision and loyally supported it when so many of his friends disapproved. In order to accompany him and be useful to him there she trained as a nurse. In later years the state of her health prevented her from living for long periods at a time on the Equator, but whilst in Europe she still worked for the hospital by giving lectures. She died on June 1, 1957, at the age of seventy-nine, having just returned from Africa to Zürich, where she visited her daughter Rhena, who is married to an organ builder there. At her funeral the officiating minister declared: 'She married not only the man Albert Schweitzer, she also married the work to which he had been called.' Through her it was given to Schweitzer to know what a lifelong unity of wills can mean.

The growth and development of the jungle hospital was not a ceaseless forward movement. The catastrophe whose approach Schweitzer had sensed did not spare him even in the jungle. The self-destruction of Western civilization and Western prestige, the break-down of moral forces, even the weakening of the instinct of self-preservation, were given symbolical expression when on the outbreak of war Schweitzer's work was prohibited and he and his wife were placed in the charge of coloured soldiers. Later (in 1917) he was transferred to an internment camp in France. When after seven years he returned to Lambaréné he found only the ruins of his settlement. Everything had to start all over again. Later on the hospital had to be built for the third time when dysentery necessitated the isolation of the patients, and shortage of food made it essential to produce at least a part of the necessary food on the spot. In consequence the hospital was shifted to a larger site a couple of miles or so upstream where it could have its own grounds. The decision to move was taken in October 1925, and during 1926 Schweitzer spent most of his time on the building site, because he alone was able to persuade the natives to do any work at all;

and further, being skilled in every form of handicraft, he was the only one able to solve the dozen and one problems which arose in the unusual circumstances. His past experience served him in good stead, because if you want to build even a hen-coop in equatorial Africa a tremendous number of extra things have to be thought of. Because of the soldier ants it has to be built on piles—with as few supports as possible. Because of leopards it has to be solidly built with a roof sufficiently strong to prevent a leopard's paw from scratching a hole big enough for the rest of its body to slip through. And the walls must be absolutely impervious to snakes.

The new hospital, a village of corrugated iron sheds on stilts, was built on the side of a hill. The stilts were decided on because of the danger of flooding from the near-by river, and to ensure relative safety from the torrents unleashed by tornadoes.

It had not been necessary to clear the original site, which was in the neighbourhood of the Mission Station, but now real pioneering work had to be done.

The first thing was to survey and mark off the government 'Concession', which consisted of about 170 acres, mostly forest and undergrowth. 'We worked our way by compass into the forest and cleared paths for the surveying. When we came across marshland we contented ourselves with ramming large posts into the swampland every twenty yards or so. Occasionally we came across a thicket in which the dreaded red ants had made a home, then White and Black rivalled each other in the speed with which they beat a retreat. These ants live in the branches and let themselves fall in swarms on anyone passing underneath.

'Even before this work was finished we started the land clearance. We had to make part of the site arable as quickly as possible in order to grow maize. Because of the chronic food shortage we shall probably have to feed our patients for a long time to come on rice imported from Europe, and this means giving them supplementary food with a greater vitamin content.'[9]

Every morning all the patients capable of standing squarely on their two feet and using their hands were mobilized for the work of deforestation and land clearance and taken to the site in canoes. But once there they had to be persuaded to start work. 'Left to themselves the men would do practically no work at all. Why should they, who just happened to be there at the moment, bestir themselves in order that those who would be there in a few months' time should have maize to eat, and even live in better hutments?'

To round off the picture here is a graphic description of such a working day. Schweitzer the musician has the floor:

'A day up there unrolls like a symphony. *Lento*: unwillingly the men take the axes and machetes I hand to them as they come ashore. At a snail's pace they finally set off to the spot where trees are to be felled and bushes uprooted, but at last every man is at his allotted post. The first reluctant strokes fall. *Moderato*: axes and machetes are wielded in very slow tempo indeed. In vain the conductor tries to accelerate it. The midday pause ends the first boring movement. *Adagio*: with difficulty I manage to get the men back to their places of work in the forest gloom again. Not a breath of air is stirring. Occasionally you hear the sound of an axe stroke. *Scherzo*: one or two jokes I manage to make in my desperation come off. The atmosphere improves. There are cheerful shouts. One or two men even start singing. It's also getting a bit cooler. A gentle breeze steals up from the river and wafts through the forest. *Finale*: everyone is in high spirits, and with one accord they all decide to punish the wicked forest on whose account they are here instead of staying behind comfortably in hospital. Wild curses are uttered, and shouting and yelling the men attack the forest lustily. Axes and matchets vie with each other now. But no bird must break cover, no squirrel put in an appearance. No questions must be asked, no orders given. The slightest distraction would break the spell. The axes and the matchets would rest, the men would stand there discussing whatever had distracted them, and no more work would be done that day.

'Fortunately there is no distraction, and so the enthusiastic work goes on. If this *finale* can be extended for a good half an hour then the day will not have been wasted. And it goes on till finally I shout: "Amani! Amani!—enough! enough!" And then the work of the day comes to an end.'[10]

When Schweitzer won the Nobel Prize for peace in 1953 (in the meantime he had reached his seventy-ninth year) he had to turn himself for the fourth time into a builder on the grand scale because the prize money, together with funds subscribed by the Norwegian people, provided him with sufficient cash to found a leper village with accommodation for almost 300 patients. Leprosy, by the way, is very widespread in equatorial Africa. At first Schweitzer treated his patients chiefly with chaulmoogra oil from India. In less serious cases many months of constant application would often bring about an improvement and sometime even arrest the development of the disease. But recently a more successful treatment has been introduced in the shape of promin, and it has proved possible to heal even severe and very painful leprous sores on the feet in a relatively short period. 'How wonderful that there is now hope for these most wretched of the wretched!' The happiness at this success was great, but no less great were the strenuous efforts necessary to find accommodation for the patients. A letter written in this period[11] allows us to sense some of the difficulties:

'Most of my time now goes in building a village for my 280 leper patients. The old village of bamboo huts has rotted and there is no point in building the huts up again. I must build other and more permanent accommodation, and more comfortable too. I have to be with the lepers all the time, because they will obey no one but me, and if I were not there they would do nothing. . . . As soon as I leave the building site work stops. It is quite disheartening. The result is that I have to be there as overseer for weeks and even months on end. During the difficult levelling of the site, when hundreds of cubic metres of earth had to be excavated and carted away, I stood there weeping inwardly at having to do such stupid work. And now the stones have to be broken up, and building materials carried to the site and up the hillside. The new buildings are being erected on concrete walls 30 cm high and 18 cm thick. The framework is of hard wood. One of these buildings is already finished, and the lepers are happy at being half-way decently accommodated at last. But that doesn't make them work any the more willingly, and they have to be urged and driven the whole time. After the evening meal I have to attend to the most urgent matters relating to the hospital, including the most pressing correspondence: orders for supplies have to be drawn up and payments made. There must be no confusion here. I seldom get to bed before midnight, and I have to get up every day at 6.15. Chronic lack of sleep often affects my own performance.'

As Schweitzer's book *Civilization and Ethics* has it, reverence for life is 'a relentless creditor'. It will allow man to show consideration to others, but never to himself.

In 1957 the hospital was extended to take another hundred beds. Apart from the leper village it was now in a position to accommodate 350 patients. The patients are treated by three or four doctors—not including the jungle doctor himself. In addition there are doctors who come in to perform serious operations as a labour of love. The rest of the hospital staff consists of about a dozen white nurses and ten native male nurses. Then there are native women who sew, patch, wash and darn; native cooks, and native labourers in the fields.

9. At the piano in Lambaréné
(By permission of Erica Anderson, New York)

The establishment of the hospital, slow, arduous difficult, starting again from scratch on three occasions, has been achieved by methods which are about as far removed from those used to build up a modern civilized undertaking as one could imagine. A follower of Jesus cannot help tackling his work in a very different fashion from that of someone who is transferring a rationalized, equalitarian, civilized undertaking into some under-developed area—whether it be a power station, a clinic or a model settlement. This sort of undertaking has to be settled in all its details, and planned and financed before it starts; otherwise it can't be done. But the follower of Jesus acts according to a very different law. He must dare to go forward into the unforeseeable, not only for himself but for his project too. He knows that he must find his way without a navigational chart; in fact he knows that with the primitive means at his disposal he wouldn't dare to go forward at all according to any detailed plan. When Schweitzer started off he had no financial reserves, and when the First World War drove him back to Strassburg he found himself penniless with wife and child. The financial resources he managed to mobilize were just sufficient for the carrying out of a minimal programme for two years only; and because he was absent from Europe he was unable to supplement his reserves by lecturing and giving concerts. But again and again, and with never a gap throughout the years, what he needed turned up. One day he went into Lambaréné to collect his letters. The first one he opened was from the bank in Port-Gentil informing him that debits for hospital supplies had left his account heavily in the red. Very depressed, he sat down on a bench and racked his brains over the problem of how to raise the necessary money. And when, in order to take his mind off the seemingly impossible problem, he turned to the rest of his correspondence, the last letter he opened informed him that a substantial contribution to his work was on the way from the United States. It was just enough to clear his deficit. When he needed a special building for consumptive patients a letter arrived informing him that he had won a literary prize in Paris; 5,000 francs in cash went with it and this was used to build the new wing. When the bamboo huts in which the leprous patients were living began to cave in, the Nobel Prize financed the building of a more permanent leper village. You have to go forward along such an insecure path with unswerving faith or not at all.

The world can show other examples of such faith. In Schweitzer's case, his Alemannic peasant temperament allows him to pitch all preliminary book-keeping to the winds and make up for it by his practical competence and his constructive sense for organic development. He goes forward without any detailed plans, he takes all the time necessary for his project, and if necessary he starts all over again—and yet again. In consequence the whole undertaking has grown naturally, like a tree adding age-ring after age-ring and developing an individuality which bears all the marks of Schweitzer's own personality and also of the environment in which it was so lovingly built up. The hospital is unpretentious, admirably suited to its purpose, and above all natural.

Frugality is not asceticism. Schweitzer has sacrificed every claim to personal happiness, and even to a personal life. But this self-sacrifice was imposed upon him by the work itself, and for the same reason it is constantly imposed anew. But this self-sacrifice is not an end in itself, and it is not from any inner urge to spiritual or physical self-mortification. Schweitzer's style of life is, for example, quite different from that of his great African brother, Père de Foucauld, the friend of the Tuareg, whose contempt for physical needs made it impossible for even the most self-sacrificing companion to stay at his side. With all his personal simplicity, Schweitzer is urbane and his style of life is determined by its purpose. In his own person Schweitzer conscientiously carries out all the hygiene regulations laid down for the preservation of health. He regards his own health as important; something to be taken great care of in the interests of the work itself. The magnificent negligence of self in a Father Damien in treating his lepers (which caused him to contract the disease himself) would strike Schweitzer as more than folly; for him it would be a positive offence, an outrage against reverence for life. His collaborators are made as comfortable as the modest circumstances permit. Importance is attached to a carefully laid table and to a cultivated and above all healthy cuisine. Feast days are celebrated in high spirits, and, needless to say, this applies to the great feast days of the Church. The birthdays of the staff are not forgotten, and each new building is joyously dedicated on its completion. And there's room for a sense of humour. When Joulot, the tame young chimpanzee, was presented with a new cage he was escorted in ceremonial procession to his new quarters, which were specially decorated with bananas for the occasion. St John's day (Midsummer Day) is celebrated with a great bonfire on the sandbank opposite the hospital.

Some critics have complained that the jungle hospital of Lambaréné is too primitive, but Schweitzer is not a worshipper of technical perfection, and so the settlement—with the exception of the operating room

—is still without electric light even today. Although he has always been troubled by writer's cramp, the Doctor attends to all his huge correspondence without dictating and without the use of a typewriter. When he goes on board ship for a journey to Europe he is always accompanied by a bulky sack containing correspondence to be attended to on the voyage. Such well-filled sacks are to be found in his room too. He also takes a number of white linen bags with him on his journeys, and each contains a supply of currency for the countries he is visiting. But if anyone concluded from all this that Schweitzer lacks common sense he would be very much mistaken. In its latest form the jungle hospital is a marvel of adaptability, thanks to long years of practical experience, which have brought numerous problems, all of which have been solved, often with unconventional ideas quite astounding in their simplicity. If you compare Schweitzer's hospital, which has, so to speak, been stamped out of the ground, with a 'Negro Clinic' set up with lavish funds and equipped with all the latest technical achievements, the superiority of Schweitzer's more modest venture soon becomes obvious. It is certainly inimitable, but in fundamentals, whose significance seems not to have been sufficiently recognized yet, it should be copied. Europeans are inclined to think that they are doing the natives a favour when they impose a civilized way of life on them, but there is food for thought in the fact that Schweitzer, the greatest friend of the natives, objects very strongly to this viewpoint.

His hospital is natural according to its surroundings. 'It must be like a big native village in order that patients should feel at home, should come willingly and gladly bring their families with them.' The 'Humanitarianism' which thoughtlessly transfers what is suitable for us to the natives is cold and loveless, because it does not sufficiently consider the human beings concerned. Schweitzer, on the other hand, knows his Negroes very well, and he therefore knows that they feel happier if they can prepare their own food in their own family circle. No institutional cooking would do them as much good as the food they are used to—though, of course, in some serious cases exceptions have to be made. In a native village each hut has its fire going day and night; the food of the family is prepared on it, it warms the hut, and its smoke is the best protection against mosquitoes. And therefore fires are allowed in Schweitzer's hospital, even in the corridors and between the sleeping quarters—only when the patients try to light them under their beds does authority intervene.

Whoever is primarily conscious of the suffering of the world, and the need to alleviate pain, finds himself in an extreme situation in equatorial Africa. Schweitzer did not deliberately seek it, hardly imagined it; it was just there. It is as though in his campaign against pain and suffering he had set up his headquarters in the heart of the enemy camp. In describing his first impressions he quotes a young Negro as saying: 'Here, among us, everybody is ill', whilst an old Negro chief declared: 'Our country devours its own children.' To make matters worse, the Negro knows nothing of any means to alleviate pain; and it is quite wrong to assume, as Europeans often do, that he is less sensitive to pain than they are.

The most widespread ordinary diseases are tuberculosis, liver, kidney and heart troubles and chronic rheumatism. And then there are the tropical diseases proper, whose proliferating excesses are reminiscent of the luxuriating tropical vegetation all around.

Leprosy, which is mentioned in the Bible as an accursed disease which cuts off a sufferer from the company of his fellows, provides the jungle hospital with the biggest proportion of its patients.

Malaria is a threat which every white man in the tropics must bear constantly in mind, and almost all Negroes suffer from chronic malaria. As it is spread by mosquitoes which are abroad after dark, people must as far as possible stay indoors after sundown and all doors and windows must be protected with a fine mesh to keep out the mosquitoes. A mosquito-net is essential for sleeping. When you enter a building in the tropics after dark you hurriedly close the door behind you, and if a mosquito happens to have found its way in a hunt is staged at once. As a prophylactic measure everyone must take a quarter of a gramme of quinine daily. Anyone who contracts the disease before his body has become accustomed to the quinine runs a danger that the disease develops into the dreaded black-water fever (so-called because the urine takes on a blackish colouring) when quinine is the medicament used.

The malaria carrier flies by night, but the daylight hours are threatened by the no less dreaded tsetse fly, which injects the parasites of sleeping-sickness into the blood. At one time this disease was invariably fatal. Today it is curable. But in order to keep it under control, doctors must visit every village in sleeping-sickness areas twice a year, and take blood samples for microscopic examination. At the slightest suspicion the same procedure has to be adopted with spinal fluid obtained by lumbar puncture. Only if the infection can be identified in its early stages, i.e. when there are as yet no outward symptoms, and treated at once so that there are no sufferers for the carrier to sting, and then transfer the sickness to healthy people, will there be any prospect of suppressing the evil once and for all. Obviously, only government action on a big scale can secure this.

An unbalanced and monotonous diet can cause beri-beri, and the disease is endemic at the logging camps where the native labourers are fed on husked rice, and those responsible are unaware that on account of the husking the rice no longer contains sufficient protective vitamins. The result is beri-beri, which can produce paralysis, the swelling of the extremities and various coronary disturbances.

Infants suffer particularly from the terrible framboesia sickness, commonly called yaws. Not that adults are altogether spared its ravages. In the early stages of this disease raw excrescences like over-ripe raspberries appear on the skin—hence its scientific name. Later on they develop into widespread sores and penetrate in depth to attack the bones.

Dysentery is one of the scourges of the jungle hospital. In addition to the micro-organism common in Europe, tropical countries also have the amoeba bacillus. The disease is caused by unicellular animalcules (amoeba) which colonize the large intestine, penetrating its walls and causing bleeding sores. A patient can suffer simultaneously from both kinds. The indifference of the Negroes endangers not only themselves but constantly threatens the whole hospital with epidemics. And what a tremendous amount of work the treatment of native dysentery patients causes! Often they are too weak to move, sometimes they haven't even sufficient strength to lift a spoon to their mouths. And they foul themselves wherever they happen to be. At the same time it is very difficult to persuade healthy natives to take precautions against the disease, and absolutely impossible to persuade them to render the slightest help in the revolting treatment required by their fellows suffering from it.

The intestines are frequently attacked by various kinds of dangerous worms. One kind attaches itself by its mouth to the mucous membrane of the intestinal tract and produces ankylostomiasis or hookworm disease. The symptoms are severe stomachic disorders and anaemia, sometimes of a very severe character. Another kind of worm causes bilharzia which leads to internal haemorrhages and tumours in the mucous membrane of the large intestine.

For some as yet unknown reason the Negroes of Central Africa are much more subject to rupture than white men, and strangulated hernia is very common amongst them. The intestine becomes impassable, gases generate, the intestinal walls are terribly distended and the sufferer undergoes great agony. After several days of torment death comes as a merciful release. At some time or other every Negro has seen some unfortunate fellow suffering from strangulated hernia, rolling in the sand of his hut, and howling with agony till death comes to relieve him.

Boils and abcesses of all kinds flourish exceedingly in the climate of equatorial Africa. Sand fleas bore their way into the soles of the feet and cause painful sores. The worst of all are the so-called phagedanic abcesses, peculiar to the tropics. These spread in all directions, and often a patient's leg will be one raw sore in which bones and ligaments can be seen as white lines. Here too the pain is intense, and, in addition, the stench is so frightful that no one can bear to stay in the sufferer's vicinity. In the ordinary way such unfortunates are left lying in some deserted hut, wasting away until they die.

Finally there are the horrifying elephantiasis tumours, and here the proliferating fantasy of tropical nature runs riot. The patient is often unable to walk and he grows weaker and weaker. One such tumour cut away in hospital weighed over 80 pounds. Another patient was accustomed to use his growth as a sort of stool to sit down on.

One could go on indefinitely in the same way, but enough horror has already been described to prevent readers from continuing to regard the jungle hospital at Lambaréné with a sort of mild benevolence. Lambaréné is a battlefield of the struggle against pain and suffering, a battlefield whose horrors are not one whit less than those of the real battlefields of the Old World. And yet it is easier to rise to dramatic events than it is to sustain the never-ending struggle with those hostile powers which beset, torture, disfigure and kill men and women like the monstrous products of some Breughel-like fantasy. The enemy may be forced back at one point, but he has simply inexhaustible reserves to call on. The prospect of eliminating sleeping-sickness from a whole area is an exception. As a general rule when the enemy forces are defeated on one front, further legions press forward to take their place. It is like a battle with the hydra-headed monster whose heads grow again as soon as they are cut off. It is a battle which knows no end, or even a temporary armistice. Inexhaustible courage is necessary to sustain such a fight, coupled with a grim persistence which never allows the sword arm to sink. It is, in fact, a truly heroic undertaking. Heroic is an expression which is justified only in exceptional circumstances, but it certainly is here. It is a form of heroism which is made up of patience, humility, silent service and never-failing human sympathy. It requires forgetfulness of self and calm resignation, because the task ahead is always vastly greater than the successes so far achieved. Not that the struggle is without its rewards: there is the tremendous joy occasioned by the frequent victories over pain. Probably Schweitzer's greatest encouragement in the inferno of pain and suffering into which his path of obedience and renunciation has led him is the consoling knowledge that medical science has tremendous possibilities of alleviating pain in equatorial Africa even with modest means. For example, strangulated hernia can be cured by a comparatively simple operation; and an injection with arsenobenzol clears up the sores of framboesia almost as though by magic. With tropical dysentery injections of hydrochloric emetin quickly bring about an improvement and usually the cure is permanent. Even with sleeping-sickness and leprosy, treatment usually secures an improvement and the spread of the diseases is arrested. Patients suffering from elephantiasis sometimes look like old men when they first come to the hospital for treatment, and they often leave it as young vigorous men. Such successes are reward enough, because love, and that is the thing which ultimately dominates Lambaréné, is not so much concerned with suffering as an abstract and therefore immeasurable and unconquerable magnitude, but with the suffering of the individual, our neighbour.

The description of this stronghold of reverence for life would not be complete without mentioning another of its particular features: it has to be reconquered every single day, because this 'outpost of the Kingdom of God' lives up to its description in the constant threat to its existence. The jungle is a relentless enemy of any form of civilizing activity. But the constant offensive of this primeval force is not all; there is the no less constant lethargy, even resistance, of the natives for whose benefit everything is done in the first place.

Schweitzer has taken the Negroes to his heart. He has discovered lovable characteristics in them. But they certainly strain his patience, and everything which requires their co-operation demands a very special form of human charity. It is, in short, 'an exhausting task'.

All the native helpers are so unreliable that not the slightest temptation may be placed in their way, and they must never be left alone. Everything has to be carefully locked away, and no stores may ever be entrusted to them lightly. For example, the cook is given only the supplies he needs for the next meal. Should a European neglect such elementary precautions then the Negro steals with a good conscience. If a thing isn't under lock and key then it 'goes for a walk', to quote

Joseph, one of Schweitzer's Negro helpers. If a man is careless with his property then anyone else is entitled to take anything he can lay his hands on. And whether the stolen article is of any use to the stealer is quite beside the point. For instance, in this way Schweitzer lost the piano edition of *The Mastersingers* and the copy of Bach's *Matthew Passion*, 'into which I had written the organ accompaniment, which I had worked out very carefully'. All the windows of the living rooms and the store rooms of the hospital have to be carefully barred with hard wood-battens as a protection against pilferers.

Schweitzer's own room (unlike the simple but comfortable rooms of the young doctors and their wives) is as bare as a monk's cell, but not so tidy. It is cluttered up with a collection of pails, baskets and tools; in fact it has become a sort of toolshed. Schweitzer himself distributes such items daily and collects them again in the evening—in order that none of the expensive and often irreplaceable objects should get 'lost'. If he handed over control to someone else the new storekeeper might content himself with just counting the number of articles. But that wouldn't do at all. In such circumstances a new matchet could easily turn into an old one so worn as to be only half the length of the new one, because, given the chance, the labourers would keep the new matchets and sell them and hand in the old ones. The same is true of the axes and saws. And the flock of hens suffered in the same way: the numbers always tallied, but the birds themselves got progressively smaller. The big European hens gradually disappeared from the hospital hen-house to end their days in one native village or the other, whilst small, scraggy native hens took their place.

The losses sustained by this indiscriminate appropriation of hospital property are made worse by an utter lack of understanding for values. Expensive planks and rafters are used for fuel in order to save the trouble of going into the near-by forest and cutting timber. The same fate was suffered by a laboriously constructed sun canopy over Schweitzer's canoe; one morning it was missing and its charred remains were found on a native fire. Similarly, used bandages are thrown away instead of being handed in for sterilization and re-use.

Further, the difficulty of inculcating even a modicum of discipline into, and obtaining a modicum of help from, the natives, particularly the savages from the interior, is enormous. On principle the natives are not prepared to do anything which is in the least repulsive. No native can be found to wash out bandages, not even for high wages. No native will do a hand's turn to help in the treatment of dysentery patients; it all has to be done by the white folk. And the same is true of any kind of labour which does not obviously belong to some recognized job. 'The cook does nothing but the cooking; the washer-man washing and ironing; and "the Boy" looks after the rooms and the fowls. Each of them, as soon as he has finished his own work, goes off to rest!' Even the most elementary hygienic precautions are neglected. Only water from the well should be used, but the well is a hundred paces away, the river only twenty. The natives therefore drink the contaminated river water.

But even more difficult to deal with than real savages are those natives who regard themselves as educated. One day Schweitzer was carrying building timber under cover at the beginning of the rains, doing the job himself because of a shortage of labour: 'I catch sight of a Negro in a white suit sitting by a patient he has come to visit. "Hullo, friend," I call out, "won't you lend us a hand?" "I am an intellectual and I don't drag wood about", comes the answer. "You're lucky," I reply, "I too wanted to become an intellectual, but I didn't succeed." '

The biggest difficulty of all is that the conception 'fellow human being' just doesn't exist for natives. Generally speaking sympathy and assistance from natives is available only for those who belong to their own tribe. Once towards evening an injured man had to be brought quickly into the examination room. A Negro was sitting by a fire doing nothing. Schweitzer happened to be treating this man's brother, and he asked him to lend a hand with the stretcher. At first the man pretended not to hear, and when Schweitzer repeated his request in a voice which made it impossible to ignore, the man replied firmly: 'No. That man belongs to the Bakele tribe, and I am a Bapuna.'

It is therefore not surprising that sympathy and despair occasionally form 'a tangled knot' in the heart of the jungle doctor. Exhausted he let himself sink into a chair in the consulting room one day and groaned: 'What an idiot I was ever to become a doctor to such savages!' To which his coloured helper Joseph observed unsentimen-tally: 'Yes, you are a big idiot on earth, but not in Heaven.'

However, what a wisely conducted Christian teaching at the Mission Stations can and often does achieve is not undone by such disheartening experiences. The way of 'reverence for life' adopted by Schweitzer does not culminate in the loving care for the individual and his well being, but in the general struggle against pain and disease. His contact with the Negroes is brought about by physical crises in their lives and it usually ends when they have been overcome, so that generally speaking it is impossible to exercise a profounder influence on them. The struggle against pain is carried on in an unending series of individual acts, and this form of charity is in complete accordance with the will ethic of Schweitzer. It demands service to threatened life and not to any individual personality. This springs from its equalization of all forms of life. With compelling logic therefore human life appears as something anonymous. The apostle of reverence for life has to bear the burden of working as a human being amongst human beings who pass before him as unknowns in a horrible procession of innocent sufferers from the self-alienation of life, hoping always that he can alleviate their pain and suffering. Attempts to present Lambaréné in pictures are variants of two motives, everything else is a side-show: scenes from the 'battlefield' under the banner of reverence for life, and scenes showing the intimate relationship of Schweitzer with his dumb friends the animals, who live with him as part of his household. These pictures are the only ones which give an idea of intimacy, relaxation and content in a heart at rest. Schweitzer himself has described the life of only one of the inmates of his hospital. The subject of this biographical sketch is a pelican.[12]

One must not conclude from all this that Schweitzer is not just towards his Negroes. He is, indeed, and the daily grind does not cloud his judgement. He discovers traits in these children of nature which he missed in his former environment, traits which he values higher than those they lack. The Negro, 'not having been artificialized and spoilt as we have been, has only elementary standards of judgement, and he measures us by the most elementary of them all, the moral standard'.[13] 'He has a natural responsiveness to the notion of goodness and all that is connected with it in religion. . . . There lives within him a dim suspicion that a correct view of what is truly good must be attainable as the result of reflection. In proportion as he becomes familiar with the higher moral ideas of the religion of Jesus, he finds utterance for something in himself that has hitherto been dumb, and something that has been tightly bound up finds itself released. . . . Never have I felt so strongly the victorious power of what is simplest in the teaching of Jesus as when, in the big schoolroom at Lambaréné, which serves as a church as well, I have been explaining the Sermon on the Mount, the parables of the Master, and the sayings of St Paul about the new life in which we live. . . . Moreover, there slumbers within him an ethical rationalist.'[14] For Schweitzer this is the highest praise.

The jungle hospital at Lambaréné is based on practical experience and it has enjoyed full freedom of development. Because of this it is an accurate reflection of Schweitzer's idea of his relationship with the natives as human beings amongst whom it is his destiny to work. But the solitude of the jungle in which he once felt himself secure has suddenly changed into an arena where the most dramatic issues of world politics are at stake—no less than the liberation of the Dark Continent. Problems have arisen whose solution will change the face of the earth for better or worse. This make us wonder about Schweitzer's own views concerning the treatment of the Negroes and their relationship to the Whites. The answer to this question will help us to understand both Schweitzer and his hospital. His reaction to politics as such and to the practical problems of treating human beings in his own sphere of experience and work is not doctrinaire. No 'idea' is allowed to plant itself between his eyes and reality. Things are seen and tackled as they really are. But this is realism of a particular kind. The only criterion is the improvement of human conditions.

Schweitzer's opinions have been formed as the result of long years of experience amongst the natives of equatorial Africa. He understands them as hardly anyone can who comes into contact with them only through politics, the civil service or economics.

His judgement on the native problem is based on a rare combination of factors: a deep belief in humanity, an absence of all racial prejudice, and a concentration on the peculiarities, needs, sufferings and well-being of the Negro, who does not represent a means to any sort of end whatever, but an end in himself. And, finally, a lack of all ideological bias. When Schweitzer talks about colonization and about the relationship between the white and coloured races, he does so, as he says himself: 'as the farmer talks about his crops'. A sense for realities and sound common sense guide him. In tackling native problems you must start from things as they are and not from abstract ideas of liberty and human rights. In this respect, too, Schweitzer clearly finds himself utterly at variance with the spirit of the age, and his opponents have not failed to exploit what appears to them a vulnerable point.[15]

What interests Schweitzer is that the natives should develop into capable human beings able to cope with the circumstances brought about by having to live in contact with the outside world, and that, as far as possible, they should themselves control and mould those circumstances. They must therefore be helped to develop qualities they do not possess in the ordinary way, or not in sufficient measure: 'Seriousness, a sense of duty, a consciousness of responsibility, love of work, devotion to their calling, an enterprising spirit, circumspection, independence—that is to say, all those qualities which produce soundness and solidity in the best sense.'[16] The awakening consciousness of an obligation towards the 'under-developed' people who have been handed their independence without sufficient preparation is certainly to be welcomed. Only when the idea of the solidarity of all mankind takes hold of the mind of man will it be possible to solve the problems which arise with the compulsory civilization of primitive peoples. Its triumph would mean the entry into a new world era. However, we are still very far removed from realizing the moral profundity of this idea. It embraces selflessness and modesty; that is to say, qualities which are not often met with in political life. The primitive stages of civilization contain elements that are superior to those of the more developed civilizations. When the Negro awakens to real independence, instead of falling victim to the superstition of progress, he realizes this. Where there is no respect for the old orders endangered by civilization then any intervention can only be destructive. With its 'development aid', which is often impelled more by political interests than by any care for the well-being of those 'aided', to whom there is no really responsible relationship, the civilized world is in danger of loading itself with a burden of guilt even greater than that imposed on the white world by the crimes of the colonizers.

Any educational efforts which are carried out without proper attention to the course of development of the civilized peoples are doubtful from the start. The missionary schools which grew up out of real love for the natives are well aware of this.

From this standpoint there is no sense in measuring the progress of civilization in Africa by the extension of a railway line to this point, or a motor-road to that, or by the establishment of an air line between this point and that. This sort of thing merely creates problems; it does not solve them.

In the same way, educational efforts which start with the struggle against illiteracy as such without taking the disparity of development into account are just as useless and even dangerous. Anyone who is in the least acquainted with adult education knows that despite a thousand years of civilized progress adult education is very far from having solved the problems that widespread literacy—using the term in the sense of being able to read and write—has brought with it. The natives are in danger of skipping the intermediate stage between their own primitive lives and that of the civilized brain worker. The 'educated' native has a great disinclination to use tools; and coupled with this disinclination is a great longing to sit in an office somewhere with a cigarette between his lips and a pen behind his ear.

But human civilization begins with tools. And Schweitzer can see very clearly that whilst the imposition of a European educational system teaches the native to read and write it also tends to make him hold working with his hands in contempt. On the other hand the natives can be helped to become capable people by religious and moral training and by working with their hands. The other things will lack all sense so long as this primary basis is not well and truly laid.

The tragic thing is that the interests of civilization and those of colonization (or more accurately, the inevitable process by which the natives are drawn into the larger world of economics and technology, whether this is brought about by colonialism or not) are not identical; indeed, in many respects they conflict. Native interests require that their traditional rights and customs should be maintained and developed, and that the existing state of affairs should not be changed without real necessity. In fact, however, modern innovations break up traditional native customs, upset the age-old rhythm of native life and destroy the old social order. The Negro is a really worthwhile person only when he is with his family in his own village, where he is morally sustained by tribal solidarity. Taken suddenly out of his natural environment he falls an easy prey to moral and physical ruin. Colonies of Negro labourers living without their families are hotbeds of demoralization. But modern commerce, big plantations and the efficient exploitation of the country's natural resources demand such colonies, since without them they could not be carried on at all.

Today it is fashionable to ignore or even discredit the achievements of the original colonizers. The European powers are urged to give the colonial peoples independence as rapidly and completely as possible. Any inclination to continue governing these peoples and guiding their development is condemned as brutal imperialism. A conference at Accra in December 1958, allegedly representing 200 million Africans from twenty-eight countries, forcefully demanded the immediate and complete liberation of Africa; full sovereignty for all African peoples; the creation of an African Commonwealth; and the overthrow of imperialism and colonialism. The conference also called on the already independent native States of Africa to support the still dependent peoples in their struggle for freedom.

There is no force that can hold up this elementary surge towards emancipation. It is creating new and violent spheres of power which are already in process of changing the face of the world. The colonial powers have given way to it without resistance because, above all, they have long lost that inner sense of security which is the preliminary condition for the exercise of any kind of authority. The apple does not fall before it is ripe. And men are anxious to divest themselves of responsibility when they no longer have strength enough to carry it. In the meantime, the primitive peoples are engaged in the most daring experiment in history and they are entering into a period of great danger—for them and the rest of the world.

Now Schweitzer would not dream of denying that the colonial powers have sinned grievously against the natives, but his profound sense of reality has taught him two things: a frank appreciation of the real achievements of colonization, and the doubtful value of the liberty which the natives are so anxious to obtain. So-called 'Imperialism' abolished the slave trade; it also put an end to the constant wars which the primitive peoples of Africa waged against each other, thus bringing the benefits of peace to large areas of the world. At the same time many governments did their best to protect the natives against exploitation by commercial interests.

Generally speaking primitive and semi-primitive peoples did not lose their freedom because their territories were occupied by some colonial power. They actually lost their freedom and independence the moment the first ship put in with white men bringing powder and shot, rum, salt and textiles. The task of political colonization was largely to act as a corrective to the evils accompanying the economic development which then opened up. And when at a later stage such a territory becomes formally independent once more the real liberty of the peoples living in it is by no means safe on that account. The farther such a territory moves away from its former primitive conditions of life the more it finds itself entangled in the web of world economy, and its economic development necessarily brings it into dependence on outside capital investors.

Modern programmes of political emancipation push forward something which really belongs in the background. 'Whoever knows the colonies and is well disposed towards the colonial peoples can never regard the speediest possible achievement of independence as the first and primary aim. This is by no means what is most needed. The primary aim should be to assist the colonial peoples to obtain what is essential and serviceable to them in modern civilization, and to obtain it in such a way that they can develop into sound and capable men and women representing a real and valuable humanity. Whether or not when they have finally arrived within reach of this aim they feel it right to rule themselves is something they must decide for themselves. But in their present stage of development it is doing them no service to egg them on to think primarily about their independence and to organize themselves to express 'the will of the people'. The more they are deluded into chasing after this secondary aim the farther will they drift away from the thing which should be of primary importance to them.'[17] It has not taken many years to demonstrate the truth of these words of a true friend of the Negro peoples.

Schweitzer's ideal is based on the ideas of freedom and human rights developed in the eighteenth century. However, when the welfare of human beings to whom he is devoted is at stake his attitude is completely empirical.

The political demands put forward by the representatives of the coloured peoples show clearly that they are not really on the way to their emancipation. Such demands merely reveal that they have been carried away by Western ideas which, though they may be valuable rightly applied, are nonsensical when applied in totally different circumstances.

The nationalistic demands put forward on behalf of the coloured peoples are based on the fiction that these peoples are comparable with the peoples who were struggling for their development in the rising national States of Europe. In reality the former colonial peoples belong together only in so far as they were subjugated by one particular foreign people, and have lived since then in what was once its particular colonial territory. One result of this occupation was that tribes which had formerly fought each other ruthlessly were now compelled to live at peace. Thus independence removes the main thing which previously held them together: the various native peoples once again feel themselves separate; their differences come to the fore; the tensions which existed between them become important once more. The classic example of this is the tragedy ushered in by the granting of independence to the Congo.

The idea that 'the will of the people' can be discovered by means of the ballot-box is quite unrealistic where the majority of the voters are illiterate. Very few can read and write, and of those even fewer are capable of forming a reasoned political judgement. Under colonization the natives were untroubled by political passions. But these passions are an inevitable concomitant of political activity. Schweitzer anxiously wondered what form they would take, and what the consequences would be. The answer was provided all too clearly by an incident which took place on February 17, 1959, in Brazzaville, the capital of the French Congo. Fighting broke out between two tribes, and according to official reports 250 natives were killed. The actual number was very much larger but impossible to estimate with any accuracy because many corpses were flung into the Congo river and devoured by crocodiles. The Negroes bedizened themselves, donned their tribal trappings, and proceeded to attack their enemies with knives and clubs. And what did they kill each other for? A debate on the parliamentary budget!

When Schweitzer returned to Lambaréné in 1924 he soon had to recognize that his hospital would not be the same as before. At that time the change was being brought about by economic developments. During his first stay in Lambaréné most of his patients belonged to tribes long established in the neighbourhood. Now many of his patients were primitive savages from the interior, homeless proletarians recruited to work as labourers in the timber camps. This gave rise to complicated social, economic and hygienic problems.

Since then further changes have called the whole structure of the hospital community into question. Gabun has changed so fundamentally since Schweitzer's hospital was founded that in the new French edition of *On the Edge of the Primeval Forest* in which he describes his early experiences the preface calls it an historical document. In tones of resignation he describes the dawning of the new era:

'At the time with which this book deals we still had the right to regard ourselves as elder brothers of the natives; elder brothers who were well disposed towards their younger brothers, and at the same time sufficiently experienced and knowledgeable to be able to judge what was best for their true advancement, and able to act accordingly. And those of us who felt like this and acted accordingly were not an isolated few. On the contrary, there were very many of us: Governors, colonial officials, missionaries, doctors, even timber merchants, traders, colonists of all kinds. And with pride and satisfaction we observed that the most sensible and far-sighted natives did, in fact, regard us as their elder brothers, and recognized that we had their well-being at heart and were doing our best for them in a spirit of justice and equity. As an eye-witness of the efforts made in those days I make bold to say that in many years of work we were often successful; not only economically but also in the establishment of a spiritual and human relationship between ourselves and the natives. A relationship based on mutual trust and confidence was developing. Despite the inadequacy of our achievements, despite lost opportunities, and despite

10. Schweitzer checking his drugs—under difficulties
(By permission of Erica Anderson, New York)

many mistakes, we had good reason to feel that we were on the right path.

'Now we have to admit that we can no longer feel ourselves as elder brothers, and we can no longer act as though we were. Today many people seem to think that the era of progress can dawn only if the younger brother is regarded as already mature and every bit as capable as the elder, and that therefore the natives should take the fate of their country more and more into their own hands. The spirit of the age has spoken. In all things, and everywhere throughout the world, it calls for the abolition of all traces of the former patriarchal system and its replacement by a non-patriarchal system, one which is difficult to define and will be even more difficult to carry out.'[18]

Schweitzer can see the problems which have been raised by the native demand for emancipation clearly enough, and he is prepared to solve them in a realistic fashion. But the very conception of the hospital at Lambaréné is patriarchal. This is first of all in accordance with the personality of its founder and director and secondly with the actual character of the people with whom he has to deal. As both one and the other have remained the same there is no room for any change in the structure of this unique formation. In fact any such change would shatter its foundations altogether. When life or death is at stake there is no room for slogans. A sort of parliamentary democracy in the jungle hospital would be impossible. According to the Afro-Asian Congress in Cairo in December 1957, 'The white man . . . must get used to living with the natives [in Africa] on the same footing and as equals', but this becomes an empty phrase when much needed and much desired help has to be brought to the natives, and when the only way to do it is authoritarian. Practical experience in the work of the hospital demonstrates this very graphically. The Negroes at Lambaréné,[19] both the savages from the interior and the semi-civilized natives from around the lower Ogowe, are just not capable of competing with the Whites in work, discipline and self-sacrifice, nor, indeed, have they any desire to do so. Thus not only have they no just claim to equal rights, but to grant them such rights would very quickly operate against their own interests.

We have now seen the jungle hospital of Albert Schweitzer at work.[20] We know how it became what it is today, a focal point of interest to the whole world. We know what goes on inside those corrugated iron huts, and we know the spirit that guides it all. But does all this make obvious the sense of the undertaking as a whole? Certainly, the curing of all those Negroes who would be helpless victims of their sufferings but for the jungle doctor appeals to us at first glance as raising no problem at all and requiring no special comment. The simplest soul can grasp it at once. It is as straightforward and obvious as the proverbial deed of the Good Samaritan. But every profound simplicity is made up of many layers and produced from the pressing of many vines. That is also true of this product of a unique combination of enthusiastic mysticism and enormous common sense, of adventurous courage and thoughtful reliability, of self-will and obedience. 'My friends have no more patience with my paradoxes. It is time for me to go' said Schweitzer shortly before his first departure for Africa. He did not leave those paradoxes behind him when he went.

The spiritual structure of the building he erected under palm trees in the distant jungle, and as it developed through the years, is far from simple. It rests, so to speak, on three pillars, though its threefold ideological foundation is not the result of any previously thought-out plan, and in all probability the founder himself had no very clear idea about it, but it does have the advantage of providing a broader support.

The main idea, deeply rooted in the early layers of Schweitzer's own nature, forms the basis of the 'Fellowship of those who bear the mark of Pain'. The importance attached to it can be seen from the fact that Schweitzer himself regards it as the dedicated pillar of the whole edifice. Schweitzer has no Church behind him, no government and no organization—even the Paris Missionary Society gives him very little practical assistance—so he applies to those 'who bear the Mark of Pain'.

Who are these people? They are not necessarily Christians, and from the very first stages of his work in Africa Schweitzer was conscious of undertaking something that extended beyond any religious confession as such.

'Those who have learnt by experience what physical pain and bodily anguish mean, belong together all the world over; they are united by a secret bond. One and all they know the horrors of suffering to which man can be exposed, and one and all they know the longing to be free from pain. He who has been delivered from pain must not think he is now free again, and at liberty to take life up just as it was before, entirely forgetful of the past. He is now "a man whose eyes are open" with regard to pain and anguish, and he must help to overcome those two enemies (so far as human power can control them) and to bring to others the deliverance which he has himself enjoyed. The man who, with a doctor's help, has been pulled through a severe illness, must aid in providing a helper such as he had himself, for those who otherwise could not have one. He who has been saved by an operation from death or torturing pain, must do his part to make it possible for the kindly anaesthetic and the helpful knife to begin their work, where death and torturing pain still rule unhindered. The mother who owes it to medical aid that her child still belongs to her, and not to the cold earth, must help, so that the poor mother who has never seen a doctor may be spared what she has been spared. Where a man's death agony might have been terrible, but could fortunately be made tolerable by a doctor's skill, those who stood around his death-bed must help, that others, too, may enjoy that same consolation when they lose their dear ones.

'Such is the Fellowship of those who bear the Mark of Pain, and on them lies the humanitarian task of providing medical help in the colonies. Their gratitude should be the source of the gifts needed. Commissioned by them, doctors should go forth to carry out amongst the miserable in far-off lands all that ought to be done in the name of civilization, human and humane.'[21]

The guiding idea at the basis of this Fellowship that 'he who has been delivered from pain' must bring freedom from pain to others is clearly a variant of the idea that originally took possession of the young Schweitzer that whoever has received many good things in life has an obligation to give as much back again.

However, the moral obligation which is advanced here as though it were a matter of course proves on closer examination not to be so matter of course at all. On its own it is not universally compelling even though it may seem obvious enough to nobler souls. Schweitzer himself regards it as an idea which must conquer the world because of its 'inexorable logic'.[22] Here too we can once again recognize the urge which is in him to present those things he regards as obvious with the authority of 'intellectual necessity'. Now although the obligation certainly makes a powerful appeal to heart and conscience, it is not all that obvious and matter of course to rational thought. The relationship it establishes between a man's own welfare and his attitude towards his fellow men, the derivation of a moral obligation from his personal well being, or his personal liberation from suffering, is obviously taken from the parable of the wicked servant (Matt. xviii. 33): 'Shouldest not thou also have had compassion on thy fellow servant, even as I had pity on thee?' The moral logic of this demand for reciprocal charity is based on the fact that the servant received charity as a gift of the Lord. It does not extend therefore to well-being which is the result of chance and is not appreciated as a gift. But this is not altogether what Schweitzer has in mind. The urge of the charitable heart needs no particular justification, neither does the need of the man made happy to make others happy. These are reactions which are spontaneous in charitable natures. They are voluntary impulses. But it does not follow from this that a winning ticket in the lottery of life imposes as an intellectual necessity a moral obligation on the lucky one to give his winnings away to others less fortunate than himself.

It is not often that the secularized expressions used by Schweitzer (Work of humanity! Human civilization!) so transparently reveal the background of Christian belief on which his thought is based. And at the same time it is not often so clear that the real significance derives from this origin; and that it can, in fact, not be replaced by any supposedly compelling logical argumentation.

The second ideological pillar of the work at Lambaréné is of local origin. It does not directly concern the suffering of fellow human beings as such but the moral obligation of the European towards the natives of Central Africa. The services rendered by the former to the latter are regarded as the payment of a debt. 'What has to be done for the suffering natives must not appear to us as "a good work" but as an ineluctable duty. . . . We are not free to decide whether we will do good to the people out there or not—we must. The good we do for them is not an act of benevolence; it is an act of atonement. For everyone who causes suffering another must go out and bring help. And yet if we all do everything which lies in our power we shall not atone for a thousandth part of the guilt.'

A great deal of suffering has been caused to the natives by the disturbing effect of colonization on their traditional lives. For example, sleeping-sickness was at one time confined to certain localities, but then it spread because European colonizers and explorers caused natives to move from place to place as members of boat crews and bearer trains. The sand flea, or 'Jigger', which is responsible for the fact that most of the Negroes of Central Africa have crippled toes, was introduced from South America in 1872, and within a decade it had spread from the Atlantic to the Indian Ocean. Tuberculosis was unknown in the French Congo until it was introduced comparatively recently from Europe. In the hot humid climate it develops rapidly and if untreated usually ends fatally. Europeans also bear a heavy responsibility for the ravages wrought by schnapps and venereal disease, both of which they introduced.

When Schweitzer went to Africa he was filled with the idea that his action was an atonement for the sins of our civilization. Now this idea is not derived from humanitarian idealism, but, like the idea of an obligation on account of favours received, from the biblical world. Guilt, atonement and vicarious sacrifice are all unfamiliar concepts for modern thought, which deliberately evades them. They presuppose some sort of mystical debit and credit balance, and this inevitably culminates in the idea of rewards and punishments which, in accordance with liberal thought, Schweitzer himself rejects as a primitive form of ethics. It is therefore natural that this non-contemporary moral pillar of the jungle hospital should have attracted least public attention.

The third pillar, the ethic of reverence for life, has, on the other hand, been almost explosive in its effect. In fact one can say with confidence that this was the factor which made the jungle hospital, despite its isolation, a central point of attention for people all over the world. Not that they bothered much about philosophical morality and its intellectual necessities. It was just that the jungle hospital gave them what they secretly longed for and what they missed elsewhere: a demonstrable unity of idea and action. The idea was clearly living up to its obligations every passing day. What was believed and what was taught was also practised. 'It is good to preserve and encourage life; it is bad to destroy and inhibit life.' In the jungle hospital people could see, so to speak, a working model of this axiom in practice. It extends 'the Fellowship' beyond those who 'bear the Mark of Pain to include all humanity, and it extends the circle of those entrusted to it to include all living creatures.

In addition, the dècor heightens the general impressiveness. One day a visitor noticed an ant on Schweitzer's collar and was about to remove it, but Schweitzer intervened. 'Leave it in peace,' he said. 'Have you learnt to pick up an ant or push it away without breaking its leg?' Such a gesture in Europe might touch an observer because of the sensitivity it bespoke, but against the fantastic proliferation of African fauna in which a man has all he can do merely to defend himself, and in which a lover of animals must appear as an enemy of the barbarous mass slaughter which piles up hecatombs of victims every year in the African jungle, it takes on the quality of a dramatic event. In short, in circumstances when this very proliferation of fauna represents a constant and extreme threat to life and limb, the ethic of reverence for life takes on a particular accent all its own.

At the same time the whole undertaking has developed against the background of two world wars and an increasingly widespread contempt for human life. It is therefore not surprising that this manifestation of reverence for life has developed into a symbol of protest against the daemonism of the age and at the same time into a symbol of faith in its ultimate overcoming.

One might suppose that with an examination of the motives which led Schweitzer to begin this work, with a description of the work itself and of the ideas which govern its operation, the reader would now have a thorough knowledge of the jungle hospital. But this is not so; there remains an insoluble rest in the test-tube which has defied the analysis. There is an element in the jungle hospital which cannot be recognized from its outward appearance, or from its inherent ideas, or from anecdotes about its founder Albert Schweitzer. Whoever knows Schweitzer and his work will feel that there is something very important which is very difficult to describe and which has, in fact, not yet been described. If anyone should doubt it there is one sure sign. A very great deal has been said and written in an effort to explain the unexplainable impression created on so many people by this magnificent and yet essentially modest undertaking. But not all of it put together provides an entirely satisfactory explanation of its magical influence. Lambaréné has become a sort of mystic formula which unlocks the hearts of men, turns strangers into friends and gives confidence to those who despair of the world. Now no matter how great the interest in an ethical idea and its practical realization may be, it is not enough to account for this. If Lambaréné were nothing more than the practical result of an ethical principle the vast influence which it exerts would be incomprehensible. But in its innermost essence it is something quite different. It is the outward expression of the fate destined for a great soul. It is the transformer which makes the tremendous power of this soul assimilable by the outside world.

There are violent elements in Schweitzer's character. His undertaking is carried forward by his will alone; it challenges conventional thought; it places a question mark against the way of the world; it declares war on the self-alienation of the will to life. Nevertheless Lambaréné is not the result of some titanic act of defiance. It was not brought about by Schweitzer, but rather through him. He is not so much its master as—to use his own expression—its prisoner. Everything has certainly been very carefully thought out, but when people try to praise his organizing ability, Schweitzer replies: 'When I think of how Lambaréné was built up it often seems to me as though I did it all half in a dream.'[23]

The salvation represented by Lambaréné has two aspects which constantly interact and intensify each other. First of all it spelt salvation for Schweitzer himself. And for him salvation could only come through action. He hears and answers the call of the earth, of his fellow creatures, of suffering human beings; he turns towards them and under his capable hands the jungle chaos becomes an orderly world subject to his own form of moral 'imperialism'. It is a world in which everything has its right place, its right weight and its right measure. The one supreme law is that of reverence for life, but here that merciless ruler which elsewhere plunges men into tragic conflicts becomes a bringer of peace. Schweitzer, who is far removed from any form of power politics, nevertheless admires colonialism because it established peace in its own sphere of influence—*pax Romana, pax Britannica.* And he himself enjoys the blessings of the *pax venerationis vitae.* He does not waste his time brooding on the misery of the world, but 'I always held firmly to the thought that each one of us can do a little to bring some portion of it to an end.'[24] To be confronted with such an endless task, and to realize the impossibility of ever doing justice even remotely to the ethical obligation involved would have made many an equally ardent nature despair. But Schweitzer was born under a different star, and his metamorphosis into a jungle doctor led to personal relaxation, and those never-to-be-resolved tensions in the sphere of thought continue to vibrate only in the intensity of the atmosphere. The jungle hospital would certainly not be what it is but for the intellectual work which went on night after night in the doctor's room to lay the ideological structure of the ethic of reverence for life. But the light which shines out from that room on to the silent hospital village does not disturb its peace; on the contrary, it watches over it.

And the power in whose service Schweitzer went out in the first place still watches over him and preserves his peace. This too he has himself confirmed.[25] 'I had to perform a very difficult operation', he writes. 'Oppressed and anxious I went into the hut where the patient was lying. Everything was ready for the operation. And suddenly the words came into my mind: "All things are possible for me in the name of him who gives me my strength, Christ!" And after that I was completely myself again. I smiled and got on with the job, operating with extraordinary calmness. And so the word of St Paul accompanies me wherever I go.'

VIII

GOETHE

Amongst the great figures whose example guides Schweitzer on his way, sustaining and strengthening him, and to whom he turns passionately in his deep need to admire greatness and live according to its light: Jesus the Master and Paul the teacher in the sphere of religion and theology; Bach the master in the sphere of music; and then there is a fourth: Goethe. What role does he play in Schweitzer's life?

The emphasis with which Schweitzer himself acknowledges his relationship to Goethe makes it quite impossible that it can be a more or less arbitrary inclination and a chance encounter. In fact it tells us that the relationship must be a very important one with a very precise significance. Now Schweitzer's attachment to those other great figures is readily understandable, but at first sight his elective affinity with Goethe must strike us as surprising, even strange. Schweitzer has never regretted the fate that placed a century between them. 'Had it been otherwise we should have been kept apart by what in each of us was strange and incomprehensible to the other.'[1] It entirely misses the mark to compare Schweitzer with Goethe and say that there is 'very little difference' between them,[2] or to seek some parallelism in their lives.[3] In fact whenever you come across any of the frequent attempts to turn Schweitzer into a sort of Goethe you can be quite sure that Schweitzer's character has been misunderstood.

By origin, social sphere, work and mission the difference between the two is about as great as possible. On the one hand there is the son of a Frankfurt patrician family, the Minister of State, and—since the Italian journey—the sovereign moulder of a 'literary existence' devoted to poetry and research, a man called to the contemplative life. And on the other there is the son of the Günsbach parsonage, the theologian, preacher, philosophizing ethicist, organist, Bach enthusiast and jungle doctor for unknown Negroes. And even apart from all this there is very little similarity in their general spiritual make up.

Goethe is the natural, creative man *kat exochén*. Whatever touches his mind is fructified. He renewed the German language. He gave love utterance in the German tongue. He inquired into the 'obvious secret' of nature, and as a poet he proclaimed and interpreted it. He drew all spheres of life into the microcosm of his work, and with this material—rich in him as in hardly any other human spirit before or after—he created a world of truth, goodness and beauty, a world which bears his name and the impress of his personality, a world which, as though by a decree of fate, took possession of the spirit and soul of his own people.

Albert Schweitzer is made in a very different mould. He is not the *uomo universale* into which indiscriminate admirers in certain circles are trying to turn him. In fact despite the multiplicity of his talents he is a personality whose strength lies in its very definite limitations. The expansiveness of Goethe's nature stands against the homogeneity of Schweitzer's. Into a ripe old age Goethe still remained open to all possibilities of human activity, whereas from his earliest youth Schweitzer's way of life was already determined. Goethe added ring after ring to his personality like a growing tree, Schweitzer's nature is more that of the solid monolith. The 'once and for all' decision which determined the course of Schweitzer's whole life is reminiscent of the monastic vow: *volo in perpetuo*. All the forces of his soul are poured into one passionate desire. Goethe lacks this 'enthusiasm'; instead there is the passionate capacity of a heart that never grew old; instead of permanency there is 'event', happening, the moment. For Goethe the all-important thing was to give permanency to the moment, which, like the form, is unique and unrepeatable. He desired to eternalize it and give it a character deriving from the eternal and the supernatural.[4] For Schweitzer the meaning of life lies in ceaseless ethical activity. He is well aware that, apart from musical improvisation, creativeness has been denied him. The sensuality which combines Goethe rhapsodically with nature 'in all her glory' is not for him. For him the creative phenomena of nature are not unique in themselves, but significant only as manifestations of the general will to life. For Schweitzer thought is the legitimate path to knowledge. Goethe attaches great importance to intuition. Schweitzer abstracts where Goethe keeps to the concrete. Schweitzer's God is the universal will to life; Goethe's world creator is a formative spirit.

This difference, even antithesis, between their two natures does not diminish the importance Goethe has for Schweitzer, particularly as it does not lie in Schweitzer's temperament to embrace a personality intuitively as a whole. His relationship is solely with the qualities and ideas with which he has an affinity. In those spheres which are of essential importance to him he finds the attraction of Goethe very powerful indeed. Thus Goethe became the friend with whom Schweitzer has conducted dialogues all his life and in whom he feels himself confirmed. 'Goethe is the personality with which I have been most deeply concerned',[5] he writes. (Jesus, as being of an altogether different rank, is not included here. He does not belong in Schweitzer's gallery of 'great personalities', as he certainly did in Goethe's, and as, in the view of enlightened liberalism, he should. W.P.) 'Paul, who, in my opinion, has had a decisive influence on me, belongs to a period which is too far away and too different from our own. The details of his life are too little known for me to be able to associate and converse with him.' What Schweitzer means is quite clear. Paul's thought has had a much more powerful effect on his own than Goethe's could possibly have had. But the more Schweitzer's own path leads him away from the beaten track into solitude the more he feels the need for human closeness and intimacy such as he is unable to obtain from the apostle Paul.

The relationship of Schweitzer to Goethe is that of one who admires and loves. He kept this admiration locked away in his heart until well into the middle years, and it might well never have become known to the general public at all but for the fact that the town of Frankfurt granted him the Goethe Prize. The honour was not awarded because of this secret relationship to Goethe, and the text of the award, which speaks of the 'Faustian metamorphoses' of this totally un-Faustian man, does not suggest any intimate understanding of the prizewinner.[6] But Schweitzer made the award the occasion for a speech with which he wished to establish a precedent, a custom on the part of the prizewinner to acknowledge publicly what Goethe meant to him. Once the secret of his inner relationship to Goethe had become known he subsequently dealt frequently with the personality of his great companion in spirit.[7] There is no question of any Goethe research on his part. By this time Schweitzer was no longer interested in increasing the sum of scholarly knowledge, but only in exercising the widest possible moral influence. What he has to say should be regarded more as an expression of his gratitude. It is a declaration of what Schweitzer himself admires in Goethe and would like others to admire and emulate. And in this sense what he has to say is—perhaps more than he realizes—a confession.

In his first speech in Frankfurt he eloquently described the spiritual encounters with Goethe, which meant so much to him.

The first lies back in his student days in Strassburg; Goethe provided the impulse for Schweitzer's rejection of the speculative systems of philosophic idealism.[8] The second encounter, which took place a little later, created—almost electrified, one might say—the human relationship. In the *Harzreise* Schweitzer read how Goethe 'set out amid November rain and mist to visit a minister's son who was in great spiritual difficulties', in the hope of spiritually strengthening and consoling him. We know already what an impression such things make on Schweitzer. 'And so whenever it happened that I had to take upon me some work or other in order to do for some fellow-man the human service that he needed, I would say to myself: this is a *Harzreise* for you.'[9] He collected evidence of Goethe's generosity, and he was delighted to learn how Goethe had helped others to keep their heads above water, how he had given money to Vogel, his doctor, in order that Vogel should help any needy people he came across during his practice.

And when Schweitzer was a parson and suffered because the many outward obligations of his condition left him so little time for intellectual work, there was once again 'Goethe, the consoler', who 'could not imagine any intellectual occupation which did not run parallel with practical activity'.

When later on—this was the fourth encounter—Schweitzer's decision to study medicine was opposed by his friends, he reminded them that Goethe made his Wilhelm Meister, who was unprepared for anything of the sort, become a surgeon in order that he too might serve.

The final biographically motivated encounter is best described in Schweitzer's own words: 'Once again I met Goethe when my laborious student years had ended and I went out into the world of medicine. It was as if I conversed with him in the primeval forest. I had always supposed that I should go there as a doctor. In the early years, whenever there was building or similar material work to be done, I took pains to pass it on to others who seemed to me fitter for it or engaged for it. Soon I had to admit that this would not do. . . . So for weeks and months I stood in the jungle trying to wrest fruitful land from it, and tormented by unruly workers. Whenever I was in complete despair, I thought of Goethe, who had imagined his Faust, in the end, busily regaining land from the sea where men might live and find nourishment. So Goethe stood beside me in the gloomy forest as the great smiling comforter who understood me.'[10]

And so 'the powerful solar disc', Goethe, gave 'the small moon', as Schweitzer jokingly but with real humility described himself, a little of its light at critical moments. But as important as these encounters were, they do not tell us the essential thing about the constellation of these two stars.

Schweitzer feels himself 'attached to Goethe in respectful friendship'. He has never attempted 'to enter the magic circle of his existence and witness the tremendous objective experience of his life', in the way that Ortega y Gasset demands of a Goethe biographer.[11] His attitude to the great figure he admires is governed by the feeling that 'A man must not try to force his way into the personality of another'.[12] At the same time the cultivation of this friendship has certainly brought a very profound knowledge of the works and life of Goethe with it. One can only be astonished once more at the tremendous intellectual energy which used the midnight hours to master this enormous material in addition to everything else. Its absorption through the medium of a great man has more to it than mere Goethe philology.

Goethe appears here as a contemporary. The publication of Schweitzer's Goethe addresses in the United States was regarded, and not without cause, as the literary event of the bicentenary celebration of Goethe's birth. But the perspective is intensely personal, and these addresses really tell us more about Schweitzer than they do about Goethe. Schweitzer is looking for affinities and he finds them in astonishing number. He feels, despite all differences, that he can recognize someone of his own kind in his friend, and so he feels at ease in his company.

The Goethe with whom Schweitzer stands on an intimate footing is a 'profound, simple man', a 'man of inner intensity', who is at the same time a man of action, and as such a personality in a powerful but unobvious fashion. In loyalty to the great humanitarian ideals of the eighteenth century Goethe represents a 'profound and simple humanitarian ideal'. He avoids daemonism and abhors the grotesque. He expresses himself quite simply in everyday language and is capable of lending it pathos. 'His ideal is the sound and reliable.' The basic traits of his character are the deep earnestness which marked him from youth on, a love of truth and a real humility. 'When he meets another genuine will and ability then he subdues his own self-confidence, and his only aim is to understand and learn.' 'He has taken up the cudgels on behalf of many men and helped their advancement, sparing neither time nor effort when he feels himself called upon to fulfil the obligation of neighbourly charity. He is moved by a profound desire to serve. He never evades any obligation which falls to his lot, or any responsibility which he feels to be his. He does the smallest thing with the greatest conscientiousness, always going to the very limit of his ability.' His word and his deed are one.

All this is true enough and it can be supported by facts. Nevertheless, it covers neither what is splendid nor what is problematic in Goethe as an individual, and in material points it can be disputed. For example, could it not be said the flight which plays such a role in Goethe's life is in reality a flight from responsibility, right up to the highest, the practical determination of his personal fate? 'He eludes the grasp everywhere,' said Schiller. And Ortega y Gasset is struck by the repeated contradictions in the ideas of the thinker Goethe about the world . . . his Spinoza-like optimism, his devotion to nature, his botanic idea of the world in which everything, including his own life, proceeds according to some benevolent cosmic necessity without fear and painful confusion.'[13] But what Schweitzer says about Goethe applies to himself trait for trait. As far as it is humanly possible, Schweitzer's admiration transposes its subject into his own key.

This becomes even more obvious with the thinker Goethe rather than the man. Though Schweitzer's relationship to Goethe is intensely human, he sees its actual roots neither in the purely human nor the poetic sphere, but elsewhere. 'What binds us together in the profoundest depths of our beings is his philosophy of nature.'[14] And what could be more typical of Schweitzer!

There are two philosophies for Schweitzer. The one violates nature and the world, and places man in relation to a world bent to his own thought. The other, the 'unpretentious philosophy of nature', leaves nature and the world as they are and compels man to find his proper place in them and keep it. The former philosophy is ingenious, the latter is elementary. Encouraged by Goethe to 'consciousness of self' and confirmed by his own medical and scientific studies, Schweitzer acknowledges the latter. It contents itself with an incomplete ideology and goes no farther than the recognition that 'nature is life and succession from an unknown central point to an unidentifiable frontier'. It rejects metaphysics. It does not attempt to raise itself above natural science by speculative thought, but holds fast to the principle of advancing in the finite to the farthest extent of the fathomable, whilst modestly respecting the unfathomable.

Schweitzer feels himself at one with Goethe in this philosophical basic attitude and finds this identity of thought confirmed in the religious sphere. Of course, Goethe presents certain difficulties. His pantheistic mysticism in which all things are in God and God in all things, so that things become a revelation of God, presupposes concrete rather than abstract thought, unlike Schweitzer's. But Schweitzer's 'Experience of thought' which perceives God as a universal will to life is also pantheistic. Goethe 'felt inclined to the assumption' that there is something imperishable in us which is destined to new activity in this or other worlds, but this appears too vague to Schweitzer to shake the assumption that his theology is rational. What matters to Schweitzer is that Goethe 'adopts the religion which has come to him by thought and which is reconcilable with natural science, and not the Christianity of dogmas'.[15]

According to Schweitzer the religion of Goethe is identical with his ideology and his general view of life. God, who is one essence with nature, is in some mysterious way quite unfathomable for us, is not only creative force but also moral will.[16] By incorporating the love of God Jesus merely reveals to us where we are carried in our thought.[17]

The identity of this interpretation of Goethe's religion with Schweitzer's own theology is so striking that Charles Joy concludes[18] that Goethe's contribution to Schweitzer's life and thought must be greater than even Schweitzer himself realizes. But Schweitzer does not acknowledge any such dependence, and his own spiritual development confirms the independence of his thought. Must we therefore assume the existence of a pre-stabilized harmony, a freak of nature establishing a twin brotherhood of two spirits separated from each other by a century, a spiritual curiosity of history of great importance in Schweitzer's life, but fundamentally speaking essentially personal? The real facts are both more plausible and more significant.

Schweitzer believes that each of the ideas expressed in Goethe's works, letters and sayings falls into place, like fragments of glass in a kaleidoscope, in a simple and unified philosophy.[19] Deeply moved he sees in it the reflection of his own thought. But the reflection is deceptive. Once again we find ourselves faced with the mysterious secret which protects him spiritually. Even in obvious error he remains attached to truth. He is mistaken about Goethe, but not about the fact that a spiritual relationship does associate him with such a very different companion.

Goethe is certainly no 'opportunist thinker'[20] even though he frequently contradicts himself, and although what he says is often dependent on the particular occasion, on his interlocutor, and on the context of affairs. Despite this, his outlook has an inherent structure of its own. His metaphysical poetry, his investigations of nature, his critique of reason and his aphoristic philosophy are all essential aspects of his striving for knowledge.[21] This totality of spiritual outlook is in accordance with the law of his being, but at the same time it forbids any strict adoption of formulas. 'We are pantheists when we investigate nature, poetic polytheists, moral monotheists'—these words, which must not be interpreted as any theologically binding 'confession', bear witness to the need of a universal spirit for ideological freedom of movement. This was the reason why Goethe, as he said himself, always 'kept himself free from philosophy'. According to Schweitzer, Goethe's philosophy consists 'in the observation of the material and spiritual phenomena of nature both within and outside us, and in the conclusions drawn from it'.[22] But even Goethe's procedure in his investigation of nature does not content itself with this 'simple way of thought' (Schweitzer). How much more inadequate must it appear then to the poet and the philosopher! The higher organs of perception do not operate in this way, and for Goethe intuitive perception stands first and foremost. He never forgot that Spinoza accepted the validity of the *scientia intuitiva*. Only intuition is capable of perceiving the form in phenomena, and amongst the forms—the peak of scientific knowledge—their origins (*ihre Urbilder*). 'I am very versatile', said Goethe of himself.[23]

Where the Highest Being is concerned Goethe's thought does not confine itself to natural philosophy. In Schweitzer's view Goethe does not seek God outside, and in addition to, but 'only in nature'. 'Like Spinoza . . . he believes in the identity of God and nature.'[24] As a philosopher Schweitzer vehemently disputes the reality of the absolute, and his own 'mysticism of reality' confines itself to the practical phenomena of being as they impinge on his own sphere of activities, but this is responsible for a deep-seated misunderstanding, which is, incidentally, widespread, and one which Goethe himself provoked by his references to Spinoza's formula '*deus sive natura*'. But at no time did Goethe believe that nature was God and God nothing but nature. Any such belief would clash with his conception of the creator of the world whom he comprehends as a formative being in analogy with his own being and in line with the analogous concept of Christian philosophy. God 'thought' man (*Westöstlicher Diwan*). Nature is

His 'organ' (*Maximen und Reflexionen*). And Goethe's later works decisively reject Spinoza's philosophy of identity. 'The Divine which reveals itself to us as nature still remains the Other which never shows itself but only calls to us.'[25] God is, of course, beyond direct comprehension, and no metaphysics can explain him by the scientific method. But the contemplative spirit, the sense of awe, extends beyond the limits set to thought and investigation. It seeks and it finds. And this too is comprehension. Youth may identify itself with the universe—'old age contents itself with Him who is, who was and who will be'. Such a saying is not, as free-thinking interpretation is fond of saying, a relapse into an outdated phase, but the final conclusion of continuous effort. Goethe's late work shows that right to the end he unfalteringly acknowledges the law by which he began. A rare boon was granted to him: in his old age he was allowed to bring in the full harvest of a lifelong sowing.

Thus Goethe cannot be understood in terms of a simple and uniform natural philosophy. Thought and inquiry are not the only means by which he approaches the secret of life. Thanks to his artistic genius he had direct access to it. The all-important thing for him is 'contemplation' rather than the results of thought. With Schweitzer it is no different.

Even the affinities which Schweitzer himself stresses, hardly support the supposed similarity when they are not isolated but regarded as part of the whole picture of Goethe. *Idem hic non est idem.* The same thing made of two different materials becomes different. What then is the deepest bond between Schweitzer and Goethe? It is first the similarity of their spiritual standpoint, and then, even more, their attitude to their destiny and the tasks it involves.

Goethe stands at the watershed between the age of Enlightenment and the scientific age. Belief in reason was shaken. It was followed by the realism of scientific thought, which based its views not on rational abstractions but on the observation and investigation of natural phenomena. The striving for truth remained uppermost. It sought new ways without at the same time abandoning the emancipation of the inquiring spirit. As the son of his time Goethe felt obliged to think out an ideology for himself and based his religious life on personal comprehension. He rejected dogmatic belief. Outward Church trappings were not essential for him, and perhaps even inimical to the spirit. The Church of the Cross was to become the Church of the spirit. Pious belief in Christ was rejected. The text of the Bible was subjected to criticism in the belief that criticism could not affect its

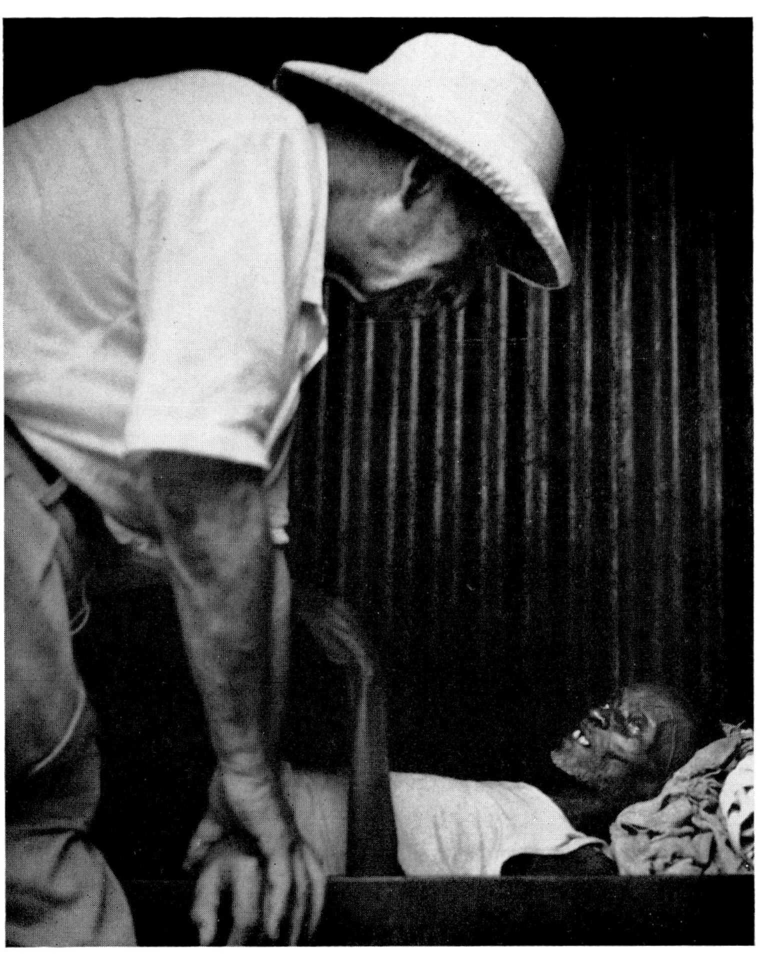

11. Visiting a patient
(By permission of Erica Anderson, New York)

'original essence'. The 'spirit' blows where it listeth. It is not limited to the 'Book of Books', as Goethe called the Bible, or to the Church, or to Christianity. 'In His essence' God remains 'eternally unknown'. In accordance with its 'negative' theology, *Gott und Welt*, the collection of poetry which is the deepest expression of Goethe's natural philosophy, offers no positive evidence concerning the unfathomable Godhead. Thought bows before the unfathomable.

This spiritual position of Goethe as a thinker is the same as Schweitzer's. Schweitzer stands at the end of that period of Western spiritual life characterized by the subjection of thought to the methods of the exact sciences; Goethe stood at its beginning. Their basic attitudes remain the same. It was not till our own day that the right of positive science to set itself up as a law-giver was called into question. The anachronistic attachment of Schweitzer to eighteenth-century thought completes the similarity. This is quite remarkable, of course, but it is based on objective circumstances. Much more remarkable, however, is their similarity of attitude in this situation. As highly personal and nevertheless essentially the same, it offers a far more satisfactory explanation of the intimacy of their strange relationship than any ideological conformity. Briefly it has three aspects.

The first is the spirit of awe which both Goethe and Schweitzer seek to attach to the enlightenment and free-thinking movements of the age. Both unconditionally demand freedom of thought, in particular with regard to the historico-critical interpretation of the Bible, but at the same time they both loathe 'unfair and jeering attacks and misrepresentations' (Goethe: *Dichtung und Wahrheit*). For both piety is supreme, and questions of belief of only secondary importance.

The second is the inner necessity by which they both break through the limits of knowledge drawn by the enlightenment movement and science, though neither Goethe nor Schweitzer questions them in principle. But whilst the former, thanks to the freedom of his formulated views and the possibility of changing to and fro between the spheres of scientific investigation, poetry and 'wisdom', creates a space in which both soul and spirit can develop free of all trammels, so the latter does the same through the 'mystique' of his reasoning thought, and, where necessary, by arbitrary inconsequence.

The third is that for them both the freedom won in this way makes a 'double ideology' possible. Herman Grimm pointed this out where Goethe is concerned, though it is probably more accurate to speak of a polymorphic ideology. 'The God he experienced had nothing to do with the God he sought to interpret. . . . Goethe's belief in God and

M

in immortality had nothing to do with his philosophy. This belief had grown up in him and belonged to him; it needed no proof, and he was not prepared to see it called into question at all.'[26] The thing is not so simple where Schweitzer is concerned because for him, unlike the poet, intuition is not a legitimate method of comprehension. In theology he remains subject to free thought, and in philosophy to 'absolutely logical thought experience', although in fact the intervention of 'experience' in the logical thought process calls its binding force into question. But when at one time he uses philosophical language and at another traditional religious language he does so in the last resort not out of consideration for the thought pattern of his audience, or out of piety, but because of personal necessity. In this way he makes it possible to express his elementary experience and to lend words to the double ideology whose existence he may not admit even to himself. Whatever his position in this respect before the bar of reason, he is right because—like Goethe—he is bearing witness to a truth of which he has become inwardly possessed by the certainty of unerring experience.

With Goethe as with Schweitzer this truth is at the same time inherited possession and personal attainment. As sons of the Enlightenment neither recognizes any obligation towards tradition or doctrinal authority. But the power of the soul tolerates no dependence on the spirit of the age. Both Goethe and Schweitzer are greater than their own time-conditioned thought. Here they are on common ground. But the dioscurian relationship indicated in Schweitzer's addresses on Goethe becomes really comprehensible only in its overcoming. It belongs to the sphere which Goethe described and treated as the sphere of the mysterious.

Goethe's description of a Christian in *Briefe des Pastors* (1772) as 'one who calls Jesus his master', rounds off the picture of this strangest of all relationships.

IX

MUSIC

Once the wanderer through Albert Schweitzer's world enters the sphere of the musician he experiences a feeling of agreeable relaxation. The passionate wrestling of the critical biblical investigations to discover the 'true' Jesus; the personal confrontation of Schweitzer with the 'Lord' in the form of a relationship 'from will to will'; the tension between reasoning thought and spiritual experience; the ethical philosophizing about the tragic contradiction of creation which makes man a kind of spiritual Marcus Curtius who must sacrifice himself by springing from the light of personal happiness into the darkness of torment as a suffering creature if he wishes to close the abyss opened up by the self-alienation of life; the choice of a form of life which exposes the compassionate heart to a permanent contact with suffering in its crassest form; the experience of the decline of culture and in consequence world-wide catastrophes; and finally profound anxiety at the threatening self-destruction of humanity—'all this rages, wrenches and strikes, stabs and burns'. But none of this finds entry into the world of sound. At the organ Schweitzer is under the protection of Johann Sebastian Bach. 'A soul which out of the world's unrest longs for peace and has itself already tasted peace' allows him to share in its experience.[1] Not that Schweitzer was at any time a man who knew no peace. He is spared this by the soverign supremacy of his character over all inner and outer convulsions, and even more by an instinctive consciousness of ultimate security. However, the peace of the soul had to be re-captured and held again and again in the violent battle of ideas, in the clash of feelings, and in conflict with the surrounding world. But one step across the frontier of the sphere of music, and the artist in him is above the battle. It is impossible to imagine how Schweitzer would ever have been able to carry the burdens of his life had he not been able to take refuge in this haven from time to time.

As amazing as it may seem in view of his multifarious activities, in the sphere of music Schweitzer is a master in the strictest sense of the term. The basis of this mastery was laid very early on. Five years' training under the excellent Mülhausen organist Eugen Münch made him a mature organist at the age of sixteen—an organist worthy of being entrusted with the splendid Walcker organ of St Stephen's Church there both for religious services and for concerts. The obituary he wrote in 1898 on the death of his teacher[2] reveals an unusual shrewdness of judgement in a twenty-three-year-old, and at the same time a very thorough knowledge of the art of the organist. By this time he had already laid a very solid foundation of musical knowledge and experience, and thereafter there was no interruption. In fact, this was not the only sphere of his activities in which there was never any interruption. The study of music, begun in childhood, was carried on into old age with a persistence and determination which brooked no obstacles.

At one point, however, even his music was called into question, and when he left for Lambaréné he feared that he would have to sacrifice his music as well. As a parting gift the Paris Bach Society presented him with a tropical piano, complete with organ pedal, as an acknowledgement of his many years of service as its organist. But at first he lacked the courage to practise: 'I had accustomed myself to think that this activity in Africa meant the end of my life as an artist, and that the renunciation would be easier if I allowed my fingers and my feet to get rusty with disuse.'[3] The reaction was as violent as the pain of deprivation. He suddenly realized that the solitude of the jungle offered him an unexpected and unique opportunity of perfecting his playing. He then decided to work through the compositions of Bach, Mendelssohn, Widor, César Franck and Max Reger one after the other down to the last detail until he knew them by heart, no matter whether he had to devote weeks or months to each piece. 'And how I enjoyed practising now I had peace and quiet, and had no need to worry about concerts arranged for me!' In long journeys by canoe to visit patients, sometimes on the way for days, accompanied only by natives, and hemmed in on all sides by the scenery of endless tropical forests, he set himself to learn the fugues of Bach by heart. To a friend he said: 'When I have lived another couple of years in inner Africa I shall feel myself the complete organist. I have found the peace and quiet which Bach needs.' It is to these circumstances that he owes 'his unique position amongst present-day organists'.[4] His jungle affinity which is amongst the profoundest traits of his character, has not only ripened his personality but it has given him the gift of musical perfection. 'O, jungle solitude, how can I ever thank you for what you have meant to me!'

Schweitzer cannot stop making music. This was demonstrated when, in September 1917, he was torn away from the jungle and carried off as a prisoner, first to Garaison in the Pyrenees—after a stay in a *caserne de passage* in Bordeaux had given him dysentery—and then to the former lunatic asylum St Remy which was made over as an internment camp for civilian prisoners from Alsace. The common-room there was already familiar to him from a sketch by Van Gogh, who had stayed in the place for a while as a mental patient. Now it was Schweitzer who walked round and round behind the high walls of the institution. The garden with its fountain has also been immortalized by Van Gogh in a wonderful drawing. Schweitzer, the upholder of the love ethic of Jesus, was scorched by the hatred between nations. Even in his far-distant oasis of humanity he was unable to escape the ramifications of the war machine, and in his prison garb, complete with clogs, as a contemporary photograph shows him, he became a symbol. The attitude of the man sitting there, a little hunched, his hands clasped, expresses resignation and at the same time inexhaustible patience. But the eyes clearly reveal the fire which is burning there, ready to be let loose to take up the struggle against 'the wicked old enemy' the moment the chains are struck off.

How did Schweitzer the musician master this situation? On the voyage from Cape Lopez to Bordeaux he was under constant observation, and it was impossible to write. So he spent his time learning Bach's fugues and Widor's sixth organ symphony by heart. In the prison camp at Garaison another opportunity arose. A fellow prisoner unexpectedly offered his services. The man's wife had been cured of an illness by medicaments which Schweitzer had thoughtfully handed over to the representative of a Hamburg firm of timber merchants before the latter was sent off to prison camp too.

Schweitzer now became the proud possessor of a table the grateful husband carpentered for him. Now he could 'play the organ' again with the tabletop as manual and the floor as pedal. Thanks to this constant practice Schweitzer was able to give concerts again as soon as the war was over; first in Barcelona and then in Sweden. The proceeds from these concerts paid off the debts which had accumulated during the war on account of the hospital. Schweitzer's musical artistry thus victoriously surmounted the double crisis of emigration into the jungle and imprisonment during the war. After that it was never again called into question.

From all this it becomes very clear that music is not just an addition to Schweitzer's rich life, but an essential element in it. His music is not a supplementary talent, a sort of astonishing 'and this too', a heading for another chapter in his biography. Such a suggestion takes no account either of Schweitzer's essential personality or of the importance which music has in his life, which, in the words of Charles R. Joy, consists of an uninterrupted chain of golden notes. If the accompanying undertone of the organ is not heard then the symphony of his life cannot be understood. The organ is the continuum in all the dramatic changes of his life. As a boy he had to grope for the wall for fear of falling over the first time he heard a duet in the school hall, and he almost fainted the first time he heard brass music. They were early signs of the role music was destined to play in his life both as destiny and rich gift.

The musician Albert Schweitzer is publicly identified, and not altogether without reason, with the interpreter of Bach. But this does not convey a real idea of the originality and scope of his musical talent. His decision to study medicine made it necessary for him to abandon his plan to write a book on Schubert, though the preparations were already far advanced. Schweitzer finds 'the nearest thing to Bach's cantatas'[5] in the accompanying music to Schubert's Lieder. As soon as he had saved up enough he would always make a pilgrimage to Bayreuth. Later he was to publish his memories of Cosima Wagner.[6] During the years which lay between his own resignation as the Director of the Thomasstift, a theological training college in Strassburg, and Schweitzer's emigration to Africa, Friedrich Curtius, President of the Council of the Augsburg Confessional Church, gave Schweitzer the attic floor of his official residence, and in the evenings, as far as his time allowed, Schweitzer would play the piano in the Curtius' domestic circle. Apart from Bach, Schubert and others, a great deal of Beethoven was played too. Gerda, the young daughter of the house, his most devoted listener and later his pupil, would sit by the piano, nursing her doll Jolanthe. It became a tradition to end the evening with an impromptu lullaby for Jolanthe, though Schweitzer never bothered to put his improvisations to paper. One evening he unwittingly caused considerable embarrassment to a highly-talented pianist, who happened to be present as a friend of the family, by suggesting that he should play a fugue on a chosen theme. It was just a mystery to Schweitzer that a musician should find any difficulty in that.

The considerable musical-historical achievement of Schweitzer is a double one. It consists in his interpretation of the music of Bach and in his contribution to the reform of organ building.

The work which led to a new interpretation of the music of Bach can be compared with the opening up of a new approach to the 'secret' of Jesus. Martin Buber calls Schweitzer a 'spiritual realist'.[7] Immediately after the publication of Schweitzer's dissertation on the Last Supper, Buber recognized the theological realist in him 'because he saw the phenomena of the spirit in relation to the realities in which they occurred'. And Schweitzer himself regards his interpretation of the life of Jesus as 'realistic'.[8] Just what that means we can see from the experience of the young student of theology on manœuvres as described in his autobiography. To look at a set of circumstances overgrown with tradition, doctrinal authority and scientific theory with fresh eyes and entirely without preconceived notions and to form a judgement based on an unspoiled sense for reality is evidence of an unusual capacity indeed. Precisely because of this capacity the young organ student burst into the sphere of Bach research no less dramatically than the young theological beginner burst into liberal research into the life of Jesus. His teacher Widor describes it for us in the preface to the German edition of the works of Bach.

Even before the beginning of Schweitzer's theological studies Charles Marie Widor, organist of St Sulpice and a prominent composer in his own right, had promised to complete Schweitzer's training as an organist as soon as the young man could manage a stay in Paris. One day—it was in 1899—the two were dealing with the choral preludes and Widor confessed that he was unable to understand the musical logic of the master in his treatment of a choral melody. The young 'realist' immediately replied: 'A good deal must inevitably remain obscure to you in the chorals because they can be explained only from the accompanying texts.' Schweitzer then translated the texts from memory into French. 'The riddles were resolved . . . I got to know a Bach of whose existence I had previously had only a vague idea. Suddenly it became clear to me that the Thomas Kantor was very much more than the incomparably great contrapuntist I had always admired, and I saw that in his work there was an equally incomparable capacity to express poetic ideas and to turn words and music into a unity.'

Widor thereupon suggested that Schweitzer should write a treatise for French organists on the choral preludes, and the young man set to work. But what applied to the choral preludes applied equally to the cantatas and the passions. The vocal pieces and the choral preludes explain each other. In this way the work gradually grew into a book about Bach, and it was published in French in 1905.[9] It made good use of the valuable experience Schweitzer had obtained as organist of the Bach concerts given by the choir of St Wilhelm in Strassburg directed by Ernst Münch, the well-known brother of his own teacher in Mülhausen; as organist of the Paris Bach Society; and of the Orféo Catala in Barcelona. The book was so successful that the preparation of a German edition was obviously called for, but when Schweitzer finished his history of the quest for Jesus and turned to this new task he found it impossible to translate his own work, so he decided to write the book all over again in German. In doing so the same thing happened to him as with the second edition of his work on the *Quest for the Historical Jesus*: a volume of 455 pages became one of 844 pages. The first pages were written right through the night until dawn after Schweitzer had attended a performance of *Tristan* in Bayreuth. By the beginning of 1908 the book was ready. Historically it was based on Spitta's classic Bach biography, but it provided a diametrically opposed Bach aesthetic, offered detailed information concerning the way in which Bach's compositions should be played, and set out—unlike Spitta, whose book is not easy to read because it is too specialized—to provide both musicians and laymen with a deeper understanding of Bach's music. The moment for such a book was well chosen. The final volume of the definitive edition of *Bach* had just appeared (in 1900), exactly fifty years after the beginning of the undertaking. Brahms declared that its completion was one of the two great events in his life. The other event he referred to was the founding of the German Empire.

Just as Schweitzer's quest for Jesus put an end to historicizing liberalism, so his Bach research put an end to the then currently accepted idea, supported by the authority of Spitta, that Bach was a completely 'pure' musician; that is to say, a musician who was free of all non-musical 'materialistic' elements, and that his music was not inspired by any pictures or ideas associated with the accompanying text. Even Spitta cannot deny the artistic strokes of composition clearly related, directly or indirectly, to the text, but for him they are 'jests resulting from fugitive impulses, and their presence or absence do not alter the value or comprehension of a musical piece in its real essence'.[10] Schweitzer, on the other hand, shows that the musical phrases of Bach are 'only the text crystallized into music'[11] 'This music reflects the text like clear moving water.'[12] It is true that Bach does not follow his text line for line, but expresses rather its characteristic feeling; the word, which appears obvious to him at once as typical of the spirit of the whole, is expressed in a corresponding motif which illustrates the melody. He developed a graphic musical expression which operates with picturesque associations. Thus the title of the French edition of Schweitzer's book on Bach is misleading: Beethoven and Wagner made poetry with music, Bach painted with it. As the most consistent representative of painting in music Bach is the antithesis of Wagner.[13]

As revolutionary as these views were, they were final. The aesthetics on which Schweitzer bases them are, of course, like any aesthetic theory, not incontestable. For one thing he underestimated what still remained to be done in the sphere of historical investigation—as its subsequent results have proved. He also did not know—and could not then have known—what the 'Art of the Fugue' means. He himself is very conscious of the fact that today after the passage of fifty years, his work, though still indispensable, needs revision.[14] But all this makes no difference to the fact that he opened up a new era in the cultivation of Bach's music, and provided unsurpassed instructions for its execution. Beyond all contemporary, time-conditioned theories of musical interpretation he revealed the reality of Bach to the whole world in all its greatness just as he had first done to Widor at the organ of St Sulpice.[15] With this Bach 'all aesthetic explanations necessarily remain on the surface'. You do not merely enjoy Bach, you edify yourself in him, for 'he experienced his art as religion'.[16]

But Schweitzer would not be Schweitzer if he behaved like those archaeologists who write about Greek temples without knowing the first thing about practical architecture. Of course, he could play the organ very well indeed, but this was not enough. From boyhood he had been anxious to know all about its inner construction. But this very urge for knowledge was to become a source of misgiving for him when two particularly loved instruments, the Walcker organ of St Stephan's in Mülhausen and the Silbermann organ at St Wilhelm in Strassburg, were renovated and modernized, and, as a result, lost their soft, rich tone. The distress this caused him was the beginning of an epic in his life: the struggle for the true organ.

The decisive experience in this respect was his visit to Stuttgart to hear the much-praised new organ of the Liederhalle there. He found the tone harsh, and during the playing of a Bach fugue by the excellent organist of the Stiftskirche he could hear only a chaos of tones in which it was impossible to detect the separate parts. His general feeling that the modern organ represented a retrograde step where tone was concerned now suddenly became a certainty. This realization of the twenty-one-year-old was summed up in the blunt formula: 'About the end of the nineteenth century the master organ-builders became organ-manufacturers.'[17] Organ-manufacturers no longer asked whether an organ had a good tone, but merely whether it was equipped with every possible modern device for changing the registers, and whether for the lowest possible price it had the greatest possible number of stops. Any organ-builder who was not prepared to join in this development faced ruin. At the same time the mass destruction of fine old organs began, and their replacement by modern factory-produced instruments.

Here, too, we can see Schweitzer's realism, though in a different sense from his interpretation of Bach's compositions. With the latter we are compelled to make the comparison with his quest for the historical Jesus; with the former the appropriate comparison is with the jungle hospital at Lambaréné. As an ideologist Schweitzer is pledged to the idea of progress. But though he greets every new medical discovery for the more effective treatment of tropical diseases with enthusiasm, he is not prepared to let himself be carried away by the perfectionism of modern clinics, because his aim is to create a hospital suited to the requirements of natives in the heart of the African jungle. He approaches the technical seductions of the modern organ in the same uncompromising fashion, even though modern organists do go down before them like ninepins—not to mention the parson and the church council! An organ is an instrument of music, and therefore the only permissible criterion for Schweitzer is: how must it be built in order to convey the art of music as perfectly as possible to the ear?

From the first moment of revelation Schweitzer was well aware that this attitude was heretical; and, in fact, when he now began to study as many old and new organs as he could, and to discuss the questions involved with organ manufacturers and organists, his contention that the old organs had a better tone than the new was rejected at first with amusement then with irritation. At that time Schweitzer was a young man and as yet unknown to the general public, so he had no prestige to support his views. Thus it required a good deal of moral courage to publish, ten years after his visit to Stuttgart to hear the new organ there, a book entitled *Evangelium der wahren Orgel* (*Gospel of the True Organ*).[18] In this new task his intimate knowledge of both German and French organ-building stood him in good stead, and at the same time he fulfilled, and in a unique fashion, the true mission of Alsace—to act as a bridge between France and Germany and their different civilizations. But now a duel opened up with a very formidable opponent, no less than the spirit of the age itself.

In this book Schweitzer handed the palm to the French organ-builders in preference to their German colleagues, because in many respects the former had remained truer to the old methods of organ-building. The deep attachment of the French to tradition was some guarantee against an uncritical capitulation to a purely technical civilization. However, when Schweitzer upheld the ideal of the old fine-toned organ he was not campaigning for an unconditional return to the eighteenth-century organ. The dogmatism of the musical historian was just as foreign to him as that of the organ manufacturer pledged to 'technical progress'. As an artist he enjoys the inner freedom which his 'free-thinking' thought sets up as an ideal even if he cannot realize it. The sphere of the organ is his sphere of liberty. Its problems are tackled practically and without preconceived ideas. As interpreter of Bach he complains: they have buried the romantic Bach only to fall victim to the 'historical' Bach. The restrained pathos of his own Bach comes neither under the one heading nor the other. As a reformer of organ-building he had to make sure that the rejection of the modern organ did not mean a return to the organ of Bach's time; though he certainly did, and does, demand that such old organs of the seventeenth and eighteenth centuries as still exist shall be preserved as historical treasures. He certainly did not fail to realize that his teacher Eugen Münch was to some extent indebted to the technical imperfections of his instrument: it compelled him to the quiet playing and the refinement of registration which lent his concerts their unique quality. However, Schweitzer did not regard the organ of Bach's day as 'the true organ' but only as its predecessor. The ideals of art are absolute and not archaic, and there was no need to scrap the real achievements of the great masters of organ-building in the first seventy years of the nineteenth century, particularly as one must remember that the great composers for the organ at the turn of the century—César Franck, Widor and Reger—would have been impossible without them.

The first reaction to Schweitzer's appeal to public opinion was not encouraging. Some organists were even so indignant that they broke off friendly relations with him; and the destruction of the splendid old organs went on; though with some difficulty he did manage to save the old Silbermann organ at St Thomas's in Strassburg. But his ideas gradually made headway. At the congress of the International Music Society in Vienna in 1909 a section for organ-building was established for the first time, and Schweitzer was invited to deliver an address on organ-building. He prepared it by conducting preliminary inquiries amongst the organists and organ-builders of all European countries. His address and the results of his inquiries led to a congress decision to draft 'International Regulations for Organ-Building'. The section, now seized with Schweitzer's own enthusiasm, sat more or less in permanence, and its members hardly had time to eat and sleep, much less pay any attention to the social arrangements of the congress. But the new 'Regulations' were drafted and agreed and circulated all within a matter of four days.[19]

Twenty-two years after he wrote his revolutionary work on organ-building Schweitzer had the satisfaction of seeing it re-published in a new edition, provided with an epilogue on the present state of organ-building, which is one of the most impressive documents we possess from the pen of its author. It is the voice of a master of the organ whose mastery extends equally to both its artistic and technical problems and is capable of finding a solution to them all. Since the year 1909 Schweitzer has accumulated a knowledge of the organs of Europe which is second to none.

It is not surprising to find that his campaign for the true organ is at the same time a fight for a spiritual ideal: 'the struggle for the good organ is to me a part of the struggle for truth'.[20] In this fight he has enjoyed the rare privilege of tasting victory. Unfortunately, of course, the organs which were destroyed have been lost for ever; and unfortunately, too, the master organ-builders, who were ruined by the score and forced to abandon their craft when the factory-manufactured organ swept all before it, cannot now be replaced. However, astonishing conversions are taking place: organ-manufacturers and organists are gradually beginning to praise what they formerly condemned. And Schweitzer was in a position to make the proud statement: 'The idea I pioneered twenty years ago has now established itself. Today the struggle has been won.' Schweitzer had given back what the organ had given to him. And that was a great deal.

The organ is the instrument with which Schweitzer finds himself in complete harmony. It gives him the opportunity of expressing himself as an artist in the way best suited to his talents. He has to thank the organ for that productive relationship to music which is essential to his life.

The organ also greatly helped Schweitzer to obtain the necessary funds for his jungle hospital.

The organ was the basis of Schweitzer's relationship to Bach, a lifelong symbiosis. Schweitzer is unthinkable without Bach, and nowadays Bach has become unthinkable without Schweitzer.

Schweitzer also has to thank the organ for making him so at home in church. It is not so much the parson who, so to speak, spends his life in church, as the organist.

At the organ Schweitzer can devote himself to the life of the soul without 'inhibitions from thought'. It is here that his basic piety can express itself without restraint. Bach as the purest personification of the world of organ music, expresses—in the words of Widor—'the purest religious feeling'.[21] And because of their piety a denigration of Mendelssohn's organ compositions is frowned upon. For Schweitzer the organ opens the way to religious meditation. Confessional differences and theological doctrines have no place here. Sitting at the organ Schweitzer can accompany a Protestant service in Günsbach or a Catholic service in the Minster at Colmar.[22]

Until well into his eighties Schweitzer gave public organ concerts. Now he 'converses with his organ'. The organ has remained his companion and consoler, and the voice of his soul.

Whoever hopes to understand the life of Albert Schweitzer must think of it as an oratorio with organ accompaniment.

X

EPILOGUE

Any evidence regarding a personality exceeding the standards normally set for human beings is necessarily inadequate. Every practical summary of qualities and achievements deepens the feeling that the real thing, as being something indefinable, is distorted rather than presented. The ultimate significance of both his actions and his life evades critical estimate. Nevertheless, at the conclusion of this attempt to interpret the real character of this much honoured and yet widely misunderstood man, the question must still be faced: Who is Albert Schweitzer? And what is his significance?

For the general public Schweitzer is the jungle doctor of Lambaréné. This greatly narrows the viewpoint, and it certainly does not suit him, because his work in Lambaréné can be understood only in relationship to his life as a whole, though it is quite true that all the elements of his make-up are concentrated there as though under a magnifying glass. Without his theology, without his ethics and without his music Lambaréné would not be what it is. And this effectively disposes of all comparisons with other jungle doctors and heroes of humanity.

The way to this heart of Schweitzer's activity passes through a heroic landscape dotted as though with erratic boulders and splendidly conceived examples of spiritual architecture. Some of them have never been completed, others have been left to crumble, because the centre of that landscape, the jungle hospital at Lambaréné, took up progressively more of his strength and energy. However, like much of the surviving evidence to the creative powers of antiquity, their impressiveness is hardly lessened by their being only torsos. And taken all together they form a whole quite astonishing in its compact homogeneity. Seen from a distance the impression is one of harmonious concordance. The frequent tensions noticeable in Schweitzer's spiritual cosmos, indeed, even essential to it, do not disturb the interlocking effect of the various disparate elements. The unity of the personality itself triumphs over all contradictions in the sphere of comprehension. Albert Schweitzer is greater than his thought. But through the strength of his spirit he influences the spirit of our age.

The contemporary significance of Schweitzer is threefold. His theology erected a barrier to modernization and psychologization in the investigations into the life of Jesus. He revealed the hopelessness of all attempts to bring Jesus Christ 'humanly closer' to the people of our own day in this way, and at the same time he exposed the violation of the principle of truthfulness they, if unconsciously, represented. He set up the principle that the quest for the historical Jesus must be carried on without regard for either theology or doctrine, and, in the firm belief that the spirit of truth is also the spirit of Jesus, must seek to establish the historical truth. He insisted that historical investigation into the life of Jesus was not only possible, but necessary, and for his part he proved it. His own investigations certainly did not reject the uncompromising procedure of the historian, but he rose above it in the firm belief that the significance of Jesus would be 'neither shaken nor confirmed by any historical discovery'.[1] Thus on the one hand he is a pioneer of '*Realtheologie*' which, after a period of scepticism towards the historical source value of the Gospels on the part of form-historical investigation, once again judged their value favourably and aimed not at a biography but at a history of Jesus.[2] And on the other hand, as a critic of 'historical theology', he is a pioneer of the newer Gospel research which seeks to free the Christian Gospel from its historical dependence and to concentrate on its timelessly valid core. His work anticipates the desirable and necessary synthesis between those tendencies of Jesus research which still seem to stand in apparently irreconcilable contradiction to each other.

The relationship of Schweitzer to Jesus is quite independent of the results of any critical investigations into his life. Schweitzer concludes his own work by dramatically casting aside the cloak of the historian and presenting himself as 'a prisoner of Jesus Christ' (Origen). This is his greatest theological achievement, because it is essential for theology that the world 'should be changed not by theologically correct thought, but by the fact that theologians themselves are the first to let themselves be freed by God to love in the world and to love the world'.[3] Thus a step which leads beyond the path of the theologian becomes his crowning glory.

Schweitzer's place in the history of Protestantism is secure thanks to the key position of his quest for Jesus; but one day the fact that by dint of unconditional questions concerning the person of Jesus, that is to say, questions free of all theology, the inquiring spirit of this 'agnostic' penetrated to the original core of Christian belief and obtained a foothold there, will be regarded as of even greater importance. This achievement of critical thought has the quality of genius—the term is to be used sparingly and only after careful consideration, but it is justified here. Its standing is higher than any result of mere scholarship could be. In the sphere of research into the life of Jesus there is nothing which can compare with it. But the most vital impression will always be that of the theologian who was swept out of his fruitful scholarship by the love of Christ into the sphere of practical Christian activity. When such a call is no longer made and followed, theology must lose its credibility.

In Schweitzer's opinion, 'the truth that the ethical is the essence of religion is firmly established on the authority of Jesus.[4] His position as a moralist is thus the logical consequence of his discipleship, though he deliberately avoids presenting his own ethical teaching as Christian teaching, in order that its influence shall not be narrowed by any preliminary assumption of Christian belief. In this he feels he is justified by Paul who wished to be all things to all men in order to win them all. And thus the theologian Schweitzer appears in the role of a humanitarian moralist, indeed, the greatest moralist of our twentieth-century civilization.[5] As such he stands in the centre of an age of moral weakness and doubt; he opposes the decline of morality both in public and private life with his own belief in 'the ethical existence as the highest manifestation of spirituality'.[6] Even more, he becomes the personification of his own belief. His demand for belief in thought and respect for truth is a flaming protest against the spiritual and moral degeneration of public life, against the surrender of the fate of peoples to shallow and cynical opportunism, against deceit and lies as an instrument of politics. The anxious question as to what outstanding and convincing spiritual substance the West has to offer against the negation of the value and dignity of the human being in the totalitarian States can be answered by reference to this phenomenon. Christian teaching has a different content, and it obtains the effect which accords most profoundly with its essence by an intensive rather than an extensive attitude. But in somnambulistically following his star beyond the limits of Christian doctrine and community, Schweitzer is answering the challenge of our times. In so doing he certainly went

12. Service at Lambaréné
(*By permission of Erica Anderson, New York*)

to the uttermost limit for a follower of Jesus. But this act of self-sacrifice—it is not particularly important that it took place unconsciously—met the need of a world which Christianity cannot directly approach but which in its present hour of danger is greatly in need of the Christian message of love. The result justifies an undertaking which one can never imagine being repeated. A strengthening, consoling, guiding light was lit which now shines out over half the world. 'There is a longing for humanitarian spirituality in the world. I have been privileged to find the word which meets this longing and lights up the darkness. . . .'[7]

By his moralism Schweitzer becomes the representative opponent of the demoralization of our modern world. By putting his moralism into effect he has given his work of love an unsought actuality. Its original impulse was his personal need for 'direct human service . . . to practise true humanity towards his fellow men'.[8] When this impulse developed into the plan to become a doctor for jungle Negroes, he realized that this was the way to make atonement to the coloured peoples. But in those years before the First World War, and during the war when the Great Powers used the natives of their colonies as cannon-fodder, thus destroying the moral basis of colonialism, who could foresee the resentment akin to hatred with which the white man would soon have to cope from the Far East to Arabia and on to the Dark Continent, a resentment which would cause the beneficial sides of colonialism, the establishment of peace, the spread of civilization and Christianity to be forgotten? The jungle hospital alone cannot—though it has been copied amongst the Indians of the Amazon—dam this rising tide. But when we read that a little while ago the son of a coloured sergeant stationed in Italy appealed through his father to the military authorities to supply Schweitzer with a certain medicament, whereupon an appeal was made to the general public to subscribe to pay for supplies, with the result that within a very short space of time quantities of medicaments greatly in excess of requirements arrived by air in Lambaréné, we get some idea of the counter-tide of humanity which Schweitzer has caused to rise. Far more than any other charitable undertakings, however worthy and numerous they are, Schweitzer's jungle hospital has brought the West to regard the African Negro as the brother to whom it is under a special obligation of humaneness because he has suffered more than others at its hands.

This is enough to indicate the fundamental importance of this 'genius of humanity' (Churchill) for our time. Where Schweitzer goes into action something essential is at stake, something which will meet an urgent need. He 'goes to the heart of the cancer of our time' (Pestalozzi). However, there are two questions asked about him again and again, and they have not yet been convincingly answered. Is Albert Schweitzer a Christian?[9] And how can his extraordinary influence be explained?

Schweitzer is an *anima naturaliter christiana*. For him Christianity is 'true and valuable for it answers to the deepest stirring of our inner will to live'.[10] He calls himself a Christian. He regards Jesus as his Lord and Master. He is 'a loyal soldier of Christ'.[11] He acknowledges his 'belief in redemption through Christ',[12] though not in the sense of any Church doctrine. Nevertheless doubts as to his Christianity have not been dissipated, and he is repeatedly claimed on behalf of a 'universal religion' which proposes to get along without Jesus and seeks to replace his teaching either by humanitarianism or by a so-called 'Christian civilizatory ideology'.

The explanation of this is to be found in Schweitzer's own utterances. Because he 'wants to give . . . and gives . . . those outside Christianity something which will serve them as religion',[13] because as a moralist he proclaims not the love of Christ but 'the philosophic equivalent of the principle of love', the specifically Christian in his thought recedes into the background; and it may be too that when the discussion enters into philosophical channels his 'free thought' seems to underline his 'unbelief'.

Schweitzer's spiritual historical standpoint makes it impossible for the sincerity of his reasoning thought to compromise with Christian dogma. However, he takes no pleasure in his unbelief and is far from congratulating himself on it, though both these things belong to Free Thought. He acknowledges 'that we wish to believe and are frightened of unbelief'.[14]

For Schweitzer the inner essence of Christianity 'is Godliness arising out of inward constraint'[15]; that urge—'We call it piety'[16]—to 'surrender ourselves voluntarily and in gratitude to a higher, unknown'—the words are Goethe's. Thanks to its profound piety, Schweitzer's religiosity rises above his own moralism as well as above all theological controversies. It flattens the theological trenches. When he was asked why he had entrusted the education of his daughter to the Moravian Brotherhood (*Herrnhuter*), seeing that their beliefs were very different from his own, he replied: 'Because they are pious.' It is piety which makes him feel attached to the monks who helped him in the days of his internment as a prisoner of war, and for years, every time he went to Europe, one of his first visits was to delight them with his organ playing.

Schweitzer is not the revolutionary renewer of Christianity some people seem to think.[17] He does not pretend to any particular comprehension of the supernatural, and what is more, he is not particularly interested in it, and, in fact, he regards the differences of belief within Christianity as of secondary importance. His definitive utterance in this respect is to be found in a passage towards the end of his history of the quest for the historical Jesus, a passage which so far has not received sufficient attention. It expresses his conviction that 'independent and committed religiosity which now go separately will one day come together. . . . The differences . . . are so obvious only because there is such a lack of elementary and vital religiosity. Two narrow streams wind independently through the stones and gravel of a broad river bed. The efforts made from time to time to break down the barriers between them and allow them to flow together in the same channel have not been successful. But once the water rises it will submerge the stones and gravel and then the two streams will be one. Independent and committed religiosity will find their way to each other when the will and the hope for the Kingdom of God and the community of the spirit of Jesus once again become elementary and powerful in them, bringing them together in ideology and religion. The differences in outlook will remain but they will be submerged as the stones and gravel are submerged when the river rises, to be visible only as things far below the surface.'[18]

For Schweitzer too the way to God passes over the flattened trenches of doctrinal conflict, ignoring all obstacles and chasms of thought. The metaphysical agnostic believes 'that we are not poor human creatures abandoned to the play of chance, but that in all being we may be certain of the infinite love of God. What do we need? Confidence in God. . . . Pray for the grace to look God, the Heavenly Father, in the face and to feel His merciful glance of love, and I think I may say that you will not have prayed in vain.'[19]

The 'Father God' has no place in Schweitzer's theology, and so he has to justify his belief in Him to his own thought by saying that the profoundest truths can be expressed only in metaphors and paradoxes. As a thinker he chooses neither pantheism nor theism. But no sophistry —and Schweitzer is not a sophist—can reconcile the God of his philosophy with the merciful Heavenly Father. The former is an experience of thought, the latter an experience of the soul. Melvin Arnold tells us that the prayer with which Schweitzer always ends his religious services in the jungle is: 'God our Father grant us the blessing of becoming Thy children.'[20] Schweitzer cannot help but call 'the eternal unnamed' (Goethe) with the name which Jesus has given him.

Therefore we can confidently leave the answer to our question in the hands of St Augustine who, during the religious disputes of the early centuries, proclaimed: 'They will cease to be our brothers (i.e. *christiani*) when they cease to say "Our Father".'

Whoever attempts to explain the essence and significance of Albert Schweitzer may well at the end of it all feel like a diver who has gone down into the depths of the sea and come up again bringing to the surface this and that which may throw light on the multifarious life in the depths of the sea. But he knows full well that what he has brought to light gives only a very faint and inadequate idea of the richness of that undersea world which he has been privileged to see with his own eyes. And so perhaps we may close this study, in which much has necessarily been left unsaid, partly on account of the restraint imposed by personal considerations, by answering the question as to whether Schweitzer is a Christian; a question with which—not without hesitation and yet with a certain knowledge of the case—we dared to penetrate into the innermost recesses of his being. But we are not relieved of the necessity of saying something in conclusion about the reason for his power over his fellow men. To some extent it is already answered by the general reference to his greatness with which we began, and to the way in which his thought and his deed meet the need and longing of the age. But a more detailed explanation and one more closely related to his personality is necessary if we are really to understand the origin of his influence. Three traits in which the outline of the whole figure is visible contribute to the explanation.

Schweitzer radiates a belief in the spirit which can truly move mountains, and carry all before it. It is a belief he has held unwaveringly through all the storms and stresses of our time. And when towards the end of a life devoted to the preservation of life and the improvement of human conditions, he saw a new and terrible danger arising for all living things in the shape of nuclear weapons, whilst at the same time the nuclear tests showed that both West and East held life in contempt, it was this belief which gave Schweitzer the strength to enter the lists once more and call upon all humanity to remember its responsibility.[21]

With the thoroughness which is second nature to him and never allows him to say anything publicly which is not based on an exact knowledge of the facts, he first made himself thoroughly conversant with all the problems of nuclear armament. And when someone objected that the problem was very complicated and difficult he replied with all the force of his great moral authority: 'Nothing is difficult to the spirit'—and with these words he tells us his conviction that the nuclear danger can be combated only by the power of the spirit and not as the result of political manœuvres, and still less as the result of fear.

'The age of the spirit will come' is a formulation which expresses his belief in the coming of the Kingdom of God in which the creative accordance of spirit and life will once again be established. An undertone of the Age of Enlightenment can be heard in this enthusiastic spirituality, but Paul, Schweitzer's great teacher, tells us its real origin in words which might almost have been spoken by Schweitzer himself: 'No man can say that Jesus is the Lord, but by the Holy Spirit'. (1 Cor. xii. 3.)

The second factor of Schweitzer's specific strength is the *caritas perfecta*. It is of a particular kind.

The perfect example of neighbourly love as given in the life and work of Albert Schweitzer as love to all creatures has caused him to be hailed as 'the saint of Lambaréné', as a sort of second St Francis of Assisi.[22] The misunderstanding could hardly be greater.

The love of Saint Francis of Assisi for men was not founded in man as man. It derived neither from brotherly feelings of humanitarian solidarity nor compassion. His love was, as he was accustomed to say himself, *per amore di Dio*. His love was an image of the power of God's love by which he knew he was loved. The material welfare of humanity and the struggle against pain and suffering represented the least of his anxieties. His daemonic nature, which the modern age honours above all other saints with an aesthetic-sentimental and thoughtless respect, ought to repel any man who thinks as our age thinks, and arouse protest precisely where his real nature, i.e. his holiness, is concerned—if we saw St Francis as he really is. He was certainly a man who loved greatly and who lived as a poor man amongst the poor. But—as cures were for Jesus—his almsgiving was above all a sign: it was intended more to strengthen the soul than to help the body—as witness those words which modern man must regard as inhumane and as running counter to all social feelings: 'Whoever has someone over him would do greater and better to be subject to that higher one than to alleviate the needs of those who stand lower. Therefore for the creature who has God above him, love (*caritas*), through which he unites himself with God, is greater than compassion, through which he alleviates the needs of his fellow men.'

The comparison with St Francis helps to make the picture of Schweitzer clearer. During the years the goodness inherent in his nature—only in this sense can development in the unchangeable be perceived—has permeated his being into its uttermost recesses like yeast. It manifests itself in the least significant word and in the most casual action. His self-renunciation is complete. His life is spent absolutely and exclusively in the service of love, *caritas*. But this, as the ethic of reverence for life clearly shows, is exclusively based on the consciousness of solidarity with everything living and the responsibility which flows from it. It is humanitarian. It is compelling not by its theoretical justification, but by its perfection. 'Whether one is a believer or an unbeliever, it is impossible to resist the example of charitable neighbourly love. If it is sincere and confirmed by life then it is the strongest weapon (*l'arme le plus formidable*) ever placed in the hands of man.'[23] This is the weapon which Schweitzer wields, and he wields it as a conquerer of men.

In addition there is a third factor which contributes to his influence: his presence.

Total presence in every situation is the infallible sign of the significant human being. Schweitzer has this sign in the highest degree. Napoleon needed an actor's training. But with Schweitzer the effect is unconscious and obtained without any gesture. During his years in Strassburg a new organ was built in the Sängerhaus according to his instructions. The organists of Strassburg came together at the inaugural celebration, and each sought to demonstrate the capacities of the new instrument and his own mastery of it. When everyone else had played his piece, the man who had created the organ walked slowly up to it in his usual fashion, his arms hanging loosely by his side, sat down at the organ and played the chorale—it was Advent—*Wie soll ich dich empfangen*—and then walked away again. And yet the one figure that moved with the least fuss is the one which remains in the memory after the passage of half a century. The photographic illustrations in the present book show the same presence—as indeed do all reports of any meeting with him, even when the witness is not talented in the use of words.

All these things are evidence of human greatness. But even the greatness of Schweitzer reveals its particular character paradoxically. It is a greatness which perfects itself in becoming small. 'To content oneself with becoming small: that is the only salvation and liberation.

To work in the world as such, asking nothing of it, or of men, not even recognition, that is true happiness . . . There are things which one cannot do without Jesus. Without Him one cannot attain to that higher innocence—unless we look to Him in the disappointments of life, and seek in Him the strength to be childlike and small in that higher sense. . . . Whoever has gone through the world of smallness has left the empire of this world to enter into the Kingdom of God. He has gone over the border as one goes over the border in a dark forest—without taking note of it. The way remains the same, the surrounding things the same, and only gradually does he realize that whilst everything is familiar it is different, that life is the same and yet not the same because of the clarity which lights up in him, and because of the peace and the strength which have taken possession of him because he is small and has finished with himself.'[24]

At the beginning of this study we set out to present Albert Schweitzer as a great man. And now, at its end we see him as one who has become small in the highest sense—'*L'humilité est la gloire de toutes les vertus*'[25] (Père de Foucauld). The boundary of the Kingdom of God has been crossed. His work—a fragment like all the works of man—is done, though the 'heavy burdens of daily trial' (Goethe) still stretch his capacities to the full. But the burden of doubt has been taken from him. At its close his life stands under the sign of service to mankind and not of knowledge. 'I am nothing else but somebody who does what is natural. The natural, however, is loving kindness.'

The first of the Beatitudes—'Blessed are the poor in spirit'—is regarded by Schweitzer as prophetic. 'The highest knowledge is to know that we are surrounded by mystery. . . . Thus we go on our way through the world not troubled about knowledge, but committing to God what we hope for,—for ourselves and the world, and possessing all in all through being apprehended by the living, ethical God.'[26]

APPENDIX

THE STORY OF THE QUEST OF THE HISTORICAL JESUS (SKETCH)

The phenomenon of the quest for the historical Jesus is unique. A religious self-examination such as that represented by historical dogma research and, hand in hand with it, the investigation of the canonical writings in order to discover the historical significance and utterances of a founder of religion, regarded as a divine being, is unique in world history. It arose from the clash between belief in revelation and scientific thought when the latter presented itself as the sole champion of truth, and decided that it was possible to detect what is 'true' from what is 'untrue' by means of scientific criteria; in other words, when it decided that truth can be discovered by the scientific method.

And thus the quest for the historical Jesus began, a figure which had been ignored by Christianity for almost eighteen hundred years. Since it already lived with Christ in the future world whose imminent coming it expected, early Christianity was not greatly interested in the history of the life of Jesus. For the same reason Paul did not want to know Christ in the flesh (2 Cor. v. 16). And later Christology turned its eyes away from the man Jesus of Nazareth. Only when the dogma of the double divine and human nature was shaken was there any reason for regarding his existence as historically conditioned and defined.[1]

Christianity is the only world religion which presupposes an intervention of God in world affairs. It originated in a personality whose appearance in a certain historical constellation changed the world. It is based on a manifestation of God in time. So a moment necessarily came when there was a need to know the personality in which this manifestation expressed itself as an historical phenomenon. And when historical thought developed, here was its greatest task. The beginning of the investigations into the life of Jesus go back to an earlier period it is true; they were brought about during and by the Age of Enlightenment, which first cleared the way for the historical investigation of the life of Jesus. It was part of the destiny of Christianity, a profoundly paradoxical religion, that unbelief was first necessary before it could develop its significance to the full.

Three motives were responsible for the launching and maintenance of this tremendous undertaking; first of all, 'in pure faith in the truth';[2] secondly, a desire to proclaim the Christian gospel in a form acceptable to modern man; and, thirdly and finally, a desire 'to see Jesus'. These were all honourable and compelling motives, and they led to a dramatic action which has no equal in the history of the human spirit. Their accent differs according to the nature of the actors and the time of their appearance. At first there was the wish to discover the historical Jesus as an ally in the struggle for emancipation from the 'theological deception' of dogma. Simultaneously there was no lack of Luciferean elements in the urge for knowledge. Schweitzer insists that 'the greatest of them [the lives of Jesus] are written with hate;[3] for example, the 'lives' of Reimarus, David Friedrich Strauss, and Bruno Bauer, who ended by denying the historicity of Jesus altogether. 'Because they hated they could see more clearly in history, and they furthered the investigation more than anyone else. Without the offence they gave, scholarship would not be what it is today.' In addition there were those who desired to 'bring Jesus to life with love' (Schweitzer). These men found it difficult to be sincere. When the struggle between belief and knowledge is transferred to an investigator under an obligation to his scientific conscience, its features are likely to be tragic. A clear example of what it can cost can be seen in the personality of the great Jena theologian Karl August von Hase, who took an active part in the investigations into the life of Jesus for fifty years[4]—and gradually saw himself compelled to abandon what he had once regarded as immutable truths. And yet he still stood firmly for 'the absolutely untrammelled freedom of investigation', the principle he had adopted at the beginning of his investigations. Finally, he could say to his students: 'It is no business of mine to be horrified at an idea, or to express it with misgiving because it is disturbing.' And Schweitzer declared: 'The world had never seen before and will never see again, a struggle for truth so full of pain and renunciation as that of which the Lives of Jesus of the last hundred years contain the cryptic record.'[5] At the same time both Hase and Strauss maintained belief in a higher invulnerability of the true life of Jesus. It will be seen whether and in what sense this belief was justified.

'The quest for the historical Jesus represents a blow for truth on the part of Protestant Christianity.'[6] Schweitzer's blunt statement is justified, but it requires explanation. The character of its theological achievement can be fully appreciated only against its background: the doctrine of the inviolability of the gospel texts on the basis of verbal inspiration, both typical Protestant phenomena, are corresponding but opposed magnitudes. The one extreme produces the other with dialectical inevitability. The theological risk taken by the former, which stakes the whole of religious belief on the investigation into the life of Jesus and puts the intellectual honesty of those engaged in it to the uttermost test, stands in casual relationship with the founding of belief on the literal text of the Bible.[7] For Catholicism belief is based on the Church and its sacral reality. The Bible receives its religious validity only from the authority of the Church. From this standpoint there is no fundamental difficulty—and there has been none since the days of Origen—in rising above the direct literal sense of the text and discarding 'the metaphorical Jewish-oriental piety in which the truth is wrapped and seeking a sense which accords with reason',[8] with the proviso of course that the dogmatic fundamental evidence may not be touched. This evidence stands in reciprocal relationship to dogma; dogma is based on it, and at the same time dogma justifies it with its own authority. The above-mentioned proviso certainly applies to those texts that are fundamental to belief, but it allows critical exegesis more room to manœuvre than is generally realized. 'Amongst the many things contained in Holy Writ there are only a few whose sense has been explained by the authority of the Church, and the points on which agreement prevails amongst the Fathers of the Church are not much more numerous.'[9] Protestants know very little about the relative freedom enjoyed by Catholic biblical exegesis since the days of the early Fathers of the Church, and those champions of enlightened thought outside Christianity know nothing at all. They still believe that all Christian thought is 'based on the evidence of the Bible regarded as truth requiring no further proof'.[10] Now the doctrine of verbal inspiration, for which Protestant theology is alone responsible, acted on the Age of Enlightenment like a provocative challenge. It was laid to the account of Christianity as a whole, which has not been altogether forgiven for it yet.

In opposition to the doctrines of the Church, Luther founded belief on the Bible, or, to be more accurate, on the word of God as evidenced in the Bible. However, he was not greatly concerned with the historical accuracy of its texts. Referring to the driving of the moneylenders out of the temple, placed by John at the beginning of the public life of Jesus and by the Synoptic Gospels towards the end, he merely observes: 'The Gospels do not put the miracles and acts of Jesus in any particular order, and it really is not of much importance. If a dispute should arise about Holy Writ and it should prove impossible to settle, then the best thing to do is just to let it go.' Only later, in old Protestant orthodoxy, did belief crystallize on 'the Word', thus leaving no freedom of movement for textual exegesis in its present-day form, and necessarily leading sooner or later to an all the more violent irruption of critical scientific thought and a collapse of the artificial dams which hedged around the sphere of belief.

The great German dramatist Lessing was the first to set the fiery torch to the tinder; and the spirit in which he did so can be seen from two of his utterances, both of which might well have been taken as terms of reference for the quest of the historical Jesus. The one was: 'If God offered me all truth in his right hand, and in his left the constant urge to truth, even on pain of repeated error, I would in all humility indicate his left hand and beg that he might give me that.' And the other: 'Christian tradition must be explained by its inner truth, and no writings handed down can give it inner truth if it does not already possess it.' It was this passionate search for truth coupled with confidence in the ultimate success of the undertaking which persuaded him, despite his misgivings, to publish the fragment of 'the Wolfenbüttel Unknown' (Reimarus, Professor of Oriental Languages in Hamburg, who died in 1768) in 1778, although he was by no means in agreement with it.

The magnificence of this opening gesture, which summed up all the motives behind the later investigations, suited the importance of the moment. 'This document is not only one of the greatest milestones in the history of the critical spirit, it is at the same time a work of world literature' (Schweitzer). Here, for the first time, a historian thoroughly conversant with the sources criticized tradition. He recognized that there could be no solution of the problem without a combination of historical and literary methods. He recognized that Jesus lived in Jewish ideas. He recognized—an astonishing performance!—that the ideology of Jesus was eschatological. Justice in view of the coming Kingdom of God was the innovation in his teaching. Justice according to the law was no longer sufficient because the Kingdom of God was at hand. A new, more profound morality was needed. Reimarus certainly misunderstood the proclamation of the Kingdom of God by Jesus. He confuses the messianic idea with the political-Davidian idea which expected the Messiah as a wordly liberator. In this sense Jesus becomes a people's leader who has failed in his mission; and his disciples become ambitious men so disappointed that they are goaded by the shameful death of their leader into playing a trick—the stealing of the body from the sepulchre—and seeking to save their faces by harking back to the second aspect of Jewish messianic hopes, the supernatural one, making a communistic society possible. With this Christianity stands condemned. The only argument which could save it would be proof that the parusia, the return of Christ, actually took place in their day. But no such proof can be produced.

Thus at the beginning of the quest for Jesus we come across a work which certainly represents a tremendous critical performance, but is blind both to the essence of Christianity and to the person of Jesus. Hatred both of Jesus and the 'deception' practised by Christianity, which refused to admit the eschatological non-arrival of the Kingdom of God, and whose teachings and history are full of contradictions, is the impelling motive here, but Reimarus aims too low to have any hope of hitting his target. He makes the whole thing banal. He is shrewd; he has a certain feeling for history, and as he is not a theologian he is free from theological inhibitions. And therefore at his first attempt he reaches the conclusion, to be buried during the subsequent one hundred and twenty years, that the historically-conditioned Jesus must be understood as the culmination of eschatological-apocalyptic Neo-Judaism. And yet he doesn't really know what he is talking about. He is not a profound spirit, and this limits his insight. He has no feeling for the grandeur of Jesus, or for the historical absurdity of an assumption that the phenomenon of the Christian world religion has its origin in a piece of trickery organized by a handful of unimportant little people whose only desire was to continue, even after their leader's death, the comfortable life his female admirers had provided—with the assistance of credulous people who were expected to share their wealth with the community. This is so-called Enlightenment in its shallowest form.

There are two things even in Reimarus which will astonish us again and again in the course of the subsequent quest for the historical Jesus. The one is the extraordinary low standard of the attacks launched against Christianity. Consider the weapons that might reasonably be brought to bear against both Christianity and its founder! But instead the attack is launched with the most inadequate of weapons. The critical thought which has proved its high quality in an examination of the texts unexpectedly deteriorates as soon as it approaches the heart of the matter, almost as though it had lost the ground under its feet. The bold attacker swipes wildly to right and left like some Homeric hero deliberately blinded by the gods. Schweitzer is greatly impressed by the Reimarus fragment, but equally by its lack of understanding for the essentials of the problem.

The other thing is that hardly has investigation released the bonds 'which bound Jesus for centuries to the rock of church dogma'—to use Schweitzer's words—than it finds itself caught up in hopeless confusion. The investigation—re-started again and again, despite repeated failure, with the unshaken confidence of the inquiring spirit—proves to be far more difficult than had originally been supposed. A new sphere of operations opens up to theology but it finds itself almost completely on its own, though philology certainly offers indispensable assistance. However, the science of comparative religion was more hindrance than help—which became very clear when the historicity of Jesus came up for discussion. Whilst history itself left theology in the lurch altogether. 'No historical school has ever laid down canons for the investigation of this problem; no professional historian has ever lent his aid to theology in dealing with it. Every ordinary method of historical investigation proves inadequate to the complexity of the conditions. The standards of ordinary historical science are here inadequate, its methods not immediately applicable.'[11] In part this is due to the lack of profane historical evidence as to the public life and fate of Jesus, which took place away from the centre of the then civilized world. And to some extent the difficulties arise from the particular character of the available sources, in which many layers are combined, and which, in addition, provide an account which aims at communicating a creed rather than providing a factual account. It was therefore from the beginning quite impossible for Reimarus to do what he set out to do—if only because he was unfamiliar with the methods of differentiating between the sources, methods which required several generations of investigators for their development. And, finally, the New Testament, which is the subject of investigation, is not an historical book in the ordinary sense at all; not in the sense of verbal inspiration which would demand belief in the totality of its evidence and make it immune to textual criticism, but for the much simpler reason that it does not concern profane historical happenings.[12] Even if we leave aside the supernatural ('mythical') evidence of the Gospels, which caused the investigation many a headache (the investigation period preceding Strauss is dominated by the problem of miracles, and even the 'solution' Strauss found was by no means final), the ordinary criteria of historical investigation are inadequate to embrace a personality who, according to the first witnesses and the biblical stories, brought history to an end and inaugurated the Kingdom of God, and with whom, according to Schweitzer, we can enter into a mystical relationship. The history of the quest for the historical Jesus is the history of the dilemma of theology: it felt itself obliged to behave as though it were history in dealing with material which is only very conditionally subject to purely historical treatment; and at the same time it found itself hampered at every turn by theological considerations.

But over and above all these difficulties, the investigations were to experience something quite unexpected, and only in part explainable by what has already been said: namely, no matter how earnestly the investigation sought the 'true' Jesus, and no matter what methods it adopted to 'outline' and define him, it found that he slipped through the mesh again and again. Despite his great discovery, which certainly revealed the central historical problem, Reimarus was never able to see Jesus. And, as we shall see, even since then, all the efforts made to reveal the figure, life and work of the historical Jesus of Nazareth have not succeeded in producing a result which can be accepted as even moderately reliable. In retrospect we can see that this Reimarus fragment, which was, significantly, written as a polemic and not as an objective piece of scholarship, foreshadows the fate all subsequent investigations were to suffer.

The work of Reimarus has no tomorrow. It 'remains on its own, uncompleted, and leading nowhere'.

The history of the quest for the historical Jesus was begun by a self-willed outsider and individual. But the time was ripe for what he did. This was also shown by the fact that almost at the same time—and certainly for the first time in the history of theology—theologians set to work to write the life of Jesus, though naturally in an altogether different spirit. 'Half-baked rationalism'—to use the words of Schweitzer—was the first to enter the arena.[13] Compared with the theologically-uninhibited work of Reimarus, it cut a very poor figure indeed in its attempts to sentimentalize Jesus, to bring him 'closer' to the age, to present him as the great teacher of virtue, and to show that his teaching was really identical with the reasoned truth worshipped by rationalism. Reimarus was not interested in consolidating the authority of Jesus by modernizing him. And this at least enabled him to think historically, whereas rationalistic theology behaves altogether unhistorically. And in presenting the teachings of Jesus it takes its obligations very lightly; in not one of these various lives of Jesus is a single one of his sayings presented in its original form.

There are two points of fundamental interest in these first theological

13. At the organ
(By permission of Erica Anderson, New York)

efforts to find the historical Jesus: the astonishingly naïve insouciance of the 'self-confident, uninhibited thought which reveals itself here, stretching and tensing its muscles' (Schweitzer) and playing havoc with the sources—and even with Jesus himself, and the supernatural elements of the Gospels. These were no such problems for Reimarus of course—as far as he was concerned Jesus did not perform any miracles at all. We have already seen, for example, how he regards the 'Resurrection'. But these others have no intention of touching the dogmatic idea of Jesus. Nevertheless, it is lapped around by rationalism like nitric acid, dissolving the outer layers, but not yet penetrating to the core, which is left untouched. The focal point of interest shifts to the doctrine, which is rationalistically presented. Jesus becomes a reformer anxious to erect a merely moral institution and desiring to succeed entirely by moral reasoning. As far as possible the number of the miracles is reduced, but the supernatural is not fundamentally excluded.

Rationalistic theology is anxious to present Jesus as the founder of a 'moral, comprehensible, spiritual' religion of reason. The inner relationship of events therefore does not matter, and thus there can be no real question of any attempt to describe the life of Christ. But newly-awakened interest in his earthly appearance necessarily produced such attempts, and at the end of the eighteenth and the beginning of the nineteenth centuries, this was catered for by the works of Karl Friedrich Bahrdt and Karl Heinrich Venturini, a couple of disoriented theologians, who wrote the first 'lives' of Jesus. The pericopes (the passages of the Gospels which are complete in themselves) are not linked together by research, but by complete fiction. Jesus is presented as the tool of a secret society, the Essenes, and this, of course, makes quite a lot of things easy. The dilettantist conclusions drawn from the discovery of the Dead Sea scrolls in our own day have given rise to similar attempts at interpretation. The miracles are explained away in a rationalistic fashion. The 'cures' were quite simple: Jesus always carried a 'medicine chest' around with him. And as for the marriage feast at Cana, he just took along a few jars of good wine with him as a wedding present and had them broached at the right moment. John 'who was perhaps just a little tipsy himself', believed this was a miracle. In any case, when he was an old man and began to write his gospel he probably mixed things up a bit. The Resurrection is similarly explained: Jesus was not really dead at all and he was released from the tomb by fellow members of the Essenes. Venturini's 'Natural History of the Great Prophet of Nazareth' was published in a new edition almost annually until well into the twentieth century. All the romantic and novelettish lives of Jesus—and they are legion—go back to this original.

Logical rationalism also paid its debt to the investigations. The one who made payment was a Heidelberg Professor of Theology named Paulus,[14] a tremendous champion of 'unbending integrity' in reasoned thought. As such he was a passionate opponent of Schelling, whose philosophy he denounced as 'an offence against reason and common sense', and whom he pursued with such bitter attacks that in the end Schelling resigned his professorship. This Paulus had a horrible fear of anything that seemed to go beyond the limits of natural thought, and so a rationalistic interpretation of the Gospels was an absolute necessity for him. As he put it himself, 'good sense must be satisfied if the validity of the cause is to continue'. His chief interest was concentrated on explaining the miracles; and yet with him, as with all the older rationalists, the question of miracles was really quite secondary. It was a firm principle for him that the religion of Jesus needed no further justification. Unexplainable interferences with the course of nature could neither upset nor confirm a spiritual truth. The systematic operations of nature were the handiwork of God. The miracles reported in the Bible were only eye-witness accounts by men ignorant of the intermediate causes. Thus there was really no miracle question at all. For any normal intelligence all that was necessary was to discover these intermediate causes and the miracles of Jesus would be explained! However, in this undertaking —the work has no less than 1,192 pages and is a compendium of rationalistic explanations for miracles—common-sense judgement does not really come into its own. The exegesis is quite arbitrary. The author remains truthful only at the expense of the actors in the drama: what is reasonable is true, and nothing else. What 'offends reason' is therefore summarily dismissed —altogether unreasonably. In the struggle for reason it would appear that whatever happens one is always on the side of truth. There is no question of textual criticism. The thing is a sort of elucidated harmonizing and reconciling, with the Gospel of St John as its basis. Paulus sketches the history of the messiah concept, and this is in Schweitzer's view a real performance. Paulus also recognizes the importance of eschatology for the sermons of Jesus.

The last word of the ninety-year-old rationalist: 'There is another world.'

The rationalistic epoch of the investigations leaves us with conflicting impressions. It is the deposit of a particularly vigorous period in human thought, and this is evidenced by the very weakness of the investigation: it lacks historical sense; in fact it is not really interested in the past at all, except in so far as it finds its own reflection there. This is not out of regard for the Gospel, that is to say, nor for theological purposes, but because it cannot help satisfying its own urge to truthfulness. It seeks to satisfy the elementary need to reconcile belief in the Gospels with belief in reason. The 'modernization' of Jesus is carried out in obedience to an absolute principle, but the result is, as later on in the liberalistic era, an adaptation to the spirit of the age. But there is a pathos in the undertaking without which the orthodox obstacles could never have been taken, and we must not forget this if we are to be just to an undertaking whose inadequacies are so obvious. Rationalism cleared the way for investigation into the life of Jesus. But that was about all. One might have supposed that a theologically uninhibited encounter with the evangelists would lead to a moving confrontation with the essential and thus provide us with new insight. But nothing of the sort came about. Some things were certainly shrewdly observed, and their importance became clear later. But on the whole, belief in reason proved itself just as great an obstacle to an understanding of the historical Jesus as church doctrine. It found no real contact with the events around the Nazarene, no matter how they were interpreted; because, in fact, Jesus has nothing at all in common with the idea of a noble and sensible preacher of a virtuous teaching based on reason. There could in any case be no true confrontation between orthodoxy and rationalism because the latter is not only unable to negate the spiritual world but even to meet it effectively on its own field. This becomes obvious from the inadequacy of its efforts to 'rationalize' the supernatural content of the Gospels. It has no relationship at all to the reality of religious phenomena and thus in any discussion with doctrinal teaching it must begin to doubt itself. This stage of the investigation is particularly associated with the names of Hase and Schleiermacher.[15]

The two great theologians, the historian and the dialectician, are sceptics of rationalism. They are unable to free themselves from the urge to explain the miracles reasonably, but they no longer have confidence in the outcome, and when it comes to the point they put a question mark in place of a solution. Both of them leave open the question of whether the Resurrection was a supernatural event or merely a recovery from apparent death. Both retain the John miracles and to some extent reject the synoptic miracles. This anti-rationalist supernaturalism of the 'Perhaps' is inferior to Rationalism in logical simple truthfulness.

Schleiermacher's life of Jesus made no impact at all because the investigations could really not be furthered with the methods of aesthetic dialectics he used—not in order to discover the historical Jesus, but to confirm the Jesus Christ of his own doctrinal teachings. In addition, because of its late publication the work was soon made out of date by David Friedrich Strauss.

Hase, on the other hand, made the first attempt at a purely historical-scientific reconstruction of the life of Jesus, and with this really creative performance he strode far ahead of his rationalistic predecessors. Thanks to his historical sense and his shrewd psychological ability he produced the first modern historico-psychological picture of Jesus, and thus became a forerunner of the liberal school of investigations. The idea, put forward with some success later on by Holtzmann, of two periods in the messianic phase of Jesus, goes back to him. In the first Jesus is represented as accepting the nationalistic ideas of the messianic age almost without misgiving; whereas in the second period, as a result of his experiences in the first, he made good this error and accepted his real vocation. This thesis introduces the idea of development into the interpretation of the public life of Jesus.

Up to the end of rationalism the investigations were dominated by the problem of the miracles. Critical thought felt acutely uncomfortable at the idea of supernatural events, and this stumbling-block turned its attention away from its real objective, the figure and teachings of Jesus, even though the investigators clearly realized that the miracles, to whose natural explanation so much effort and fantasy was being directed, were of no importance for a religion of reason. In the end rationalistic investigation of the life of Jesus, which had set out to make an end of supernaturalism, foundered on this very problem. It was unable to allay the natural anxiety that little would remain of the historical life of Jesus as the basis of religion if it dared to apply the idea of mythos consistently; with the result that it ended in a series of logically untenable compromises. This was inevitable because it was unable to find any explanation of problematical happenings which could stand successfully before the bar of its highest court, reason; or which could do justice even remotely to the sense of the biblical accounts. If any solution were possible at all it could be obtained only by the elimination of the supernatural from the historical account in a very different fashion, namely by consistently differentiating between the historical and the mythical source elements. However, this was not done under the aegis of rationalism, which had no feeling for either the historical or the mythical, but under the influence of Hegel. According to Hegel's dialectics, mythos is introduced into the interpretation of the Gospels as a synthesis of supernatural and rationalistic interpretation. This was the achievement of David Friedrich Strauss.

Like Bruno Bauer, Strauss was a casualty of the quest for the historical Jesus, and in a double sense at that. Both men were thrown out of their course because they stood unshakably by their convictions. Bauer, who was a theological lecturer at Bonn, had to abandon his career at the age of thirty-three and turn to profane history. When later on he returned to theology his work was ignored. The two men were practically the same age, Bauer was born in 1808 and Strauss in 1809. From the beginning Strauss had to contend with both inner and external difficulties. As he wrote in a letter in 1833: 'What interests me in theology is what is offensive; and what isn't offensive doesn't interest me.' In 1839 he was appointed to the chair of dogmatics in Zürich, but the orthodox and the pietists objected so strongly that the Government had to cancel the appointment. After this first failure he never succeeded in securing any office at all. However, he rose superior to his fate with dignity. 'I might blame my book' (his life of Jesus) he wrote in the prefaces to his *Gespräche des Ulrich von Hutten* (*Talks of Ulrich von Hutten*) published in 1860, 'because it has certainly caused me a great deal of trouble'—and rightly so! shrieked the pietists. 'It has caused my exclusion from all public teaching, which I would have liked, and for which I perhaps have some talent. It has dragged me out of conditions natural to me and thrusts me into unnatural ones. It has made my career a lonely one. And yet when I think what would have become of me if I had suppressed the voice which sounded in my soul, if I had dismissed the doubts that arose in me—then I bless that book which damaged me outwardly but preserved the integrity of my soul and spirit; and, I think I can say that with satisfaction of some others as well.'

But another and truly tragic fate weighed even more heavily on both these men as the price of their search for 'truth': it was the loss of their Christianity. When they first applied the critical probe to the biblical texts they had no idea of what lay ahead of them. Bauer believed that he was out 'to save the honour of Jesus by putting his personality back into the framework of life and once more giving it that living relationship to history . . . it once had.' But finally he came to the conclusion: 'There was never an historical personality Jesus.' His urge to demonstrate the historical untenability of the sources and thus to cut the ground from under the feet of the theologians developed into a mania. It gave him a daemoniacal pleasure to tear to pieces what he regarded as the deceitful web of that 'infernal spurious science' theology. And this hatred of theology developed into a hatred of Christianity, 'because it was the false expression of truth'.

Much the same sort of thing happened to Strauss. He started his investigations in the firm conviction that they would not affect Jesus as the creator of the religion of humanity; indeed, it was this conviction which gave him the courage to undertake a critical analysis of the Gospels. In doing so he based himself on the Hegelian conception of the relationship between idea and reality. According to this the divine-human as the highest idea of human thought is incorporated in the historic personality of Jesus. But whereas inhibited thought supposes that this realization must be complete as a phenomenon, that thought which is raised to a higher unhibitedness by honest criticism knows that the truth of an idea does not depend on the proof of its perfectly natural presentation, but that its completion comes about through the contribution the idea makes to history, or through the fashion in which history itself is raised to the idea. The fact that Jesus represented this idea and brought it to life in humanity was a reality not to be negated by any criticism. It lived on and it would live on in all eternity.

Such were the ideas of the author of the most famous of all the 'lives' of Jesus. But his final judgement on the personality in whom at that time he saw the incorporation of the 'highest idea of human thought' was:[16] 'A being I can see only in vague outline, one who remains unclear to me in fundamental respects, can certainly arouse my interest as a subject for scientific investigation, but cannot be of much practical help to me in life. . . . The Jesus of history, of scholarship, is simply a problem. . . .' When Jesus had ceased to mean anything of importance to him, Strauss ended, like Bauer, by passionately rejecting Christianity.

It is one of the characteristic aspects of the quest for the historical Jesus that such victims fall by the wayside. More is at stake than a mere chapter in scholarship.

Strauss's life of Jesus (1835–36) raised three problems: the relationship between mythos and history; the relationship between Jesus and Christ; and that between the Synoptic Gospels and the Gospel of St John. The pupil of Hegel justifies the critical investigation into the life of Jesus in relationship to Hegel's religious philosophy, by claiming that from its standpoint the happenings recorded in the Gospels are of no fundamental importance; they might well have happened in that way; on the other hand, they might not. One way or the other, it could be left safely to the judgement of historical criticism. This establishment of the relationship between the historical Jesus and the idealistic Christ was of great importance for the Strauss of that period because in his view it also justified his undertaking, but it was irrelevant to the history of the investigations into the life of Jesus. However, all the more important is Strauss's solution of the problem of miracles, at which he arrives by the consistent application of the mythos concept as the historical guise of religious ideas, formed in an unintentionally poetic saga and consolidated in an historical personality. All unexplainable, supernatural events are regarded as mythical components of the sources and as such they have no place in an historical presentation. This bars the way both to their rationalistic explanation and to their supernatural interpretation, but it permits their interpretation as symbols of religious significance. Modern theology has retained this basis down to the present day. Strauss was the first to introduce the non-miraculous conception of the life of Jesus, and since his day the principle has been generally recognized in Gospel exegesis.

The third basic problem raised by Strauss's life of Jesus was the question of John. Up till his day biblical exegesis had treated the four Gospels as historical sources of equal value. Indeed, naïvely, the Gospel of St John was more acceptable to the rationalists than the others were because there were not so many miracles in it.

There are few passages in the history of these investigations in which one feels so strongly what a great achievement each step forward in the field of the spirit really is. How the pro-consuls of reason clung to outward signs and overlooked discrepancies in the evidence which should rightly have given them pause! Herder, who belongs in point of time to the period of older rationalism but was never mentioned in that connection because his profundity and the greatness of his artistic understanding set him apart from his theological contemporaries, was the first, and the only one before Strauss, to recognize that the life of Jesus could be presented either according to the Synoptics or according to John, whereas a life of Jesus based on all four Gospels could not stand up to critical historical investigation.[17] What Herder appreciated more with the sensitiveness of the poet, Strauss understood by his critical sense. He pointed out that although the Gospel of St John records fewer miracles, it underlines them so intensely that their miraculous character cannot be disputed, whilst at the same time there is a parallel moral or symbolic significance. It is thus no longer an unconsciously developing saga, choosing, moulding and grouping, but a definite apologist dogmatic tendency. John represents an advanced stage of mythos formation because he has replaced the God-son idea of Jewish Messianism by the Greek-metaphysical concept. Because of his own knowledge of the Alexandrinian Logos doctrine he has even made the Lord apply the Greek-speculative idea of pre-existence to himself. The question is therefore settled: as an historical source the Gospel of St John is far inferior to the Synoptics, but theologically and as an apologia it is far more interesting than they are.

Strauss's work provoked an unusually wide discussion. Schweitzer himself lists sixty books that have been written about it. But it was also a remarkably unfruitful one. 'The fructifying rain produced only toadstools.' Despite the best efforts of the 'mediatory theologians', whose subterfuges were first revealed in their true light, his 'solution' of the question of miracles by eliminating them from historical research was accepted. But very few people understood what he meant by mythical historical explanation, and the general view was that he had reduced the life of Jesus entirely to myths. Strauss was not altogether blameless in this respect, because he overstrained his principle and pushed the mythical frontier forward to the detriment of historical facts. In addition, his 'cross-examination' of each pericope to discover the presence of mythical elements led to a complete dissolution of all coherence. This proceeding turned the Synoptics into mere collections of tales and sayings (just as form-historical research was to do later) and made it almost impossible to grasp what Strauss was really aiming at. Although in this question certain results were arrived at, and results of far-reaching importance at that, Strauss was ignored when he put forward the relationship of the Gospels to each other as historical sources as a matter for discussion. But here he stood in his own light in consequence of his strange dislike for Mark, whom he regarded as a kind of satellite of Matthew. There is a certain humour in the fact that whilst the Gospel of St John was acceptable to the Rationalists because it contained fewer miracles, this anti-rationalist was averse to the Gospel of St Mark because its graphic descriptions, for example, of the restoring of the blind man's sight in Bethsaida (Mark viii. 22–6), facilitated the rationalistic explanation of miracles. And theology was not short of arguments to justify the inclusion of the Synoptic accounts in the St John plan. But the important thing was that Strauss did not maintain his own position. In the third 'corrected' edition of his life of Jesus (1838–39) he tolerates untenable compromises. He has become uncertain. 'It is not that I am convinced of its authenticity,' he wrote about the fourth Gospel, 'it is just that I am no longer convinced that it is not authentic.' In the following edition (1840) he does withdraw this compromise, but in order in the end to write a 'liberal' life of Jesus.[18] Thus the positive solutions which were visible in prophetic outline behind his negative criticism were not developed, and even the author himself did not sense their scope.

Though Strauss certainly carried the quest for the historical Jesus a good step forward, the Hegelian formulas he adopted barred all understanding of the historical content of the synoptic sources. He was less interested in the latter than in their 'de-mythologization'—not the term, but the idea became visible here for the first time. No further attempt was made to deal with the miracles by the methods of the rationalists, who always had a reasonable explanation for everything supernatural. Instead the interpretation was based on 'mythical idealism'; a process which was reproached—and not altogether without reason—for allowing the violation of history by philosophy. And as before, *a priori* rejected parts of the Gospel accounts were sacrificed to a principle which arbitrarily distorted the texts without seriously examining them for a possible content of historical fact. In the words of Christian Hermann Weisse, this procedure certainly cleared the old theological forest away, but it did not help historical investigation.

As the immediate successor of Strauss, Weisse was himself a pioneer.[19] As a historian he seeks the general connection in the traditional Gospel accounts which provides what is historically well-founded in the life of Jesus, and this sets a limit to mythological interpretation. In this way he comes to the conclusion that St Mark was the original evangelist and that the two other synoptics based their Gospels on his. Further he adopts the hypothesis that, in addition, Matthew and Luke made joint use of certain sources which have since been lost. This divinatory insight of Weisse was raised to the level of exact scholarship by Christian Gottlob Wilke,[20] who approached the problem from the literary angle. This so-called 'double-source theory' or 'Marcan Hypothesis', which was argued once more in Holtzmann's book *Die synoptischen Evangelien* (*The Synoptic Evangelists*) (1863), is amongst the few results of the whole investigation which are regarded as well founded and, as such, accepted by most investigators. This theory lays the basis for the text-critical analysis of the synoptic Gospels.

But not even his independent and eminently shrewd inquiring spirit could save Weisse from the theological noose. He felt himself obliged—as did subsequent upholders of the Marcan hypothesis down to the end of the century—to wage an obstinate struggle against eschatology in favour of a 'spiritual' conception by Jesus of his messianism. The idea that Jesus had lived in an apocalyptic-Jewish world of ideas seemed intolerable. Weisse therefore saw the chief task of scholarship in the provision of proof that Jesus was free of 'the fantastic errors of that Jewish thought'. 'The whole struggle around eschatology,' says Schweitzer, who took a leading part in it, 'is nothing but a progressive discarding of Weisse's ideas.' With the arrival of Johannes Weiss, Christian Hermann Weisse was exploded.

We are now approaching that period of liberal investigation from which Schweitzer himself developed and which he concluded. But first of all we must deal briefly with a phenomenon which played a special role in the architectonic structure of these investigations, which seemed to develop according to some inherent law. This was Bruno Bauer. Even before the attempts of David Friedrich Strauss, Christian Hermann Weisse and the Rationalists had led to broader efforts to construct the life of Jesus on the basis of scholarly investigation, the most brilliant and complete compendium of all the difficulties of the undertaking had already been written. Once again, its importance was not recognized, largely owing to the fault of its author.

Bauer chose the literary approach, and he followed it unswervingly to the end. In a preliminary work[21] he examined the Gospel of St John and came to the conclusion that it was a work of art shot through from beginning to end with the views of its one author. He then went on to deal with the Synoptics,[22] and discovered a difference, not in kind but only in degree. With this he found himself on the path which led logically to a denial of any historical findings.

The literary solution of the Marcan hypothesis put forward by Weisse and Wilke questioned the significance of tradition for the creation of sources. But if the whole Gospel tradition originates in one writer who has created the connection between the individual events, then how far is it to the assumption that the events themselves must be put down to his account? And further, Matthew and Luke, as literary followers of Mark, must, like him, be literary products. In this case there is, of course, no tradition at all, but just one author of the Gospel story, which thus becomes useless as an historical source. The mythos concept adopted by Strauss cannot be reconciled with this interpretation. In its place comes the deliberate crystallization of general ideas by one creative personality, in other words, 'reflection'. But then what this creative personality puts forward is not the life of Jesus at all, but that of the community. With this line of reasoning Bruno Bauer became a forerunner of the present-day form-historical method which largely determines modern Gospel exegesis, as exemplified in particular by Bultmann—though of course without its highly-developed methodological apparatus.

A malevolent fate seemed to hang over Bauer's own theological work. In the end the personality of Jesus which he was anxious to restore to its living relationship with history, escaped him altogether; and he became an enemy of Christianity, filled with a daemoniacal itch to rob theology of its content; finally he even lost his own scholarship. Now whoever rejects the Gospels as historical sources is under an obligation to offer an historical explanation for the rise of Christianity without this basis. Bauer undertook just this task in his critique of the Epistles of St Paul (1850–52) and in his last work *Christus und die Cäsaren* (*Christ and the Caesars. The Origin of Christianity from Roman Hellenism*). (1877.) His explanation is not to be taken seriously.

Schweitzer compares Bauer with Reimarus: 'Both had a shocking and numbing effect on their age. No one saw the tremendous complexity of the problem of the life of Jesus quite as they did. They therefore felt themselves compelled to seek the solution outside the sphere of controllable history: Reimarus by basing the life of Jesus on a deception practised by his disciples, and Bauer by inventing a history-producing original source evangelist. In this way they both came to grief. Their contemporaries condemned not only their solutions but also the problems which had led to them; they condemned them because they were unable either to understand the difficulties or surmount them.'

In the sixties a new period opened up in the quest for the historical Jesus, the so-called 'liberal period'. The age of the great pioneers was over. The pathos of the campaign against supernatural 'deception' had died away. Critical theology was still interested in 'the truth', but it was no longer a question of the triumph of reason, but of the attainment of scholarly knowledge. In place of fanfares there was now a programme of study; instead of belief in reason there was now a conscientious obligation towards methodical textual criticism. And the investigations were no longer carried forward by outsiders of theological or non-theological origin such as Reimarus, Strauss, Bruno Bauer and the philosopher Weisse. Professional theological scholars now had the investigations in hand. Although the struggle between belief and knowledge went on vehemently, still to the accompaniment of extravagant attacks on Jesus and on Christianity, within the academic and theological sphere it now all went off harmlessly and in civilized forms. The liberal outlook, which accorded with the spirit of the age, had won recognition even in theological circles, and its representatives were no longer regarded as rebels. To criticize the Gospels no longer meant to risk one's career, and the investigations no longer resulted in personal tragedies, because the liberal outlook, now quite socially acceptable, was disinclined to relentless logic and its dramatic consequences. The last 'case' which arose during the course of the investigations (before the bombshell at the beginning of the twenties, the forthright contention that Jesus had never historically existed at all), was the *Charakterbild Jesu* (*Character of Jesus*), not a very important work, by Professor Schenkel of Heidelberg (1864). It was a storm in a teacup and the background was chiefly a matter of Church politics. The culprit was subsequently only too anxious to tone down the impression his book had created, and he remained in office and in honour. There was no need for him to end his days—as Bruno Bauer had done—as a greengrocer. All the same, it was the last time for almost half a century that public opinion reacted with any vehemence to such publications. This does not mean that the interest of non-theologians in the investigations had diminished. On the contrary: a stage had been reached at which the latter could count on wide interest in their results. Previously, even when the aim of the investigations was to settle conflicts between the thought of the age and the Christian religion and thus facilitate access to the latter, they were essentially concerned with themselves. Principles of thought and methods of investigation were at stake, and thus nothing much of interest to wider circles was likely to result. But now interest was turning to the 'personality' of Jesus; that is to say, to a subject most eminently exploitable from the literary angle. The period of the 'life of Jesus' in its real sense was now beginning. It extended from Ernest Renan to Gustav Frenssen. It was its misfortune to be typified by the works of two writers, the most successful of its popularizers, who demonstrated to what grotesque lengths the attempts to modernize Jesus and 'bring him closer to the age' could go.

By origin Ernest Renan was a Frenchman and a Catholic,[23] but a study of

German theology made him doubt the truth of Christianity and its history. He became the first man to introduce the whole educated world to a problem which up to then had occupied the attention of theologians almost exclusively. He did it in a very striking way, because he was a very talented writer and his book is on a high literary level. However, according to Schweitzer's judgement at least, it is 'Christian art in the worst sense of the term'. As a matter of fact this judgement is hardly too severe. But the general public enthusiastically adopted the 'Jesus of the fifth Gospel' which Renan affected to descry through the Gospel accounts, the 'charming' prophet beloved of women ('those beautiful creatures'), who rode from city to city on a gentle mule, preaching the 'engaging theology of love'. But this idyll did not last long. When the inexhaustible gentleness radiating from the young carpenter did not have the desired effect, the moralist in him decided that a world revolution was needed before he could triumph. His character deteriorated. In order to clinch the impression he made he had already begun to adopt 'innocent artifices, such as Joan of Arc used later'. He then even saw himself compelled to make his mark by performing miracles. But even this did not get him very far, and finally he was compelled to recognize that he was coming to the end of his tether. And so he sets off for Jerusalem, outwardly a hero, but inwardly already half-broken. There Judas betrays him out of jealousy of John. The game is up. In the Garden of Gethsemane human feelings arise once more in a man who had finished with all earthly things. 'Does he remember the clear wells of Galilee in which he might have refreshed himself? The virgins who might perhaps have been ready to give him their love? Does he regret too elevated a nature? A victim of his own greatness, does he shed tears because he has not remained the simple carpenter of Nazareth? We do not know.'

There were two reasons why the unconsciously blasphemous contribution of Renan to the quest for the historical Jesus could not be ignored. Its immediate success, not entirely explained by the literary talent of its author, showed that his biography of Jesus met the need of the time. Liberal bourgeois society, now approaching its zenith, set great store on the development of the individual. In 1841 Carlyle had published his book *On Heroes and Hero Worship*, putting forward individual insight and initiative as the mainsprings of history. Nietzsche was about to take the centre of the stage in Germany, and for him the culmination of history was genius. But nowhere was individual brilliance more publicly honoured than in France—Renan himself was buried with great pomp in the Panthéon. It is therefore quite logical that the first man to use the material provided by German theology to erect a literary monument to the founder of the Christian religion should have been a Parisian, an inhabitant of the town in whose saloons any talented personality could be sure of attention. Though neither this nor any subsequent attempt provided a heroic life.

Secondly, the striking and at the same time illuminating reaction of German Protestant theology gives food for thought. Its investigations into the life of Jesus were discredited by this sentimentalized 'hit'. Some people saw this clearly enough, but on the whole the critics were appreciative, they even admired the historical achievement. Even an investigator like the Tübingen theologican Weizsäcker, who, thanks to his *Untersuchungen über die evangelische Geschichte* (*Investigations into Gospel History*) (1864), was in the front ranks of the liberal phalanx, expressed his admiration. And David Friedrich Strauss, who was about to conclude his own *Leben Jesu für das deutsche Volk* (*Life of Jesus for the German People*) hailed Renan in the preface as a 'congenial spirit'. But by adopting this attitude liberal investigation into the life of Jesus condemned itself before it had even entered the lists. It betrayed an extraordinary lack of understanding for the greatness and directness of the ideas of Jesus, a deficiency from which, according to Schweitzer, *all* the liberal lives of Jesus suffer. 'What else was to be expected? They had to turn a heroic-fantastic ideology into a sensible bourgeois one.'

The life of Jesus published by Strauss in 1864 was a surprise; not so much because of his failure to do what he had set out to do: 'write a book for Germans in the same way as Renan has done for the French'. Strauss was, in any case, too much of a scholar to have been able to do this; he was quite incapable of sensationalism and popularization. His new work also lacked the spontaneity of a first attempt. Fundamentally it was a popularized summary of the previous thirty years of investigations into the life of Jesus, whereas Renan had written his book in the enthusiasm engendered by a visit to Palestine. But during the course of a generation Strauss had lost not only his freshness and originality, but also his own firm beliefs. How vacillating he had become was seen with depressing clarity in his subsequent development, which culminated in the publication of *Alter und neuer Glaube* (*Old and New Beliefs*). In 1835 he had recognized eschatology as the decisive element in the world of ideas of Jesus, but in the long run this strange and unfamiliar Jesus, whose ideas could not be reconciled with modern thought, proved intolerable. As his later surrender to scientific materialism showed, he was possessed by an urge to be in harmony with the spirit of the age. And thus we find the one-time Hegelian amongst the Liberals. In his life of Jesus he set himself the task of 'spiritually' re-interpreting the synoptic Jesus; before Jesus 'was taken up with the Messiah idea, the idealistic trait, the inner guidance . . . the serene certainty that he could attain peace with God and himself in a purely spiritual fashion' must already 'have reached a certain inner maturity' with the result that he now desired to be the Messiah 'in the sense of a quietly effective, patient teacher'. Strauss then went on to dispose of the problem of miracles by ruthless 'spiritualization' instead of by the mythical interpretation he had formerly adopted. Where these new methods lead can be seen from his interpretation of the reply given by Jesus to the messenger of John the Baptist: 'So you miss in me the miracles that you expect from the Messiah? And yet daily I open the eyes of the spiritually blind, open the ears of the deaf and make the lame to walk upright, and give new life to the spiritually dead. Whoever sees how much more these spiritual wonders are, will not regret the lack of physical wonders. And only such a one is ready to receive the salvation I bring to Man, and at the same time worthy of it.' In this way of course everything awkward is conveniently eliminated, but at the same time historical interpretation goes by the board and all textual responsibility is jettisoned.

From the beginning Strauss was more a critic than an historian, and what we now have to face is the remarkable fact that in liberal hands the life of Jesus as a whole until beyond the turn of the century bears the same traits. Whether the individual investigator prefers the literary or the historic approach makes very little difference. The whole discussion about the sources bears only a very loose relationship to the quest for the historical Jesus. From the beginning they all harmonized it with the spiritual atmosphere and the religious horizon of their own time. The most important of these biographers of Jesus, Heinrich Julius Holtzmann—whose brief description of the life of Jesus in his work *Die synoptischen Evangelien* (*The Synoptic Gospels*) became 'positively dogma for the subsequent decades of the investigation' (Schweitzer)—stood guarantor, because he extracted this aphoristic conception with a high degree of artistry from the Gospel of St Mark. It is quite obvious that this sort of thing just cannot be done without internally and externally violating the texts, arbitarily distorting the contexts, and creating new associations. In addition, too, it requires the assistance of 'supplementary historical knowledge'—as Schweitzer ironically calls it. The whole thing recalls an observation of Carl J. Burkhardt:[24] 'I find historical reconstruction a highly doubtful procedure; this jigsaw puzzle, this detective work, this interpretation now according to the gentleman's own spirit, now according to the spirit of the times in which they lived.'

This comment of a highly-educated man, who has proved himself to be an historian, indicated the difficulties of historical investigation, not from 'the spirit of the age', but from its subject. The application is general. Each age understands the past in its own fashion—even Mommsen liberalized his Caesar. But theological liberalism raises the problem of historical investigation in a specific and unusually difficult form. It started off on a quest for the historical Jesus and sought to provide a 'real' picture, that is to say a picture in accordance with his life on earth. Thus the task was dominated by the demand for truthfulness which, in whatever form, dominates the whole of critical theology. Its aim was therefore to discover the essence and nature of an historic personality. But the subject resists historic understanding, a point we noted earlier on when we were dealing with Schweitzer's own investigations into the life of Jesus.

Another factor must also be taken into consideration: in considering the history of this whole investigation we must always bear in mind that the theological character of its subject necessarily involves an attempt on the part of the investigator to establish a highly personal relationship not only for himself but for others too. In the last resort this particular urge is usually more powerful than the search for truth as such. The great historian of that theological generation, Adolf von Harnack, lets us into the secret of this peculiar variant of historical investigation when he writes in the preface to his lectures on the *Wesen des Christentums* (*Essence of Christianity*)[25] that he had 'not set out to describe the teachings of Jesus in their historical form'. The aim of these lectures had been to present the 'essential' nature of the phenomenon. This was the task of the historian, since the historical understanding of a great phenomenon began only when its essence was 'freed of its time-conditioned guise', and naturally 'many original traits must be sacrificed'. Thus von Harnack describes a Jesus completely rooted in his own time, and the things which seem essential to him; a man whose 'free and vigorous spirit' was far from rejecting this world; a man who had no ascetic, heroic or ecstatic traits, and who spoke 'like a man who enjoyed peace and quiet of soul and who was able to comfort others'.[26] The disturbing strangeness both in the figure of Jesus and in early Christianity is eliminated by a, so to speak, automatic process of adaptation. There is no need to fear conflicts here, no decisions are called for. The Christian ideology is brought into harmony with that of Goethe.

As far as von Harnack himself is concerned the whole procedure is to some extent redeemed by wide knowledge, elevated thought and deep piety. But just what can happen to it in other hands we can see from a book which was published at the end of the liberal period of the investigations. This was Gustav Frenssen's *Lebensbild des Heilands* (*Portrait of the Saviour*) which, so the author tells us himself, he wrote 'making conscientious use of all the results of scientific investigations into this question'. It seems a little unfair when Schweitzer makes the Germanic spirit responsible for this particular distortion of the personality of Jesus, as though it gave us a Germanic Jesus instead of a liberal Jesus. The Teutonic heathen theatrical props—Wotan's Mount, Hun graves, oaks which whisper to the wind of 'saintly heroes'—have nothing to do with the Germanic spirit—or indeed any other. In the person of Eduard von Hartmann the Germanic spirit does clash with Christianity, but Frenssen is an epigone of liberal theology, and his hero, who, after the temptation on the mountain, 'crouches against the rock, a poor lonely man torn by terrible doubts', and who in the Garden of Gethsemane 'takes his quivering, groaning soul into both hands', represents the ultimate belittlement of the modern historical Jesus of Nazareth when the standard taken is that of puny present-day man.

The circle, which leads back to Renan, is closed.

But in the meantime something of importance had taken place, though it aroused comparatively little interest at the time, and—because Schweitzer had not yet written his history of the quest for the historical Jesus—even less understanding.

All the liberal lives of Jesus were anxious to present the sermons of Jesus as something which in the last resort was not affected by any considerations of time. This was part of their urge to release him from his own age and modernize his personality. The eschatological elements of his teaching are 'spiritualized', arbitrarily interpreted, or eliminated from the texts altogether. At first the very great progress made in the fifties in research into Jewish apocalyptics made no difference. Scholarly achievements, opposed by both the spirit of the age and the needs of theology, found it difficult to secure acceptance, but in 1892 the problem was raised by Johannes Weiss in a relatively short pamphlet, and in a form which could not be ignored.[27]

Schweitzer regards this as one of the most important works of historical theology and compares its significance to that of Strauss's first life of Jesus.

Weiss confronts the investigations with the third great set of alternatives. The first was put forward by Strauss: either purely historical or purely supernatural. The second was forced through by the Tübingen school and by Holtzmann: either the Synoptics or John. The third set was: either eschatological or uneschatological. All modern ideas, even in the subtlest form, must be eliminated from the idea of the Kingdom of God. It is entirely a matter of the future. Jesus knows no other presence of the Kingdom but a future one. There can be no question of its 'foundation' and development in this world. This was the first time this idea had been expressed again since the days of Reimarus.

Liberal investigation goes on undisturbed by this challenging formulation of the problem up to the end of the century—as one can see from von Harnack's *Wesen des Christentums* (*Essence of Christianity*) in which, probably for the last time, a great representative of modern historical theology naïvely interpolated modern ideas into the mind of Jesus. But in 1901—the history of the investigations never lacked dramatic effects—two works with almost similar titles appeared on almost the same day. Both attacked modern historical theology though from opposite angles, and threatened its whole position: *Das Messianitätsgeheimnis in den Evangelien* (*The Messianic Secret in the Gospels*) by the Breslau theologian William Wrede, and *Das Messianitäts und Leidensgeheimnis* (*The Messianic and Passion Secret*), *A Sketch of the Life of Jesus* by Albert Schweitzer. The one is written from a literary-critical standpoint, the other from an eschatological-historical standpoint. The results arrived at are contradictory, but the observations on which they are based are identical. The investigation was now faced with its fourth set of alternatives: 'either the Marcan text is historical as such, in which case it can be retained; or it is not, in which case it must be rejected in its entirety. But any attempt to tone down the text, and anything secured by so doing, is unhistorical.' (Schweitzer). Up to this time every investigator had 'sifted the traditional texts for what suited his own construction of the facts and his own conception of historic possibility, rejecting the rest'. (Wrede.) This pseudo-scholarly method of subtraction and re-interpretation was impermissible. The psychological motives and the connection of the events and actions the investigators tried to find in Mark, whose Gospel was taken as the basis for the reconstruction of the life of Jesus, just did not exist. There was not a word to be found in Mark about any development of Jesus, or his disciples, or of the exterior circumstances, it was desired to read into the Gospels. If the pericopes were subjected to the acid test of critical scepticism or eschatological fire, then the connecting links dissolved and they fell apart. Thus—according to Schweitzer—there remained a choice between two possibilities: 'The eschatological solution, which immediately raises the undiluted, disconnected and contradictory Marcan version to the level of history; or the literary solution, which regards that which is dogmatic and unfamiliar as an interpolation of the evangelist himself into the tradition of Jesus, thus rooting messianity out of the historical life of Jesus altogether.'

Wrede adopted the second alternative. In his view messianity as presented in the Gospels is the result of a communal theology interpreting history to suit itself. In this sense the Marcan Gospel belongs to the history of dogma. The 'Resurrection' is the real messianic event in the life of Jesus.

Schweitzer puts forward serious objections to this viewpoint. What interest could communal theology possibly have had in pre-dating the messianic Jesus into his worldly activity? What interest could it possibly have had in publicly proclaiming him as the Messiah and letting him die on account of this claim? How could the appearances of the resurrected give the disciples the idea that the crucified one was the Messiah if he had been no more than a 'teacher' for them during his life, and had given no indication of his real dignity even to his most intimate associates? And finally, why refuse to explain the teachings of Jesus against the background of Neo-Jewish eschatological ideology, whilst, very soon after, accepting it for the disciples and for Paul? Wrede makes no attempt to minimize the difficulties presented by the Gospel of St Mark. It bars the way to any modernization of Jesus, but in doing so it raises new and considerable difficulties of interpretation, and presents Jesus as an almost colourless ethical preacher with no specific basis in time. The critical performance here is very considerable, but the practical result is unsatisfactory.

Schweitzer's solution is very different, and the difference goes far deeper than that between the literary and the historic method. His sketch of the life of Jesus is in an entirely different key, and this applies not only to Wrede's work, but to any previous or subsequent work attempting a critical investigation of the teachings and acts of Jesus. Granting all the theological scholarship and all the exegetical shrewdness involved, it is, for the first time in the history of the investigations, not merely a question of solving a problem of scholarship but of understanding a superhuman personality, or at least descrying its outline behind the veil of secrecy, by a will possessed by it and directed to moral action, by a passionate spirit sensitive to greatness. The aim of the book is 'to depict the figure of Jesus in its overwhelming heroic greatness and to impress it upon the modern age and upon modern theology'.[28] This was the important thing for Schweitzer. The dogmatic, historical or literary criticism which might be advanced against his ideas troubled him relatively little provided it left this objective

14. Schweitzer at the age of seventy-nine
(By permission of Arne Svendsen, Oslo)

undisturbed. In fact he even hoped that such criticism might help to clear up the exegetical details, because it was his intention to develop the 'sketch of the life of Jesus' with which his investigation of the secret of messianism and the passion ends. The abandonment of this intention was one of the sacrifices he had to make when he left Europe for Africa—the *Geschichte der Leben-Jesu Forschung* (*The Quest of the Historical Jesus*) goes beyond the *Sketch* in its explanation of the solution provided by logical eschatology, but it discusses only the problems involved and does not give a presentation of the subject itself.

Schweitzer adopts a black and white technique, and the advantages of this will soon become obvious. A 'Life of Jesus' in the sense of an attempt to 'paint' a portrait of the Redeemer was not to be expected, since his history of the investigations into the life of Jesus concluded that this was in any case an impossible undertaking. It is therefore unthinkable that he should follow up this doubtful undertaking with another. When he uses the title *The Life of Jesus* he has something different in mind. A 'Vita' can hardly come into question when only a few months are taken as the basis for historical investigation, when the inadequacy of the sources for a full reconstruction of even such a short span of public activity is recognized, and when the psychological retrospective analysis, with which the historic-modern attempt at a solution operated, is fundamentally rejected as unsuitable where this particular personality is concerned. Its fundamental motives are a secret. And thus in the last resort the word *Sketch* in the title tells us more than that Jesus made a secret of his messianism and of his passion. Further, it should be remembered that Schweitzer has not the gift of seeing things plastically. His strong point is rational construction. Methodically speaking his 'solution' is remarkable because it lifts the work of a whole generation of historians off its hinges—not by any superior capacity to understand historical happenings, but by the logic of his own rational thought, which had courage enough to place the thought of Jesus against the ideological background of its time and to explain it from this standpoint.

The quest of the historical Jesus set out to uncover the picture of Jesus in accordance with the historical truth which lay under the theological palimpsest. This involved the replacement of a dogmatic by an historical conception. But the theological magnetic field in which the investigations were conducted repeatedly caused the compass needle to swing away from its historical pole. The rationalists entered the lists brandishing the weapon of reason against 'superstition', and they fondly believed that when they more or less consistently exposed the irrational elements in the Gospels they had done their work. They tackled the problem of miracles by presenting the events in the life of Jesus as natural happenings and Jesus himself as a moral preacher striving to establish a new moral order. In their opposition to any supernatural interpretation they concentrated their attention on the rational interpretation, whether there was any historical basis for it or not. David Friedrich Strauss made a vigorous start with the historical investigation of the life of Jesus. But even his 'mythical' solution, which amounted to a synthesis of the supernatural thesis and the rationalistic antithesis, remained caught in the theological pros and cons. The modern-historical attempt at a solution suffered the same fate. It persuaded liberal investigators to substitute the figure adapted to the times for the abandoned presence of Christ, and persuaded them to feel that it was objectionable that the personality upon which the teachings of Christianity were founded should be the prisoner of an ideology having its roots in the Judaism of his day, and to whom, in consequence, modern man could have no access. In addition, liberal theology could not conceive of any kind of thought which accepted dogma as an expression of truth. Now the truly remarkable feature of Schweitzer's 'solution' lies in the fact that, having gone through the school of liberalism and being a free thinker opposed to any kind of dogmatism, he nevertheless dared to contemplate the idea that the key to the life and teachings of Jesus may lie precisely in his dogmatism and nowhere else. Johannes Weiss and his followers allowed Jesus to think and express his teachings eschatologically in one or two main points, whilst for the rest interpreting his teachings just as uneschatologically as modern historical theology did. But the eschatological teaching of the coming of the Kingdom of God 'is nothing but dogmatic history which penetrates into ordinary history and negates it' (Schweitzer). Jesus not only thought dogmatically, but he made dogmatic history—such is Schweitzer's thesis.

Schweitzer's short sketch of the life of Jesus was very properly written in the consciousness that it removed the treatment of the subject to another plane altogether. His heroic-dogmatic interpretation of the life of Jesus represents the highlight of the whole investigation, and at the same time its end. In consequence it is no longer possible, or at least no longer permissible, to continue the investigations in the same naïve fashion as before. As the investigations derived from an obligation to search for truth with all the means of modern scholarship, i.e. an extra-theological motive, it was immune to theological counter-arguments—only to see itself defeated with its own weapons.

Schweitzer was very well aware that 'the all too sharply profiled picture of Jesus as provided by thoroughgoing eschatology'[29] would give offence, and he did not claim that it was valid in all respects. Everything was staked on one card here, and naturally the daring of it appeared suspect to scholarship, which demands the careful examination of every pro and con. Nevertheless, isn't there always need for the pioneer who refuses to let himself be daunted by the objections of critics who are often unable to see the wood for trees, and is prepared to open up a new vista? 'Whoever discovered a new principle without violating truth?' (Schweitzer). Whatever one may advance against the hypothesis put forward by a thoroughgoing eschatology, the extent to which it meets the demand to reveal the inner relationship between the accounts, sermons, acts and events recorded in the Gospels remains astonishing. More than one 'impossible' in the previous investigations now loses its force; and more than one problem which had previously resisted all attempts at solution now finds its interpretation. What had apparently been chaos now falls into order. Words and happenings which had been bled white by modernizing interpretations are once more filled with exciting significance. Pass what judgement you like on the picture which emerges in the process of Schweitzer's 'solution', you will still have to admit that it is complete in itself and that there are no blurred edges, although Schweitzer strictly disciplined himself to permit neither retouching nor the arbitary elimination of things which did not fit into his intention. In this respect, Schweitzer's 'sketch' is unique in the history of the whole investigations. The daring experiment of granting the validity of the sources allowed the figure and acts of Jesus to be reconstructed from them; and the result was, if not beyond all dispute, at least certainly not contradictory.

The Jesus presented to us in this way is all will which fulfils the will of God. He is about as different as possible from the mild humanitarian and moralist presented to us by liberal theology. One could no more assume a 'development' in him in the sense of modern psychology than suppose that success or failure could have any effect on him. He is solely conditioned by 'revelations'—by the revelation of his messianic nature during his baptism in the Jordan and, later on, by the revelation that the coming of the Kingdom would have to be brought about by his vicarious suffering—'as an act of mercy'—since it was not brought about, as had been expected when the disciples were sent out, by a movement of repentence, and since the prophesied latter-day tribulations had not come about.

Jesus appeared in order to announce the Kingdom of God and the Atonement. The morality he preaches is 'interim morality', since the Kingdom lies beyond sin and therefore beyond morality. It is a supra-moral magnitude. It does not develop within the world; on the contrary its coming breaks over the world like a cosmic catastrophe.

Thus for Jesus there can be no morality of the Kingdom of God. But precisely because the morality of Jesus culminates in this supra-ethical idealism it takes on the quality of the absolute. It is unconditional, because only unconditional moral renewal can bring about the Kingdom of God. As the morality of the latter days, i.e. just because it is rooted in the ideology of the people and time of Jesus, it is not bound to any ephemeral here and now.

Eschatological expectation includes the demand for certainty of salvation. The idea of a sign and a sanctification related to the coming salvation goes through the whole of apocalyptic literature. Both Baptism and Last Supper derive their real sacramental significance of a 'salvation' from what is coming. They are not symbolic actions in the modern sense. Right from the very beginning Christianity was a sacramental religion, which explains why it appears as such to Paul and to ancient theology, and why as the religion of the historically revealed mysteries it could win the minds of the East and of Greece. Thus the history of dogma is freed from the necessity of assuming that a theology which was 'purely' unsacramental in the beginning 'descended into the depths of magic ideas'; for which neither reasons nor evidence can be produced. Only in this way does the free dogma-historical investigation gain access to the origins. The thoroughgoing eschatological solution thus proves itself extremely fruitful in the religious-historical sphere too.

The Jesus of Nazareth who appeared as the Messiah, preached the morality of the Kingdom of God, founded Heaven on earth, and finally died in order to sanctify his work, thus never existed. It is a figure drawn by rationalism, given life by liberalism, and provided with an historical cloak by modern theology. But the Jesus who as the future son of man fulfilled the Atonement in himself and thus 'did actually die for the sins of men',[30] 'continues notwithstanding to reign, as the alone Great and alone True in a world of which he denied the continuance'.[31] The ultimate phenomenon of the contradiction between natural and spiritual truth which lies at the basis of all life, has become history in him.

The unprejudiced reader will inquire with some interest about the effect of this 'heroic' interpretation, since for the first time critical investigation produced something commensurate to the influence of the person of Jesus through the ages; a thing which could hardly be said of any of the 'lives' produced in the liberal period, or of Wrede's conclusions either. One would certainly have expected a vigorous reaction, particularly as the uncomprising formulation positively challenged it. But nothing of the sort happened. Schweitzer's book certainly delivered the funeral oration of liberal-modernizing investigations into the life of Jesus. Attention was drawn to the eschatological motive in the thought of Jesus; though, of course, Schweitzer was not the first to do so. But on the whole New Testament investigation just ignored this solution put forward by thoroughgoing eschatology, and proceeded on its way undisturbed. After this unique concretization of the figure of the historic Jesus there was even a swing of the pendulum of unexpected violence. First of all, the historicity of Jesus was denied altogether; and then form-historical analysis radically questioned the usefulness of the sources for the purpose of historical investigation. If we are to understand Schweitzer's theological-historical standpoint, then developments after and beyond him must at least be indicated. We are now faced with a conditional question: have the total results of the *Quest of the Historical Jesus* summed up by Schweitzer in his history really been reduced *ad absurdum*? If not, what, in the last resort, has positively emerged from the investigations now that they would seem to have exhausted all their possibilities?

The denial of the historicity of Jesus is nothing new. We meet it with the French authors Charles François Dupuis (1742–1809) and Constantin François Volmey (1757–1820), and after that, as we have already seen, with Bruno Bauer. The first two contend that the Gospels represent a myth of a primarily astral nature, whilst Bauer declares the personality who was honoured in early Christianity to be a mere personification of the ideas which led to the founding of the new religion. The former interpretation can be described as mythical, the latter as symbolic. Both contentions rely on the fact that profane history offers little practical evidence for the existence of Jesus. The ordinary means of historical investigation are not able to provide proof for the historicity of Jesus. In addition, as Schweitzer pointed out even in 1913,[32] theology itself accepts the fact that there is very little reliable information concerning Jesus. The significance of the activity and teachings of the Jesus described by the Synoptics receded more and more, and this gave general encouragement to doubt.

But the impelling motive for denying the historicity of Jesus is very interesting, and those who do so act from religio-philosophical compulsion.

Even with Hegel the notional conception of religion and the historical phenomenon of Jesus as a religious authority stand in such a relationship to each other that the latter appears superfluous if not even a nuisance. This circumstance is made less obvious by the fact that Hegel does not arrive at his idea of Jesus empirically, but creates and forms it in accordance with his own views.

But when historical investigation became independent, religion on the one hand and the person and teachings of Jesus on the other fell more and more apart. Those who identified the veneration of Jesus with religion appeared to be hampering progress, particularly as they also ignored the higher religion of salvation adumbrated in the ancient myths, and present to elementary thought as the ultimate perception. Such people were reproached for believing that religion took its historical origin from some teaching or other, whereas, of course, it was timeless, continually renewing and consolidating itself in that will and understanding directed to the infinite world whole. Those who deny the historicity of Jesus attack historical religion in the name of absolute religion. Schweitzer acknowledges the fundamental justice of their case.

The attack was first launched at the end of the nineteenth century in England (J. M. Robertson; W. B. Smith; J. Whittaker) and then taken up in Germany by Peter Jensen. With the appearance of Arthur Drews' *Christusmythe* (*Christus Myth*) in 1909 it became a popular sensation, and in the following year the book appeared in three further editions. The whole thing created a tremendous stir. The representatives of this heretical thesis, very conscious that they had a mission to fulfil, sought to win the general public to their views, whilst on their part the theologians argued the contrary thesis with a tremendous expenditure of polemical effort. The attack came from outside the sphere of theology: Robertson was a writer; Jensen was a Professor of Semitic languages at Marburg University; and Drews was Professor of Philosophy at the Technical High School in Karlsruhe. Others now joined the fray, and in 1912 a German officer named C. P. Fuhrmann, published *Der Astralmythus von Christus* (*The Astral Myth of Christ*). A Pole, A. Niemoyevsky, published a book cumbrously entitled:

The God Jesus in the light of Home and Foreign Investigations together with an Account of the Gospel Astral Data, Astral Scenes and Astral Systems, which was subsequently published in translation. All in all, the affair was quite an epidemic, one might almost say a fashion. There is a mysterious phenomenon in the scientific world which produces the simultaneous arrival of topical ideas and discoveries without any demonstrable connection between each other. This phenomenon finds itself caricatured in the rise of merely fashionable trends, though these too present themselves as the product of original research and are announced to the world as apochal revelations. When they spring up, as they did in this case, so to speak overnight, and in large numbers like mushrooms, then their nature is sufficiently indicated.

As far as the things at stake were concerned, the rapidly dying tumult was not to be taken very seriously, but one significant thing is worthy of attention even today, and that is the still vigorous attraction of the old appeal to truth. The new prophets found a hearing because they loudly insisted that they alone had the courage to uphold the truth, whereas the theologians, whether from narrow-minded prejudice or fear, still clung to the old exploded belief in the existence of Jesus and did not dare to accept the unavoidable conclusions from the latest scientific investigations. Incidentally, the new champions knew nothing at all about either the positive or negative results of theological investigations in general and into the life of Jesus in particular. Even more: fundamentally they heartily despised all the critical principles laid down as a guide to investigation. This of course made things very easy for them. For example, Peter Jensen had no scruples about assigning the 'mythical figures' of Jesus and Paul to the Gilgamesh epic, although its contents are about as different from those of the Gospels as could possibly be imagined. Drews preferred an astral interpretation. Jesus was identified with the Orion constellation because it hangs in the heavens with outstretched arms in the form of a cross, a sort of 'world tree' in the Milky Way.

There is really no need to go any farther. In the second edition of his *Geschichte der Leben-Jesu-Forschung* (*Quest of the Historical Jesus*) Schweitzer deals at some length with this new movement, which had arisen since the first edition of his book, but in this he really does it rather too much honour. Three considerations may have guided him in this: the realization that critical theology was to some extent responsible for the whole rubbish, whose German protagonists were, regrettably, university professors; the vehemence of the discussion which arose and happened to coincide with the revision of his own book for its second edition; and finally the question as to whether the historicity of Jesus is of any fundamental significance for belief, which Schweitzer denies. In this respect, incidentally, he finds himself on common ground with Arthur Drews, who also feels that 'religion is essentially independent of all history'.[33]

The second of the two matters to be dealt with here, was not touched on by Schweitzer at all, because it came to the fore after he had withdrawn from the investigation altogether.

The introductory chapter of his book[34] declares: 'We are now once more in the midst of a period of great activity in the study of the subject. On the one side we are offered an historical solution on the other a literary. . . .' The question at issue 'will be discussed in all the critical studies of the next few years. Once clearly posed it compels a decision.' Since these words were written half a century has passed. Schweitzer's diagnosis has not been confirmed. It is as though the tremendous outburst at the beginning of the twentieth century exhausted the passion which was concentrated on the investigations into the life of Jesus. The dramatic action broke off just when the tension had reached its highest point. The formulation of the problem had been intensified to the utmost. One would like to assume—with Schweitzer—that the investigations will not stop half-way, and that they will grapple directly with the questions at issue. But should they take a different turn after all then it is worth recalling that in his own book Schweitzer himself sounded, so to speak, on a second manual, the diversion from the quest for the historical Jesus.

The chaos he thought to observe in 1950[35] did not come about. Schweitzer himself has pointed out that the course of the earlier investigations into the life of Jesus were anything but chaotic, and that, if we ignore the undergrowth of non-essentials and the inevitable detours and blind alleys, we shall detect a logical development guided in part by the spirit of the age and in part by the immanent logic of the subject itself. This is in fact the basis of his own work, since his method is to formulate a question and answer it as resulting logically from the work of his predecessors. Thus to follow the critical path up to the extreme negation in the denial of the historicity of Jesus appears as inevitable and significant. The history of the quest for the historical Jesus has a shape and a profile which are not diminished in the upshot.

What happened thereafter may be described in a certain sense as the triumph of Wrede over Schweitzer. The literary-critical method dominated the scene to such an extent that there was no serious discussion of Schweitzer's theses at all. But it no longer sought, as Wrede still did, for a solution of the problem of the public life of Jesus. In place of the question as to the historical Jesus came a critical analysis of the Gospel texts, and in the period that now opened up the investigations into the life of Jesus were temporarily suspended. By 1957 it was possible to make the—perhaps too pointed—observation: 'In the past fifty years (i.e. since the appearance of Schweitzer in the field) things have become very quiet in this sphere. . . . The investigations into the life of Jesus in the Protestant tradition in Germany have ceased.'[36] Source exegesis now had the floor instead. The 'form-historical method', developed in particular by Martin Dibelius and Rudolf Bultmann, started out on its triumphant path. Its guiding principle was to interpret the Gospels as a deposit of the belief of the early Christian community. According to this theory, the historic core not only of the Gospel of St John, but also of the Synoptics, had been distorted to the point of unrecognizability by the influence of theological and dogmatic tendencies.

It was, of course, accepted quite early on that the Gospel accounts were influenced by communal theology. Even Bruno Bauer based his first sceptical life of Jesus (1841–42) on the assumption that the earliest evangelist set down the experience of the community. This text and its continuation and development in Matthew and Luke was to be regarded as the work of creative writers, as 'religious art'. The Atonement on the Cross and the Resurrection were the central core; everything else had crystallized around this. Pfleiderer, Johannes Weiss, Bousset and others also accepted this influence of communal theology but in a less radical form. Even Schweitzer's own 'sketch' is not based on any naïve trust in the historical character of the texts, but seeks to take into account the laws according to which early Christian ideas of the personality of Jesus must have influenced the story of his life and work. However, Schweitzer concludes from the essence of early Christian belief that it has not interfered with the basic features of the public life of Jesus, whereas Wrede regards the Gospel of St Mark as mere 'pale remnants of an historical idea of the real life of Jesus', and classes it with the history of dogma.

Wrede's death prevented him from working out his theory in any detail, and in his study of Mark he suggested rather than developed it. Here is where the form-historical method comes in. With the aid of an increasingly involved historico-literary apparatus it sets out to prove that the synoptic Gospels represent a collection of texts formulated in order to satisfy specific needs of the community, and never intended as an authentic record. With this there remains nothing to investigate as far as the life of Jesus is concerned. 'There is no longer any point in asking whether this or that were at all possible, and whether it really happened, but only how, since when, and to what purpose the story was handed on in that form.'[37] It is true that the question as to the historical reliability of tradition cannot be silenced altogether, but in view of the procedure adopted the net results must necessarily be so sparse and so doubtful that the historian can really do nothing with them. For one thing 'how can there be any criterion by which the investigator can separate the historical facts from tendentious dogmatic presentation in the Jesus tradition with any degree of certainty?'[38]

The arrival of critico-literary scepticism in this radical form spells the end of modern historical investigations into the life of Jesus, and this is quite in accordance with Schweitzer's own views, since, after all, he welcomed Wrede as an ally in his own criticisms of it. 'Modern historical theology' (Schweitzer) is destroyed. It is no longer permissible to tone down the texts, eliminate at will, and 'interpret' the rest.

But at the same time Schweitzer's own solution is excluded from the discussion; precisely because of its formalism, the form-historical method sees no reason to discuss the serious objections he bases on the texts themselves to the assumption of any material influence exercised by tradition on the Gospel accounts.[39] The approach is so different that no contact is possible. The assumption that the pericopes can be classified in detail according to formal criteria and thus used systematically as historical sources clearly obviates any correction from the angle of the historian. Exegesis is removed altogether from his scope.

According to Dibelius, who may be regarded as the pioneer of the form-historical method, we must distinguish three form elements of the Synoptic Gospels, which must be regarded as early Christian 'minor religious literature', directed to a small audience, and not to be compared, it is stressed, with 'literary' works: the sermon instruction (paradigma), the broader relationship of the story (fiction) and the paranesis, the didactic exhortations and teachings in the form of the words of Jesus.

Taking the eschatological pronouncements seriously has led to something as unexpected as it is far-reaching; namely the assumption that these men of a new kingdom in the old world can be credited with only one form of religious expression; namely, propaganda. According to this therefore such unlettered men waiting for the end of the world could preserve traditions of the life of Jesus only in connection with the sermon.[40] In other words, the oldest stratum of the sources, precisely the paradigma, is propaganda material which was handed to the missionary preachers (not excluding Paul himself), and may therefore be compared in our own day with material such as is 'issued to win an election or to persuade people to invest in war loan.'[41] These unlettered men can hardly be credited with the ability to express in their own words what was in their hearts. 'They were bound to what had been given to them or their predecessors to an even greater extent than the present-day "speaker". This material was the suitable form of the story for missionary purposes—a sort of predecessor of the "Notes for Speakers" we know today—and it was handed on from propagandist to propagandist.' It is, therefore, hardly possible to tell now to what extent historical tradition went into the deliberate drafting of these texts, but a relative criterion can be applied. The thesis reads: the nearer an account approaches to the sermon, the less it need be suspected of having been changed by fictional, legendary or literary influences. The telling of the story as such was not the important thing for these early Christian missionaries, and so where we can take pleasure in the actual story, or in the strange or miraculous, indeed wherever we find ourselves interested in the persons as such, then this is unfamiliar to the paradigma and strongly suggests that the text belongs to a later stratum; in other words we are verging on the Christian legend.

Christianity won a foothold in the world, with the result that there was room for other things besides propaganda. The missionary was now joined by the storyteller and the teacher. 'Stories' were created to meet the pious need to know more about it all, to impress and elevate the Christian, and also to give Christian miracle workers examples and guidance. They deal with Jesus the Thaumaturgist, and 'in the best case' they are more remote from historical events than the paradigmas, whether their basis be a Christian or a foreign idea (Old Testament stories, Greek myths and simple fairy tales). In Mark there are eight such 'stories': the storm on the lake, the Gadarene swine; the daughter of Jairus and the woman with the issue of blood; the feeding of the five thousand; the walking on the water; the deaf and dumb man; the blind man of Bethsaida; and the epileptic boy. 'The historian need expect no harvest of facts from such stories, but the harvest of the saga and fairy-tale investigator is all the richer.'[42]

Even these edifying stories did not entirely satisfy the needs of the community. Originally they were written as for the end of this world and not for the continuance of life in it. Thus they lacked 'exhortations for everyday life'. But there was material to hand, Judaism had already done the spadework. Its proselytizing exhortations, often based on Hellenistic predecessors, needed only a little re-arranging and revising in order to serve perfectly well for Christian usage. Then there were the sayings of Jesus originally collected for paranesic purposes and not at first for their christological interest. Matthew in particular has a number of these arranged in great sermons.

The foregoing is a brief description of the three elements which compose the Synoptic Gospels according to this kind of textual criticism, and whether in the meantime its schematism has been extended, modified or relaxed, and to what extent, is unimportant here. What matters is its influence on that problem child of the investigations, the question of the 'mythical' components of the Gospels. Approximately a hundred years after David Friedrich Strauss put forward his 'mythical explanation', the investigation into the question of miracles is back where it started. What it finds unexplainable, either because it cannot be reconciled with modern scientific thought, or because it does not fit into the investigator's idea of Jesus, is simply described as 'mythical', though the scope of the mythical has widened in the meantime.

Strauss set out to make all explanations of the miraculous in the life of Jesus unnecessary, but not by trying to make them understandable in a rationalist sense as natural happenings. Since then the matter has not advanced one single step. It is true—in particular after the psycho-therapeutic curative successes of the so-called '*Überwältigungstheorie*' or over-mastering theory—that investigations are prepared to form a more optimistic judgement in respect of the historicity of certain miracles; for examples the healing of the lame, or of the dropsical man. However, where the miracle cannot be explained by natural causes it is briefly dismissed as unhistorical.

But the process of 'de-mythologization' as practised by the form-historical method goes farther. It is extended to cover all accounts in which Jesus is presented not as a kind of teacher, but as a God. This applied in particular to anything relating to his messianic consciousness, which Dibelius has the questionable taste to dismiss as 'self-recommendation', going on to say: 'The conjunction of self-recommendation and preaching is the typical characteristic of the divine or semi-divine vessel of revelation in Hellenist piety, that is to say, a mythical person.'[43] As far as Dibelius himself is concerned, the history of Jesus is not of mythical origin, and its historicity is not called into question. But this sort of thing plays into the hands of those who do deny it.

Even the theological layman can see easily enough that it must lead to a threefold result; and it has, in fact, done so.

The first result is a denigration of the Gospel texts, and not only in their quality as historical sources. In an effort to protect them from any assault on the part of critical reason, the doctrine of verbal inspiration declared them to be 'the Word of God', thus taking up an untenable position by no means favourable to their living influence. Critical theology has now arrived at the opposite pole. The relationship between Enlightenment enthusiasm and belief in authority was tense from the start. Its textual criticism was the working off of a feeling of resentment, and to a certain extent it was at loggerheads with the biblical word. It launched its attack with all the historical, text-critical and fundamental objections of modern science available at the time, and in so doing, though without intending to, it underlined the importance of the biblical word. Later on, in a more relaxed atmosphere, liberalism proceeded more cautiously, more respectfully, and not without theological inhibitions. This attitude was determined by its relationship to the person of Jesus, and its investigations of the Gospel texts were guided by this search for his nature, his teachings and his life. Whoever witnessed this period of the investigations will always retain a fruitful memory of the way in which investigators worked longingly, ardently and lovingly to piece together a picture of the historical Jesus. In Schweitzer we find a unique combination of qualities: the determination of a seeker after truth, humble veneration, enthusiasm for enlightenment, Jesus mystique, critical acumen and a respect for the Gospel texts. Schweitzer embodies a synthesis of the driving forces of that movement. After him the form-historical investigation comes as an anti-climax. Despite its epochal significance and despite the high standing of its advocates, it gives the impression of being a very sober academic affair; until later on Bultmann gave it an exciting turn with his attempts to exclude mythology. Nothing remains of the pathos which ennobled the previous investigations, and the general tone is altogether lower. Bultmann's book of Jesus is clear evidence of this. It expressly avoids presenting Jesus as great, his words as profound or his teachings as compelling.[44] By adopting this attitude the investigators believe that they are outdoing the historians who allow themselves 'to give marks', whilst 'only formal estimates of the importance of a phenomenon or a personality for the historical connection', are permissible.[45] With its critical investigation theology is to some extent atoning for its previous uncritical acceptance of the canonical texts and for the untrammelled flow of religious life into their interpretations, but in its critical zeal it falls over itself both in its over-estimation of the objections of scientific thought, and in its excessive insistence on maintaining an objective attitude towards historical phenomena. Every profound historical insight is won by a synthesis of objective conclusions and personal involvement.

Bultmann certainly regards deep emotional interest on the part of an interpreter as a condition for any recognition of 'real history'. But this living relationship with the reality to be understood, which Dilthey demanded earlier on, does not aim at the understanding of historical phenomena. The question is not—as in Ranke's formula—'how it really was'. The reality of history as such is not the interesting thing. It is narrowed down to the 'factors' of a personal existentialist decision resulting from an encounter with the historical phenomenon. Thus the ground is cut from under the feet of historical understanding from two sides. On the one hand, the obligation imposed on the historian to confine himself to merely formal evaluations, gives him no chance of any essential comprehension of its object; and on the other its substance is frittered away by reduction to the scope of personal existence. Compared with the fullness of meaning the Gospel texts take on in Schweitzer's interpretation, this procedure applied to the quest for Jesus bleeds it white. The outlines become blurred. The critico-literary problems which arose in great number may well be fascinating, but it really doesn't matter much whether, when or how they are solved. They are not part of an historical structure and thus no total solution stands or falls by the answer to them. Clearly the accounts of the sayings and doings of Jesus must lose their specific gravity if their direct relationship to what was really said and done is fundamentally in dispute—or indeed when the relationship is not even bothered about!

This decline of significance becomes poignantly obvious in the rarefied liberalism of Dibelius. Indeed, the decline is even zealously accelerated by means of banal analogies, though without any visible motive—unless we count the obsession of the investigator with his scholarly results, and a professorial incapacity to understand a phenomenon altogether outside his own world of ideas and experience. But the process continues even in a changed theological atmosphere. If the Synoptic Gospels are mere tendentious tracts to propagate the belief of the early Christian community then in the last resort the only thing that matters is their belief itself. By comparison with this all other questions recede into the background—much to the relief of the investigator, since he cannot answer them. The cardinal historical problem as to whether Jesus regarded himself as the Messiah is of secondary importance to Bultmann.[46] Even the burning question of intellectual integrity—what is one to make of the miracles?—loses its last significance: 'There is not much point now in examining in detail how much of the Gospel miracle stories are historical.'[47] In his modernizing paraphrase of the Gospel of St Mark, Bultmann's pupil Bartsch puts the following interpolated commentary on the story of the Transfiguration into the mouth of the Evangelist: 'I do not desire to attach too much importance to this. You know, all this is not so important.'[48] And when the question of the empty tomb arises (neither Bultmann nor Bartsch regards a happening like the Resurrection, which cannot be explained in terms of natural science, as an historical event worthy even of discussion) the evangelist soothingly assures his audience: 'Brothers, you may think what you like about it. You may regard us as dreamers who tell others their dreams.'[49] The style is reminiscent of Gustav Frenssen. But at least Frenssen did believe naïvely that superstition was at last being overcome by truth, whereas here everything is left in doubt. We know what the encounter with the urge to truth of liberal theology means to Bultmann. He insists that the sermon may not 'leave the hearer in doubt as to what he is to regard as true and what as false'.[50] But how is this to be brought about when, in view of the impossibility of 'speaking directly and objectively about the actions of God',[51] the preacher is 'under the objectively conditioned necessity of talking a mythological language' and this mythological language then overlays what is 'actually to be regarded as true'? What is a man to make of an announcement which he may not take at its face value?

If the historical problems which passionately engaged the investigations into the life of Jesus for generations are dismissed then the pathos of truth-seeking loses all its force. The texts no longer have any significance. To what extent this is so we can see from the frank statement of Bartsch that as the total result of the quest for the historical Jesus the whole of his preaching has 'boiled down to a few commonplaces which are by no means original'—with one exception: namely, that with Him the Kingdom of God dawned.[52] Eschatology is no longer the key with which to interpret the life of Jesus; it takes its place.

The second inevitable result of abandoning the control afforded by historical research, is that under the form-historical method the process of arbitrary elimination, which has always played such a dubious role in the quest for the historical Jesus, is given a free hand. Schweitzer has dealt in detail with this sort of thing. Each investigator racks the texts to make them fit on to a procrustean bed of his own devising. Wrede also writes: 'In the last resort each investigator delves in the traditional texts for what suits his own construction and his own ideas about historical possibility, and discards the rest.' Whatever doesn't fit into his scheme, whatever clashes with his own subjective opinions, whatever does not support his own hypothesis, and, above all, whatever goes beyond his own understanding, is *a priori* 'impossible', and is therefore ruthlessly blue-pencilled. But in the earlier quest for the historical Jesus the responsibility for such things was individual and textual criticism as a whole was still subject to historical control. But with the form-historical method of investigation the texts as a whole are called into question, and the process of elimination is free to do its worst. Dibelius has certainly expressed the hope that the adoption of formal criteria will prevent that 'subjective arbitrariness, which, as experience shows, only too readily affects any examination of the historicity of the Gospel texts'.[53] But even if it were possible to establish order amongst the pericopes according to the degree of their historicity, which is open to doubt, the form-historical method allows everything in the least degree questionable to be put down to the account of communal theology, because the method lacks any criterion for effectively separating historical facts from dogmatic or propagandistic tendencies.

The third and most important feature of the new tendency is the decline in the importance of Jesus as a person.

This loss clearly demands some compensation, and Bultmann's demythologizing theology provides it by shifting the accent to 'the message originating in the Easter events', 'the proclamation of the act of God in Christ'. Just when the critico-literary method has arrived at a point where the texts are no longer of any value whatever as a source of information about the acts and words of Jesus, so that the investigation is in danger of losing everything, a theological solution unexpectedly crops up and makes it possible to book the loss as a gain. Something which is now of purely theological interest needs no confirmation in fact, and thus belief is saved from the temptation to base itself on 'historical factuality'.

Bultmann derives from the old traditional liberal-critical school. If Schweitzer can be called its grave-digger, then Bultmann is its heir and 'testamentary executor'. (Stauffer.)

Their common theological and moral historical origin—Bultmann is also influenced by the Rationalism of the eighteenth century, and attached to the thought processes of natural science—results in important similarities, though up to the present the radical difference in standpoint both in source investigation and in theological-philosophical speculation has caused this to be overlooked.

Both Bultmann and Schweitzer are guided by the most uncompromising demands of Gospel criticism. Bultmann's desire for scientific integrity and loyalty to the texts causes him to demand an analytical and inductive method of textual criticism very different from deductive method of Dibelius.

Both Bultmann and Schweitzer refuse to recognize traditional dogmas. 'The reproduction of traditional dogmas is not the language of belief.' (Bultmann.)

Both for Bultmann and Schweitzer, a happening reported in the Gospels is no happening at all if it contradicts the findings of natural science—or even seems to do so. This prepossession is common to them both. However Schweitzer enjoys greater freedom towards the texts in so far as his exegesis is influenced neither theologically nor hermeneutically.

Speculative thought plays a minor role both with Bultmann and Schweitzer. This results in a remarkable agreement in the reduction of human self-understanding to action and decision. 'The actual essence of man . . . is will.' (Bultmann.) Schweitzer has said much the same thing.

Schweitzer's idea, based on this standpoint, that the relationship to Jesus is one 'from will to will' finds an analogy in Bultmann, but with one fundamental difference: Bultmann is primarily interested in a teaching behind which 'the teacher' disappears, whereas Schweitzer is primarily interested in the person of Jesus. But both unquestionably accept the significance of the teachings of Jesus as eschatological (Bultmann: 'Jesus . . . brings the announcement of the coming Kingdom of God').

But more important than this difference between them is the similarity of their analysis of liberal theology, made first by Schweitzer and then by Bultmann from a different theological angle, thus underlining the conclusive nature of their results; and their uncompromising complaint (Karl Barth describes it as one of their most valuable achievements) that liberal theology causes us to despair of the possibility of any scholarly (indeed, any human support whatever) for Christian belief. In consequence the urge to remove Christian teaching both from the relativity of historical happenings and from all doubts arising from textual criticism, has become irresistible. Perhaps the most important result of the quest for the historical Jesus is that, since Schweitzer, critical theology no longer tolerates any complete dependence on the investigation of the sources. Schweitzer himself solves the dilemma by his Jesus mystique, which leaves the historical investigation in force and preserves the central position of the person of Jesus of Nazareth. The de-mythologization theology does the same by substituting the faith of the disciples in the resurrected saviour as the centre of belief instead of the person of Jesus.

De-mythologization theology has a double origin and thus presents a double aspect. On the one hand it is a problem of textual interpretation, and on the other, the 'actual intention of the whole undertaking' lies in the teaching,[54] indeed, in the renaissance of belief. On the one hand it restores the old aim of the Enlightenment movement, to deal satisfactorily with those parts of the Gospels which contradict scientific thought, in order that modern man may have access to their teaching; whilst on the other hand it regards itself as 'a necessity of belief itself'.[55] It claims to be 'in the sphere of knowledge the logical fulfilment of the Pauline-Lutheran teaching of justification outside the law through belief alone'.[56] Teaching and belief are indissolubly connected. The logos becomes essential 'only by its saying, or through its being said',[57] by the event of concrete pronouncement in the concrete situation. In the New Testament we are dealing 'first of all and exclusively with the testimony to the beliefs of the first community', that is to say with its pronouncement.[58] This is the only thing of importance for us, and this alone can be taken from the sources.

De-mythologization theology, assisted by the form-historical method, reaches its objective by an arbitrary act, namely by 'rejecting all historical contact, including that with Christ in the flesh', and by concentrating the act of belief on the one fact of the Easter faith of the Apostles and the Gospel word which springs from it: 'God is Jesus'[59] and 'The Word was made flesh',[60] which is certainly unexplainable, but equally certainly not to be called into question by any textual criticism.

The positively explosive affect of this synthetic mixture of Enlightenment and Orthodoxy clearly shows us the pressure built up under the level of consciousness in the liberal camp by the need for belief. Now there seemed a possibility of saving the kerygma without abandoning scientific thought. The critical theology of the nineteenth century disposed of 'the kerygma itself—the essence of the teaching—when it disposed of mythology'.[61] The interpretation of the mythological accounts was now to take the place of their elimination. The mythologies of the New Testament—according to Bultmann 'mythos' is the mode of thought and speech which objectivizes the unworldly to the worldly, the hereafter to the here and now[62]—are not examined from the standpoint of their objective meaning, but from that of the 'existentialist understanding' they express. Within the framework of the quest for the historical Jesus two things are of interest in this theology: the way it deals with the 'wonder world' of the New Testament, and its relationship to history and thus to the historical Jesus.[63]

The theology of demythologization takes its name from the first of these problems, a negative term which gives no indication of the scope of its programme. Nevertheless it is illuminating because it indicates the impulse which led to the development of this theological teaching: the misgivings aroused by the miracles, and by everything deriving from a 'mythical world picture'. New Testament mythology, including not only the miracles, but also the sacramental teaching, is not acceptable to a form of thought which has been 'irrevocably formed by science'.[64] The thought of 'modern man', conceiving himself 'as a homogeneous being ascribing his feelings, his thought and his will to himself' is unable to accept the idea of any intervention on the part of divine powers in the inner unity of his circumstances and his actions. 'Man cannot make use of electric light and the wireless, and, in the event of sickness, have recourse to modern medical and clinical aids, and at the same time believe in the wonder world of the New Testament.'[65] Bultmann's assurance that de-mythologization is not trying to make the Gospels 'acceptable to science' is justified to the extent that his 'existentialist interpretation' relates largely to that evidence of Holy Writ which need not justify itself at the bar of objective scientific knowledge. But his retreat to this position is enforced by his subjection to scientific thought.[66] Theologically and historically the de-mythologization procedure represents the last act of the dramatic conflict between belief and knowledge, in which the forces of enlightened thought, already overtaken by the spirit of the age, rally for a new attack, whilst belief is on the point of taking up an invulnerable position on the heights above the battlefield. The spectacle is an impressive one, and important enough to take its place amongst the highlights of the quest for the historical Jesus. Bultmann stands 'at the highest peak of a theological paripeteia' (Hedwig Conrad-Martius). But 'when we theologians try to be modern we always come a season too late'.[67]

Schweitzer distinguishes two periods in the investigations: pre-Strauss and post-Strauss. The first period is dominated by the problem of miracles. How can an historical account come to terms with supernatural events?

15. Portrait
(*By permission of Erica Anderson, New York*)

Strauss eliminated the mythical components of the sources from his historical account, and after that the problem of miracles was more and more ignored. For the phase of investigation which began in the middle of the sixties the problem was already unimportant. As we have already pointed out, the principle of the non-miraculous historical conception had already been generally accepted so that the historical account did not bother about miracles either positively or negatively. Schweitzer records this fact, and regards it as quite natural in itself, but he adds one of those observations which have been too little regarded, although they bear witness to the profundity of his insight: 'That does not mean that the problem of miracle is solved. From the historical point of view it is really impossible to solve it, since we are not able to reconstruct the process by which a series of miracle stories arose, or a series of historical occurrences were transformed into miracle stories, and these narratives must simply be left with a question mark standing against them.'[68]

But in the long run merely to ignore the problem could not prove satisfactory. When we recall the vigorous attack of scientific materialism on religious belief in the second half of the nineteenth century, and the extraordinary vehement polemics it led to, then the calm in the sheltered academic world in which the investigations take place is not easy to understand: a problem is regarded as settled although it has disrupted Protestant theology on cardinal points of Christian belief, and although every preacher of the Gospels must feel it is almost too hot to handle. De-mythologization theology deserves credit for bringing an unsettled question up for discussion once more. Its arguments show that a theological task of first-rate magnitude still awaits solution, and that the cue could not have been given at any earlier period in the history of religious thought.

The starting point of de-mythologization was thus well chosen, and its motive entitled it to the closest possible attention. It is 'the most dramatic appeal to the conscience of theology which has been issued for a long time'.[69] What theological historicism regarded as a mere problem of the history of religious thought, and assumed to be soluble with methods appropriate to the latter, was now recognized as a problem of doctrine. By the split into a liberal and an orthodox camp—here unprejudiced investigation of the truth with all the means of critical scholarship; there a dogmatism which dare not submit itself to scientific methods, and was thus dismissed reproachfully as blind authoritarian belief, if not intellectual dishonesty—Protestant theology became bogged down in the sterility of a pseudo-peace between two opposing forces. But in the long run this was an intolerable hiatus within the body of the same Christian community, and Bultmann sought to overcome it by the synthesis of a third position.

He certainly succeeded in bringing the petrified fronts into movement, but he did not succeed in advancing beyond the dead point towards a solution of the problem of miracles, because he himself is convinced of the authority of scientific thought as a final court for the discovery of truth—as his example of the supposed irreconcilability of modern wireless apparatus and the 'mythical' statements of the Bible demonstrates in an uncompromising form. Zealous but naïve believers who feel that they can descry the approaching dawn when they learn—without really understanding—the latest results of investigations in theoretical physics, should be warned against premature conclusions which can only compromise belief by supposing that it needs such support. However we are certainly entitled to ask whether the latest developments of science have not developed beyond 'Nature' as understood in the nineteenth century so that the 'possibility that the whole of nature can be transcended both spatially and in time can no longer by regarded as either senseless or impossible'.[70]

That 'modern man', who was credited with such an influential role for theology, is, if not a myth, then a fiction, or at least an anachronism. The outstanding characteristic of modern man is no longer his belief in science, and the scientific superstition Bultmann indulges in, and assumes that the hearers of the Christian Gospel indulge in, too, has been fundamentally overcome. By putting the principle of knowing into practice convincingly, authentically and methodically science becomes conscious of its own knowledge, and is well aware that it is unable to perceive the essence of being anywhere. In consequence it is unable to deny the reality of transcendental being. Such a thing lies beyond its scope.

The second characteristic of de-mythologization theology, the 'flight from the historical as something past',[71] transpires as a logical consequence of the investigations into the life of Jesus. It is the antithetic reaction to the over-exaggerated importance attached to the objective reality of the events recorded in the Gospels. Now disputed, now upheld, they obsessed critical theology far too long and caused true theological interest in the content of the Gospel teachings to recede into the background. It should therefore not surprise us, and we should not fail to recognize its grandeur, when one day a representative of textual critical investigation comes forward and summarily disposes of the whole hundred-fold-sifted material and all its infinite problematics with an act of radical historical resignation. The synoptic Gospels are almost completely abandoned as an historical source, though, now as before, any attempt to describe the teachings of Jesus is still dependent upon them. And instead—who would have thought it possible after Strauss, Bauer and Holtzmann!—the foreground is occupied by the Gospel of St John. And that is because the process of de-mythologicalization finds in it—as in Paul—a confirmation of its idea that belief is the subjective way to attain salvation. Whether or not the traditional content of the Gospels really goes back to Jesus is declared to be unimportant. Unimportant, too, are the events in the life of Jesus, and you will look for them in vain in Bultmann's book. Not even the teaching of the 'historical' Jesus is considered, only that of the Jesus as preached by the community.

In place of the criterion of objective reality we have the 'existentialist interpretation', through which, for the first time, 'the actual intention of the biblical writings is given effect',[72] since 'the appropriate question in relation to the Bible is the question of human existence'.[73] Belief is 'to be brought back to a radical consciousness of its own essence'.[74] 'It is not a question of regarding historical facts as true, but of existentialist decision.'[75] The metaphysical understanding of belief is held to have become impossible, but it cannot be replaced by the results of historical investigation. Theology can understand belief only 'historically'.[76] But this historical understanding —and here the de-mythologization theology borrows the existentialist philosophy of Heidegger—does not consist in man's making himself the subject, and regarding history as his object. It realizes itself in the here and now of direct contact. Historicity emancipates itself from history. The revelation of God cannot be traced historically. It operates only in the here and now of existence as an 'eschatological' event, creating eschatological existence in so far as the day of salvation has dawned for believers. 'Salvation' is not an identifiable process. God's action is not perceptible outside the existentialist event. Thus the evangelists cannot report it as an historical happening, but only vouch for it in the form of teaching. Existentialist interpretation replaces the 'no longer valid salvation story'.[77]

Schweitzer declared the results of the quest for the historical Jesus to be negative.[78] It led to the conclusion that the figure of Jesus 'as designed by rationalism, endowed with life by Liberalism, and clothed by modern theology in a historical garb' had never really existed. All the same, it never entered his mind that the search for this figure could be abandoned, and in the same breath he speaks of the 'historical Jesus which investigation will sketch against a background of the recognized and admitted problems'.

As early as 1892 Martin Kaehler[79] pointed out that it was impossible to write a life of Jesus in the sense of a biography of Jesus of Nazareth according to the standards of modern historical science, and with this he was merely repeating an earlier observation of David Friedrich Strauss.[80] If attention had been paid to this, theology might have been spared more than one Jesus 'biography' which merely compromised it. Despite the misleading sub-title of his 'Sketch', Schweitzer was, of course, well aware of this. Nowadays everyone is agreed as to this one result of the investigations.[81] Opinions are still divided as to whether it is possible to reconstruct the public life of Jesus. The decision is an internal affair of the professional investigators, no matter how important it may be to the layman. But now we come up against something fundamentally different and really astonishing. The investigation of the Gospels has led to the admission that many people think that in all honesty 'the once so confidently sketched map should be left blank as far as the actual history of Jesus is concerned'.[82] This need not have prevented efforts to sketch the 'picture' of him whose word has been handed down to us: 'Who has seen me has seen the Father.'[83] But instead comes the strange, even amazing, fact that 'interest in the personality of Jesus is excluded', which is what Bultmann tells us when he introduces his book on Jesus.[84] To what extent the community may have retained an objectively accurate impression of Jesus and his personality is 'not of any real importance'[85] for Bultmann, though Kaehler feels that 'it must have impressed itself on their hearts and minds with incomparable, ineffaceable and illuminating clarity'.[86] The subject of Bultmann's book is not 'this(!) 'Jesus', this something which the reader is invited to set in inverted commas at will, but 'a complex of ideas', which exegesis must now uncover from amongst the oldest deposits of tradition.

With this the quest for the historical Jesus has arrived at a total negation of itself. Its subject has drifted completely out of reach. It had shifted the accent from the traditional content of Christian belief, the 'saving acts' of God, to an historical figure. Here, too, Schweitzer draws the ultimate conclusion: 'Our faith is built upon the personality of Jesus.'[87] The reaction leads to the opposite extreme. The philanthropist and moral teacher in modern form appealed to men's mind, but the picture was revealed as an unconscious forgery. The protagonist of thoroughgoing eschatology found little attention outside theological science. Now the helm was pushed hard over. Jesus of Nazareth as a person disappeared from the view of the leading school of critical theology. It is a question of much more than a rejection of the historicism of the 'Quest'. Kaehler also does this, and, in fact, the new tendency likes to appeal to him. But whereas for Kaehler 'every trait that one can discover (of Jesus) is dear and significant',[88] the investigators were now indifferent to his life altogether; this 'simple life, which differed from the lives of innumerable others only by its tragic end and the things which brought this end about'.[89] The abandonment of the historical inquiries inevitably resulted in a misunderstanding of the historical phenomenon. It is no longer felt that Jesus is present in every word and every scene in direct sovereignty.

As far as the personality and the life of Jesus are concerned, the result of this combination of the form-historical method and de-mythologicalization is thus a disappearance of substance, and it is not compensated for by an existentialist interpretation which leaves in being only the historical existence as such and the death on the Cross. By the laws according to which it set out, the investigations with their 'continual experimenting' (Schweitzer) must necessarily pass even this dead point one day. Extreme situations provide valuable experience. One such experience teaches us that this much canvassed and much disputed life conceals its real nature as soon as it is no longer taken seriously. There is then a failure to recognize that an existence which represents an end and a beginning in the history of humanity cannot be compared with the lives of others. And its end, the death on the Cross, cannot be separated from the rest of it. If ever a man died his own death it was Jesus of Nazareth. There is even reason to believe that he deliberately brought it about. But whether this was so or not, it was certainly no tragic end, because in him, as the Easter experience of the disciples proves, the tragedy of human existence was negated.

Thus the question of the person and fate of Jesus is not disposed of when historicism is rejected. Attention is once again drawn to the investigations which have been called into question. Have they been proved empty, and is therefore Schweitzer's own investigation no longer valid? And how does Schweitzer's solution fit into the general history of the investigations?[90]

The first thing which remains quite certain is that Christianity will not, and indeed, cannot, abandon either the picture of Jesus of Nazareth or the knowledge of his thought, his acts and his words. The desire of 'certain Greeks': 'Sir, we would see Jesus' (John xii. 21) will always remain vigorously alive as long as there are Christians. The critical Gospel investigations, often contradictory in their results, have certainly not proved that such a desire cannot be fulfilled. Christianity has its origin neither in a mythology nor in a doctrine of ideas, but in an historical personality, and it realizes itself in 'following' (*imitatio*). The Church's dogma of God made Man has preserved this essential element of the Christian religion throughout the centuries from its absorption by Christology. The acknowledgement of Jesus as Lord and Master is the general common denominator of all Christian beliefs, and not even Protestant Liberalism has abandoned it. A theology which abandons the early Christian kerygma of the earthly Jesus; which turns its face away from the figure which, however one may theologically interpret this personal appearance of a divine being on earth, represents the original picture and model of Christian being; which no longer seeks access to the heart 'which loved men so much' (Saint Marguerite-Maria Alacoque) has no hope of ever becoming a recognized Christian teaching. It may have a mission to fulfil, but it will remain a mere episode.

Secondly, whoever does not investigate the life of Jesus as an historian, but regards only the so-called 'salvation process' as of theological importance, will soon find himself up against the fact that its understanding presupposes the whole matter of the Gospels. The whole report contained in the Gospels is part of the message. The Cross logos grows from the words and acts of Jesus of Nazareth.[91]

Thirdly, these words and acts are of decisive importance for Christian piety. They have had their effect and they will continue to have their effect whenever man is able to accept freely what is written 'as it is written'—which does not mean that the texts should not be subjected to critical examination. Thus there is freedom of reception whenever an open mind lets the Gospel stories exercise their direct effect. They are reconcilable with every possible degree of theological-philosophical training and education. At the beginning of his history of the investigations, Schweitzer warns the theologians not to stand between man and the Gospels.[92] 'There is no necessity for any detailed differentiation between the ephemeral and the abiding in the phenomenon of Jesus and his teaching. As though on their own his words translate themselves into the form which they must take in our imagination. Many words which at first sight seem strange become true for us too in a profound and eternal sense if we make no attempt to narrow the power of the spirit which speaks in them.' Just let Jesus preach the Kingdom of God, and there is no need to bother about making his teaching understandable to and significant for modern man.

All the same, we must not make light of the difficulties which have arisen with the rise of scientific thought and the development of methods of historical and textual criticism. They have set theology a tremendous task. The 'act of truth' which consists in subjecting its basis to a scientific examination is and remains an irrevocable necessity both for the sake of conscience and for the sake of credible teaching. This theological self-examination soon found its reward, irrespective of the validity of its results, by seeing the figure and the history of Jesus of Nazareth become the centre of attention as never before—and not only in Protestant theology. It was recognized that 'no single incident in His life, or fragment of His teaching, if it can be isolated from its context and detached can be rendered intelligible'.[93] And not only this. At the same time attention directed to the person of Jesus could not fail to observe with misgiving that the traditional teachings of both confessions represented a retouched and painted over picture, and that misinterpretation of the texts was common. The modernization of Jesus by historical theology was not necessary in order to eliminate those pregnant traits from his picture and his teachings which disturb the natural man, and made the Jesus of history a scandal to his contemporaries by presenting him as the Lord and Master of a New Order, which he himself described as the Kingdom of God.

In such a situation it is one of the most important obligations of Christian theology to use every available scholarly means to discover the historical content of the Gospels. Whoever regards this as a hopeless undertaking is certainly logical in excluding the person of Jesus. *Tertium non datur.* An 'inadequate or false reconstruction of the history of Jesus of Nazareth cuts at the heart of Christianity'.[94] It is true, of course, that historical knowledge can neither strengthen belief nor confirm disbelief. Its task is to clarify the facts, nothing more. But this is precisely the point. If the kerygmatic character of the sources excluded any historical investigation into the life of Jesus then theology would find itself in a really tragic situation. Although a unique happening in time represents the core of Christian teaching theology would be refused all access. However, there are objections to this view.

The literary school, which declares it impossible to discover the history of Jesus, is not interested, for theological reasons, in historical problematics.[95] It deliberately refrains from investigating historical facts, regarding them as unimportant, and it even objects to the 'historical character' of the story of salvation. But where no questions are asked no answers are possible. An exegetic method whose results conform with such automatic accuracy to theological requirements must necessarily come under suspicion even when those who use it insist that none of its results shall be anticipated.[96]

A theologically unprejudiced inquirer will not easily be convinced by any amount of textual interpretation that the Synoptics were not really interested in setting forth 'a declaration of those things which are most surely believed amongst us' (Luke i. 1). They obviously do attach importance to setting forth these happenings, and they 'attempt only to recount events as they took place'.[97] Schweitzer's contention that a creative tradition alone would have taken far greater liberties with its material, moulding it 'much more boldly and logically . . . that is to say, much more arbitrarily and consistently'[98] remains unanswered.

The critical assumption of the form-historical method in dealing with the texts; namely, that the expectation of the imminent end of the world must have overshadowed all recollections of the life of Jesus, because 'that which was to come was naturally . . . much more magnificent than everything which was past',[99] underestimates the compelling effect of a masterly personality, which could not be nullified apocalyptically. If the over-estimation of the eschatological motive in Jesus can be advanced as an objection to Schweitzer's solution, then it can be said here that the now admitted importance of eschatological thought both with Jesus and early Christianity, leads to an over-exaggerated estimate of its influence on the attitude of the early witnesses. At the same time, the assumption of an exclusively eschatologically determined consciousness of Jesus in connection with that of sole responsibility for the coming of the Kingdom in an individual has greater probability in its favour than the transformation of a plurality into eschatological precision apparatuses. The idea that these men of a new Kingdom in the old world knew only one activity: propaganda for their belief,[100] is a logical abstraction. Men of flesh and blood do not react with such clear-cut logic. The assurance in the Acts of the Apostles (iv. 20) 'For we cannot but speak the things which we have seen and heard' is not as Dibelius assumes, evidence in support of this alleged propagandist tendency. On the contrary, with moving simplicity it gives the real reason for what they have to say: their hearts are full to overflowing, as the story of the appearance of Jesus on the way to Emmaus suggests. One simple fact is quite sufficient to reject this theology: Jesus of Nazareth was loved by those who followed him as no other man has ever been loved either before or since. Such love will have stamped the picture of the man indelibly on the minds of his followers, together with their experiences in his company, and what they learned from him. The splendour of the Kingdom of God was present for the early Christians in the person of Jesus. A reflection of this love glows on in the quest for the historical Jesus as its contribution to Christian religiosity. But such a love asks nothing either of Heaven or earth. It demands only the real presence of its object. It preserves all the treasures of memory and presses them to its heart. The idea that the Christian sources were not interested in the life and personality of Jesus[101] presumes that the theological significance of the Easter happening smothered this fire. But the assumption flies in the face of all psychological experience.

Where historical investigation succeeds, through the discovery of new sources, by excavations, or other ways, in providing objective proof for previously disputed facts relating to a far-distant past, we find again and again that popular traditions, once despised as legendary, turn out to have been well-founded after all. Collective memory at primitive stages of society is extraordinarily tenacious and reliable. The suggestion that the Gospel texts are an exception to this general rule cannot be proved exegetically. The deeper the impressions made, the more likely they are to last. And where in the whole history of humanity can you find a more impressive happening? The systematic opening up of new sources uninfluenced by Christian tendencies, and therefore free from the suspicion of being dogmatically influenced, has produced some very remarkable results which have confirmed the texts in matters which critical theology long ago rejected as refuted. In our own day the Dead Sea discoveries have lent a new interest to historical inquiry.[102] And so, despite all objections, the idea is once more gaining ground that the early Christian Jesus tradition is 'chock-full of history'.[103] Theologically unprejudiced historico-critical work on the New Testament never doubted it, not even in the years when the form-historical method came to the fore, and achieved such influence.

The summary drawn up by Hoskyns of research conducted over a hundred years (from David Friedrich Strauss on) in the quest for the historical Jesus[104] is regarded even by those theologians who would demythologise it as 'the best résumé of New Testament investigation'.[105] Hoskyns declares that the historical problem is solved, and so does Schweitzer.[106] That is to say: a critical examination of the Gospel texts enables the historian to descry a clearly-defined historical figure. He can make this figure understandable, and, above all, he can make the rise of the Church from this figure comprehensible. The writings of the New Testament must be examined with the instrument of modern criticism, though this produces the apparently paradoxical situation that whilst on the one hand confidence in the suitability of the critical method increases, on the other, the more this is so the more we must doubt whether it will ever be possible to arrive at a simple series of 'confirmed results'. No investigator can decide with final certainty whether the individual events reported in the Gospels really did happen as they are said to have happened. . . . No New Testament account of a happening, or even reference to a happening, is a mere reporting of the happening itself, because all happenings are brought into a theological relationship and set down with theological intent. But we are not entitled to assume from this that these happenings took place in any way other than that in which they are reported to have happened. Historical and literary criticism of synoptic tradition cannot prove at any stage that an originally non-christological history of Jesus was subsequently given a christological slant. The matter itself is christological (even amongst Bultmann's followers there is in the meantime a growing realization that the eschatology of Jesus contains an implicit Christology).[107] The idea that the Old Testament is fulfilled in the history of Jesus of Nazareth goes back to Jesus himself. It determined his life and his death. He knows that by the will of God the laws and the prophets point to him and only to him. Miracle stories, and the parables and sayings of Jesus are understandable only as pronouncements of the Messiah who is bringing the Kingdom of God. Jesus acted and spoke in this way because he was conscious of fulfilling an obligation imposed on him by God through the Old Testament. He went to Jerusalem and died there not because the Jews drove him to Jerusalem and brought about his death there, but because he was convinced that as the Messiah he had to go to Jerusalem in order to be betrayed and to die there. This violent but voluntary death is the *opus operatum* that ushers in the beginning of the new order. The historian has no alternative but to confirm that both the homogeneity and the uniqueness of the Nazarene's claim are historical facts.

Jesus cannot be associated with any humanitarian idealism or any other time-conditioned evolutionary teaching, and it is no business of the historian to interpret the New Testament to suit modern thought. The historian discovers a Jesus who challenges modern thought; has nothing to do with modern philanthropism or the brotherhood of man; whose teachings cannot be related to modern ideas about humanity and humanitarianism; and whose history is determined by the claim that it is itself an act of God. The historian cannot provide a biography of Jesus, but on the basis of his critical method and his historical investigation he can provide a clearly outlined and really historical figure.

A double criterion applies to this task.

'We have a really historical picture only when the unity of the whole material is such that each fragment is not only a part of the whole, but this whole appears in each fragment . . . that all fragments have not only a common background, but that this common background is visible in each fragment. Whoever demonstrates this unity with this background discovers the Jesus of history.'

But if the historian succeeds in making the figure of Jesus understandable, then over and above this he ought to be able to show understandably how the Church took its rise from him. The task of the historian is to solve the theological riddle of the relationship between Jesus of Nazareth and early Christianity.

In the generation which has passed since then the quest of the historical Jesus has arrived at results which confirm the diagnosis put forward by Hoskyns and largely agree with Schweitzer's fundamental position. It is on the way to a rediscovery of the historical Jesus. This does not mean a reversion to the historicism of the liberal epoch. It no longer bothers about the historicity of the salvation event as a safeguard of belief. And not only is it recognized that a chronologically reliable biography of Jesus is impossible, but there is no longer any interest in it. This is in accordance with a changed outlook on history, which is no longer primarily interested, as the positivist historians were, in collecting and classifying facts, but is interested in their meaning. This shift of accent led for a while to the supplanting of historical reality by the kerygma. In the meantime there has developed a realization of a correspondence of historical writing and kerygma, which both seek to convey the significance of historical facts. The existentialist interpretation of the New Testament is outdated. The kerygma itself gives an historical person as the place of the salvation event; indeed, the development of the significance of this person is its content. After all the peripeteia of critical biblical exegesis the existence and history of Jesus are now regarded, and probably for good and all, as accessible to historical investigation. The Evangelists 'undoubtedly attached importance to stressing the importance of the story for belief' (Robertson). The authenticity of the sources is now more favourably regarded. With this—as with Schweitzer, for whom the core of the historicity of Jesus is the announcement of the Kingdom of God—eschatology is made the cardinal point of Jesus' message, and with it the claim 'that lies in all his sayings, actions and attitude, which cannot have been invented by others, but which goes back to him'.[108] The much disputed Son of Man words of Jesus are recognized as authentic. He appears as 'the one in whom the last decisions are taken'. He stands as security for 'God's last word to man'[109] 'The place of direct contact with God is the succession of Jesus.'[110]

The reader who has taken the trouble to accompany us through this account of the quest for the historical Jesus will find himself rewarded by the result.

Certainly what has been achieved is very far removed from what the original pioneers had in mind. They hoped to find confirmation for their own ideas, and they sought to harness the authority of Jesus to their own wagon. These attempts have finally failed. A theology, anxious about Christian teaching, sought to make the Gospels acceptable to the ideas of modern man. But what the Gospels tell us contradicts the ideas of the age and refuses to submit to its laws. The actual difficulty of the Christian Gospel does not lie in the scientific sphere at all, but in the strangeness of Jesus: 'And they understood not the saying which he spake unto them' (Luke ii. 50). The difficulty can be toned down only at the price of weakening this Gospel. The hope of arriving at a final solution of the problems of the investigations into the life of Jesus, whether by literary analysis or historical investigation, or a combination of both, has not been fulfilled, and is probably impossible of fulfilment. Where investigation recognizes these facts it has become modest. In so far as it has become clear-sighted it is beginning to recognize its own limitations. The naïve optimism of the early days was replaced by a resignation which occasionally went even too far.

The quest for the historical Jesus arose from the clash between belief and knowledge and in an attempt to settle it within the sphere of theology by playing off knowledge against belief. The principle that truth must authenticate itself to science was applied to a subject which resisted its application and finally reduced it to absurdity. The truth to which the Gospels bear witness is of a different character to the truths of science, which can be proved at any time. In this sphere, in which the question relates to being in its highest power, the question of truth directs itself to the experience of belief, which alone can answer it. Its answer expresses a certainty, but not one whose validity can be objectively proved.

The critical investigation into the life of Jesus, which repeatedly tackled so many difficulties, is only now beginning to become aware of the real difficulty, which lies in the fact that its subject matter is made up of two essentially different components. As veins of quartz are found running through rocks, so this material is shot through with deposits of a greater transparency which cannot be affected by the acid of critical investigation. The duty of a scholarship conscious of its limitations is not to withdraw in face of a sphere declared sacrosanct, but to define precisely the limits of its own sphere. Up to now the investigations have made no attempt to define their limits—indeed, they were not even in a position to do so, because the critique of the conception of truth with which the scientific method is accustomed to operate was only in its beginnings. The question of the relationship between truth and science, 'the real basic question of our time',[111] has hardly been formulated, much less answered. Only its clarification will bring the conflict between belief and knowledge to an end. The investigations into the life of Jesus will then enter into a new phase. It will become possible to separate the wheat from the chaff and bring in the harvest.

'Critics have wished their work to be immediately fruitful, and have desired to present assured results which they think may be acceptable to the modern world, or may relieve the tension between the Church and Modern Thought. The moment the critic surrenders to such a desire, he ceases to be a historian.'[112] 'The New Testament critic has far too often constituted himself the arbiter of faith, and claimed a peculiar ability to deal out to the modern world what it may believe and what it may not. This is, however, wholly unjustifiable.'[113]

As an offspring of the Enlightenment movement, the quest for the historical Jesus has been particularly tempted by this arrogance. However a warning voice must be raised against the present fashionable contempt for the Enlightenment; it should not be forgotten that in the fire of its belief in the human spirit it forged an element into Western thought which will never be eliminated. Part of its heritage is the intensification of intellectual conscience, and the obligation to examine and sift the store of theology according to rational principles. We have already seen how inadequately the rationalist lives of Jesus satisfied scientific requirements, and we are not likely to see any more such products, since they demand a self-confidence as naïve as it is vigorous. But down to this day Gospel investigation violates the principles of scientific thought by exceeding its own proper limits even though it does appeal to science. To grant totalitarian rights to science is not reconcilable with its own philosophical self-understanding, though it is up till now approved by the majority of scientists. The decisive step remains to be taken: science started out with the avowed object of attacking superstition; it must now free itself from its own superstition, and objectively examine its own store. What a role the *a priori* 'impossible!' has played in the investigations into the life of Jesus! What difficulties it created for textual criticism, and how largely it allowed itself to be influenced by it! But nothing is *a priori* impossible for the critical historian: 'He must ask how it happened, and not how can it have happened, or how must it have happened.'[114]

The quest for the historical Jesus still has the same task. It must prove itself more unconditionally critical than ever before; it must not uncritically condemn what is not in accord with present-day ways of thought, and, conversely, it must not first ask if its results will be acceptable to modern man, or if they will prove theologically pleasing.

To claim that Schweitzer's results are of epochal importance does not mean to claim that his attempt—like any attempt at the solution of an insoluble riddle—is not open to objections, or that in some respects it is not already out of date. We must not ignore the exegetical progress made with regard to the Gospel texts, even when we put exegesis into its proper place as the handmaid of historical investigation, and recognize that literary criticism needs the assistance of the historian, and may not behave as though it had nothing to do with history. 'The decision is handed over to the historian.'[115] The opening up of previously unknown sources and the investigation of late Judaism[116] has cast new light on the Jesus tradition. This or that fact or saying which Schweitzer regarded as historical may have turned out to be unhistorical after all. More than one of the pericopes is likely to resist all attempts to remove it from the twilight of uncertainty. The sum will hardly work out a second time in such an astonishing fashion, leaving nothing over, as the hypothetical solution of thoroughgoing eschatology has done. But all these things aside, thoroughgoing eschatology towers like a great peak above the critical investigations into the life of Jesus, a landmark to serve either as a guide or a warning in the tremendous task which still lies ahead.

For the first time in the history of the Quest for the historical Jesus Schweitzer dared to pursue his investigations without allowing himself to be side-tracked by theological or modern thought. Schweitzer was the first, and so far as he has remained the only one whose interpretation of the texts, although open to criticism, reveals a common background of all the source fragments, and at the same time demonstrates this background in each fragment. Against all customary usage he adhered to the principle of historical investigation by assuming the authenticity of the sources until they were disproved.[117] And he remained true to this principle even in cases when his own enlightened thought must have suggested that this or that account of an incomprehensible happening ought to be dismissed without more ado as unhistoric. In fact he owes his successful results to this refusal to take the easy way and indulge in methodological slovenliness. Examples of this are his interpretation of the feeding of the five thousand, and the account of the transfiguration of Jesus on the mountain, which do justice both to the text and to his own logical thought. He had the human stature to appreciate Jesus of Nazareth 'as a figure of overwhelming greatness intimidating to modern thought', and to present it uncompromisingly to the spirit of the modern age and the spirit of modern dogmatics—unlike historizing liberalism, which sought to make it presentable by reducing its size, whilst existentialist theology, for which decision constitutes existence, attributes 'decisions' to Jesus, thereby running the risk of modernizing, even psychologizing him, anew in its own way.

Julius Schniewind once expressed the conviction that careful historical investigation must reveal the epiphany of God in the man Jesus. This is exactly what takes place—though in an undogmatic form—when Schweitzer's *Quest* culminates in the representation of the historical Jesus as 'the only Great and the only True'. No quest for Jesus will ever surpass this result.

DOCUMENTS

16. In the sun at Altbirklehof

ALBERT SCHWEITZER: SERMONS

I. JESUS THE LORD

Sermon delivered at St Nicolai Church in Strassburg on May 27, 1906

'Let this mind be in you, which was also in Christ Jesus: Who, being in the form of God, thought it not robbery to be equal with God: But made himself of no reputation, and took upon him the form of a servant, and was made in the likeness of men: and being found in fashion as a man, he humbled himself, and became obedient unto death, even the death of the cross; Wherefore God also hath highly exalted him, and given him a name which is above every name: That at the name of Jesus every knee should bow, of things in heaven and things in earth, and things under the earth; and that every tongue should confess that Jesus Christ is Lord, to the glory of God the Father.' (Phil. ii. 5–11).

Last Sunday we considered the scene when, after the transfiguration of Jesus, a man came to him to ask him to cure his son, and the Lord placed him as third between himself and the child he was to help, asking: 'Hast thou faith?', and made it depend on this whether he should succeed in curing his son or not. And we were moved when we considered the matter, because we realized that when Jesus asked the man about his faith it was not out of severity, and in order to put the hard-pressed man to a new test, but because he was obeying an iron law which required that in order to go over to other men his power must go through other men; he needed a third person to place between himself and others, a person to whom he had to say: 'Now it depends on your faith whether it is possible to help this creature, whether my spirit in you can master the evil spirit of this world.'

And at the same time we were shocked because each of us recognized himself as the third man, parents towards their children, and all of us towards the people with whom life brings us into contact, together with an obligation to help them spiritually, the seekers, the exhausted, the despairing, the embittered, the tempted....

And thus all of us are faced with the question: have we sufficient faith that we may strengthen them, so that the words that proceed from us are not empty, but full of strength?

If we are honest with ourselves then we must confess: 'We are of little faith. Our faith fights with difficulty against unbelief and is almost devoured by it.' The confession of the man who said: 'I believe, Lord; help my unbelief!' is our confession too. And the Lord accepts our confession and does not cast us out—no matter how weak it is, so long as it is honest and true. That is to say, it depends, and it depends only, on whether a man can say: 'I believe in Jesus as my dear Lord', but in such a way that it is really true for him. And then in this belief he has all belief, even though he may otherwise doubt in matters which belong to the iron core of belief. . . . If only he believe in Jesus Christ as his Master then he is on the way to true belief, and it is unimportant how far his belief matures in clarity and perception in this world, in which, after all, we perceive everything only in part; the one of us perhaps more clearly than the other, but all of us only according to the words of Paul: 'For now we see through a glass, darkly. . . .' Where there is true belief in Jesus, there is the real power of belief, the keystone that carries everything.

What does it mean for us: I believe in Jesus Christ as my Lord and Master? We must understand this clearly.

And here again I believe that I am repeating only what you all have often thought when I say: it is not a matter of externals. At one time men disputed greatly as to how the divinity of Jesus was to be understood. I believe that if Jesus had thought it necessary that all men should hold the same views he would have given us such a word in the Sermon on the Mount. It is no different when we have to accept a human and a divine nature side by side in him, or how and when we have to think of him as a spirit. Some people will think of him, as the early Christians did, as a being who sits in space at the right hand of God the Father, ruling and reigning with him; whilst others, who see God more as a spirit in which we live and move, a spirit which permeates everything and is everywhere, will also think of Jesus more as a spirit which is present wherever his word fills the hearts of men.

I believe that there are many questions which are no longer important; not because they have been answered, or because men can no longer discuss them, but because life has gone on beyond them to still other questions. We are all aware that our world will not be converted to belief in Jesus as the Lord because we explain it and make it clear to the world, because perhaps we turn old formulas into new, and think we have made progress thereby.

Recently I read a book by a great contemporary thinker who wrote: 'Jesus is not the Lord, but a profound and brilliant Jewish scribe who was in some respects ahead of his time, but in others was still steeped in its prejudices. He is not the spirit who can dominate our age and help it.'

And I realized that this was a man who knew Holy Writ, and I imagined that by chance we might meet somewhere and talk to each other. How should I prove to him that he was in error? And the more I thought about it the more I realized that with words alone I should be helpless; that I could say no more to him about what Jesus was than he had already read for himself.

And I feel the same discouragement where those people are concerned for whom Jesus is nothing but a man of the past, people who are unwilling to bend the knee, people whose tongues are not prepared to recognize that he was given a name above all other names, that he is Lord and Master.

And about yourselves you know that if he is your Lord, he has not become so because you have thought the matter over, because you have compared him with other great men, because you have weighed his greatness. No! it was because you suddenly realized quite definitely: this is my Lord and Master whom I must obey. Or perhaps it was not suddenly at all; perhaps the idea slowly matured within you; perhaps it is even yet not altogether clear and mature. But you circle round him as though in a spiral whose voluted course will ultimately bring you to him.

This is the only responsibility you bear. Whether he is your Master, or whether you know that you are on the way which will lead you to acknowledge him as your Master. He is revealed to the unbelieving and indifferent world as Lord and Master through those over whom he rules. And if there are no more than a hundred people in each town: those people who bend the knee to him in obedience are the beginning of his glory, because through them, and only through them, is he revealed as one who reigns.

But may we say of ourselves: we believe in Jesus as the Lord because he reigns supreme in our hearts? Wouldn't that be too much, perhaps far too much for us? When may you say such a thing of yourself? Let us take some other life, one of the many we can see from outside, the lives of people we know. Can one see that there is a master in that life? Should not the life of a man of whom it can truly be said: 'Jesus is his Master' be something quite different, something quite out of the ordinary run of lives, a life in whose every action it is clear: this is done by the will of Jesus?

This is no easy question to answer. I am sure that if Jesus were truly Lord and Master, many lives would take on a quite different aspect, and run along quite different lines. How shall I put it?—that through the will of Jesus many more people would be called away from their families and their planned careers to do the work he considers necessary. Much more activity on behalf of Jesus would be visible to the world. We must none of us deceive himself about this or gloss it over with excuses.

And then again I believe too that there are many lives which would retain their unpretentious outward appearance, plodding on in the daily jogtrot, and showing no outward sign of activity in obedience to Jesus—and yet be lives in which Jesus reigns as Lord and Master.

And therefore we cannot say from outward signs: Jesus reigns in this life but not in that, because this is something which each knows only for himself, because only he can see his inner life. And each of us must decide, as a matter between him and the Lord, whether his life is lived in accordance with this higher will, or whether he will no longer be in a position to utter the word 'Lord' because Jesus does not determine the course of his life. No one else can add or subtract a word. The responsibility is his. He alone must bear the responsibility, and account before the face of the Lord every single day for his doings as for a talent entrusted to him.

But once you have this feeling that you must account to the Lord every day, then already Jesus is becoming your Lord and Master.

And if one may speak for many then I should like to say that in the life of each of us there is greater obedience to the Lord than is outwardly visible, and that in truth he reigns in our hearts to a greater extent than others can see in us or we in them.

But we also know, more than others can know of us, or we of them, how much disobedience there is in our lives towards him we call our Master, when in full consciousness we act against his will, whose laws we know and feel clearly within us. There is no need for me to expatiate. Who amongst us lives a single day on which he can look back and say that he feels no need for depression at the shame of having a Lord, knowing clearly what he should do, and nevertheless not doing it? Have you not sometimes gone home in the evening and found it difficult to mount the stairs because on each step you felt like pausing because of disobedience to some word of Jesus, having dismissed it during the day with the words: 'Be quiet; leave me to my own devices!' having excused yourself and thought to have got rid of it—only to meet it again in the evening like a friend with a reproachful countenance?

There too no one can help you. No one can save you from the gnawing doubt as to whether Jesus is really still Lord and Master in your life.

But let us struggle to make it so. And so long as you feel an obligation which first edifies and then shames you, so long as you go on struggling, so long may you acknowledge Jesus as your Lord and Master, and your acknowledgement will serve as belief in his eyes; and your weakness, because you feel that you are weak as one who in truth desires to serve him, is your belief in him. . . .

2. PAUL THE LIBERATOR

Sermon delivered at St Nicolai Church in Strassburg in 1906

'Stand fast therefore in the liberty wherewith Christ hath made us free, and be not entangled again with the yoke of bondage.' (Gal. v. 1.)

I do not know to what extent he has become the personal liberator for each of you, the Christian brother one finds when one is weary and sore oppressed, because he himself almost gave way under the burden of weariness and oppression; one who takes you by the hand as though to say: Come out into the light with me, and I will lead you towards the sun; the one who makes us free with his glorious words from that which oppresses us, the one who makes us peaceful and happy.

But what we want to talk about now is that he has become our joint liberator; that everything which has ever called itself Christian and will ever do so in the future, owes him a debt of gratitude because he freed Christianity from the chains of an external law.

But I have no desire to talk about it as someone who is talking about past things. To what purpose? What is past is past, and will hardly come again in the same way. I cannot of course know whether you have yourselves sufficiently considered, and can judge for yourselves, what a tremendous thing it was when this man faced the disciples and the oldest Jewish Christians, men for whom the law was something inviolable and sacrosanct, the law which even Jesus himself had not touched, and dared to demand freedom for his Gentile Christians. And went on to win this freedom! Consider: the centuries have left the Jewish religion untouched. It has passed unchanged through changing times and changing peoples, and stands today just as venerable and just as implacable in its laws as it was in the days of Paul, the only one who ever wrenched anything from it.

But let us speak here not of the past, not of what Paul was for his contemporaries, but of what he is for us. When he wrote to his Galatians: 'Stand fast therefore in the liberty wherewith Christ hath made us free', he could not realize what these words would mean for all coming Christian generations; he could not realize that the struggle for freedom would not be at an end with the winning of freedom from the law, but that it would persist through the whole history of Christendom, to break out now here, now there, and always when something, perhaps venerable and good in itself, appealed to the authority of age and became a drag on new life.

We are now in the midst of such a period of struggle. An old ideology in alliance with old and venerable symbols and formulas of Christian belief has raised itself to a law against a new conception of the Gospels which seeks to be free from the pressure of all traditional ideology and from the tutelage of all formulas. The struggle has been going on for three generations now, and it does not affect us all in the same way. Some do not feel the burden of tradition as heavily as those others who realize that the future and the very existence of Christianity depend on liberty. Many have grown tired of the dispute and feel that the squabbling must be brought to an end so that the world may not be scandalized at the disunity of Christendom.

Let Paul, who as a prophet for all coming ages dedicated himself to freedom with the words 'Stand fast therefore in liberty', now interpret the signs of our time for us and tell us how we should behave. Let him tell us what is false peace and what is true, what is false sufference and what is true.

At the first glance one might even count him amongst the intolerant. How often must his opponents have appealed to him to give way and end the discord amongst the followers of Jesus, since really it was only a question of externals, and it could make little difference to his Gentile Christians if they accepted the law under which the Lord Jesus himself had lived. But he refused to give way, and he did not pause until they had agreed to accept those Christians who did not accept the law as their brothers too. He was like one whom they wished to bind and he fought tooth and nail against the bonds. He was not meek, but consumed by a hot passion, and he was harsh to the point of injustice. Read his epistle to the Galatians, written in the heat of the struggle. Right at the beginning he describes how he rebuked the apostle Peter. Peter had gone to Antioch, in Syria, and at first he had sat down at the same table with Gentile Christians. But then the apostle James, who was a stern stickler for the letter of the law, sent messengers to him to reproach him because of his lax attitude, whereafter Peter absented himself from the common table. Only to be attacked in holy indignation by Paul who rebuked him sternly before the whole community because of his ambiguous behaviour.

Thus Paul is intolerant when the cause of liberty is at stake, when false burdens are made up to be laid upon the backs of others. But once he is granted the personal liberty he demands then his heart is open to all.

He knows securely that in the new world which has come about by the death of Jesus the old law is no longer valid. But he finds no word to say against those who as Jews, as children of the law, having adopted the Gospel, continue to live according to the law. And in order to scandalize no one, he too lives strictly according to the law, taking vows according to the Jewish custom, and making pilgrimages to the Temple on feast days. At the close of the eighteenth Chapter of the Acts of the Apostles we learn that he travelled from Corinth to Jerusalem in order to celebrate the feast, probably the feast of Pentecost.

And read Chapter xxi Paul is in Jerusalem for the last time. A great meeting of the community is about to take place and the other apostles fear that the old conflict may be renewed when those believers who still hold to the Jewish law find themselves in the presence of the apostle who preaches freedom from the law. Peter and James now come to him and beg for some public sign that he is not the despiser of the law he is thought to be. There were four men there who had made a vow, and Paul should share this vow with them in the manner customary amongst pious Pharisees; that is to say, he should purify himself with them, fast with them, go before the Priests with them, and share the cost of the sacrifices.

When the apostles mounted the steps to their brother Paul with this embarrassing request they were probably feeling a little uncomfortable. What would he say to them? They thought already to hear his thunderous words on the liberty of Christian men. . . . But when they brought forward their request—Paul agreed willingly. He was to pay for it, because when he left the Temple after that visit, the Jews stirred up the people against him and laid hands on him, and in the end he found himself a prisoner of the Roman Governor.

Or read Chapter viii of the First Epistle to the Corinthians which is completely dedicated to tolerance. From Corinth the following case is placed before him: should one eat meat originating from burnt offerings to idols? Because not all of it was burnt or eaten, what was left came on to the market in the usual way and was sold for food. To some people, they called themselves the strong ones, it made no matter. There were no such gods, they said, and therefore the meat was the same as any other meat, and one might eat it without scruple. The others, who were called the weak, were still steeped in their heathen prejudices and they felt that some curse rested on the meat because it had been offered to idols, and they did not dare to eat it.

And now listen to the answer of the apostle: for him the meat is meat like any other, and he grants the strong their point: they are right to refuse to believe that there is a curse on the meat; they are quite right to be prepared to eat it as ordinary meat. So far so good, but at the same time he imposes an obligation on those who are free from prejudice to respect the prejudice of others, and to refrain from eating such meat in order not to scandalize their weaker brethren. Listen to his words: 'But take heed lest by any means this liberty of yours become a stumbling block to them that are weak. . . . And through thy knowledge the weak brother perish, for whom Christ died. But when ye sin so against the brethren, and wound their weak conscience, ye sin against Christ. Wherefore, if meat make my brother to offend, I will eat no flesh while the world standeth, lest I make my brother to offend.' (I Cor. viii. 9, 11–13.)

A few years later, in Chapter xiv of the Epistle to the Romans, he is once again appealed to as an arbitrator in similar questions of superficial liberty and he gives the same answer, the stronger should show consideration to the weaker; and he sums the matter up in the words: 'Let us therefore follow after the things which make for peace. . . .' (Rom. xiv. 19.)

And you know the words from Chapter ix of the First Epistle to the Corinthians in which he sets out his own attitude: 'And unto the Jews I became as a Jew, that I might gain the Jews; to them that are under the law, as under the law, that I might gain them that are under the law; to them that are without law, as without law (being not without law to God, but under the law to Christ) that I might gain them that are without law. To the weak became I as weak, that I might gain the weak: I am made all things to all men, that I might by all means save some.' (I Cor. ix. 20–22.)

Thus was the Prophet who in the early days of Christianity won liberty for the religion of Jesus. If you look at him superficially you might well suppose him a weather-cock, a man without character or consistency. Men who adapt themselves to everything and who fit themselves into everything are the opportunists of our time, and a man is highly thought of if he understands this art and offends no one. And the apostle Paul will certainly have heard people say that he lacked consistency. We can read it between the lines of his epistles to this day—particularly in his Second Epistle to the

Corinthians. It would seem that people had reproached him because his yea was not a yea, and his nay was not a nay, that he was courageous with his pen but that when he met people face to face he gave way feebly. You feel sympathy with him when you read in his epistles how contemptuously he was sometimes treated by people in his beloved communities. What must he have heard from Galatia before he wrote the epistle to the Galatians! And what must he have heard from Corinth before he picked up his pen to write the Second Epistle to the Corinthians! Read that epistle again, and feel sorry for the apostle who has to justify himself to his own community.

And this man, now so steadfast and then so yielding, was the pioneer of the struggle for the liberty of Christianity. But what was the right attitude then is the right attitude now, and I wish that everyone who fights for the freedom of the Gospel today, whether against some other confession, or inside Protestantism, may be steadfast in the same way, and in the same way conciliatory in the extreme, even to the point of inconsistency. Steadfast where liberty is threatened in matters of high importance, yet urged to give way by love. Those who have no convictions, and who feel that every opinion is on an equal footing with all others, will not bring us religious peace. It is rather those who hold a conviction, and care for it, and fight that it may have liberty of expression; and then, as men to whom a conviction is sacred, but are moved by love, can exercise only tolerance, and thus win others by their generosity.

No one can lay down rules for you in such matters; only you can decide when it is necessary to be steadfast, and where charity demands that you should be conciliatory. It will bring you into difficulties; people will reproach you with inconsistency. Bear it patiently, whether they reproach you as friends or enemies. The apostle Paul himself had to suffer in this way, yet he was the true pioneer of liberty....

(Marginal note on the manuscript: 'The only thing that matters is that Christ is preached! Don't discuss!')

NOTES

TRANSLATOR'S NOTE

Whilst everything has been done to meet the desire of the author that the page references in these Notes should be to the English translations where such exist, this was not always possible—particularly where *The Quest of the Historical Jesus* is concerned, since there is no complete English translation of the original German edition from which the author worked, and some of the references are to material not embodied in the English translation. The English references are printed in italics.

TITLE ABBREVIATIONS OF THE WORKS OF ALBERT SCHWEITZER MORE FREQUENTLY MENTIONED IN THIS BOOK

KG *The Mystery of the Kingdom of God;* the Secret of Jesus' Messiahship and Passion, A. & C. Black, London 1925, and Macmillan, New York 1950. (*Das Messianitäts- und Leidensgeheimnis,* Eine Skizze des Lebens Jesu, Verlag J. C. B. Mohr (Paul Siebeck), Tübingen 1901.)

HJ *The Quest of the Historical Jesus.* A Critical Study of its Progress from Reimarus to Wrede, A. & C. Black, London 1910, and Macmillan, New York 1948—the enlarged edition has not been published in English. (*Geschichte der Leben-Jesu-Forschung,* von Reimarus zu Wrede. *Eine Geschichte der Leben-Jesu-Forschung,* 2nd ed., Verlag J. C. B. Mohr (Paul Siebeck), Tübingen 1906.)

B *J. S. Bach.* A. & C. Black, London 1911, and Macmillan, New York. Revised and enlarged version of the German edition. (*J. S. Bach,* Verlag Breitkopf & Hartel, Leipzig, 1908.)

PI *Paul and his Interpreters.* A Critical History, A. & C. Black, London 1912, and Macmillan, New York 1948. (*Geschichte der Paulinischen Forschung von der Reformation bis auf die Gegenwart,* Verlag J. C. B. Mohr (Paul Siebeck), Tübingen 1911.)

PF *On the Edge of the Primeval Forest.* A. & C. Black, London 1922. (*Zwischen Wasser und Urwald,* Verlag Paul Haupt, Berne 1921—from 1925 on also Verlag C. H. Beck, Munich.)

PC I *The Philosophy of Civilization—The Decay and the Restoration of Civilization.* A. & C. Black, London 1946, also Allen & Unwin (Unwin Books), London 1961. (*Kulturphilosophie I: Verfall und Wiederaufbau der Kultur,* C. H. Beck, Munich 1923.)

PC II *The Philosophy of Civilization—Civilization and Ethics.* A. & C. Black, London 1946. (Also Allen & Unwin (Unwin Books), London 1961 (*Kulturphilosophie II: Kultur und Ethik,* C. H. Beck, Munich 1923.) Also I and II by Macmillan, New York 1939 under the title *The Philosophy of Civilization.*

CRW *Christianity and the Religions of the World.* Allen & Unwin, London 1923. Also Henry Holt, New York 1939. (*Das Christentum und die Weltreligionen,* Verlag C. H. Beck, Munich 1923.)

CY *Memoirs of Childhood and Youth*, Allen & Unwin, London 1924. Also Macmillan, New York 1925. (*Aus meiner Kindheit und Jugendzeit*, Verlag C. H. Beck, Munich 1924.)

LT *My Life and Thought*, Allen & Unwin, London 1931. Published in the U.S.A. under the title *Out of my Life and Thought*, Henry Holt, New York 1933. (*Aus meinem Leben und Denken*, Verlag Felix Meiner, Leipzig 1932, later, Verlag Richard Meiner, Hamburg.)

MP *The Mysticism of Paul the Apostle*, A. & C. Black, London 1931. (*Die Mystik des Apostels Paulus*, Verlag J. C. B. Mohr (Paul Siebeck), Tübingen 1930.)

G *Goethe*. Four Studies, the Beacon Press, Boston 1949. (*Goethe*. Vier Reden, Verlag C. H. Beck, Munich 1950).

INTRODUCTION

1. Rudolf Grabs, *Albert Schweitzer, Denker aus Christentum*, Max Niemeyer Verlag, Halle 1958.
2. Ibid., p. 37.
3. Here are the editions of some of Schweitzer's books: *Memoirs of Childhood and Youth* 137,000; *On the Edge of the Primeval Forest* 213,000; *Philosophy of Civilization*, Vol. 1. 50,000, Vol. II, 40,000; *My Life and Thought*, 450,000. These books have been translated into many languages; these are the figures for the German editions only.
4. Rudolf Grabs devotes part of his study (p. 45 et seq.) to an examination of the question: 'Is Schweitzer a Christian?', and succeeds only in providing a very involved answer. He regards Schweitzer's thought as part of the coming 'World Philosophy' (p. 374).
5. George Seaver, *Albert Schweitzer. The Man and his Mind*, A. & C. Black, London 1947, *p. 227*.
6. HJ, *p. 1*.
7. Viktor von Weisäcker, *Zwischen Medizin und Philosophie*, Vandenhoeck & Ruprecht, Göttingen 1957, p. 19.
8. Gerhard Szczesny, *Die Zukunft des Unglaubens*, Paul List Verlag, Munich 1959.
9. Ibid., pp. 21, 59, 134.
10. Ibid., p. 58.
11. HJ, *p. XVI*.
12. Letter October 31, 1918.
13. Werner Picht, 'Albert Schweitzer', in *Wort und Wahrheit*, Monthly for Religion and Culture, Verlag Herder, Freiburg im Breisgau, August 1953.
14. Letter to the author, September 18, 1953.

FUNDAMENTALS

1. LT, *p. 254*.
2. Ibid., *p. 111*.
3. PC I, *p. 36*.
4. PC II, *p. 214*.
5. Ibid., *p. 215*.

6. Despite Schweitzer's intense interest in German literature—at the turn of the century he gave lectures before the Paris 'Société des Langues étrangères' on Nietzsche, Gerhart Hauptmann, Sudermann, Goethe's *Faust* and so on—he never occupied himself with Stefan George. And, in fact, any direct relationship between Schweitzer and a man who was necessarily utterly foreign to him because of his pathos and his priestly attitude is unimaginable. Nevertheless, in 1899 Schweitzer was a regular listener to Georg Simmel, the great sophist of Berlin University, who had made it his task to use his professorial position to proclaim the significance of Stefan George, who was not very well known at that time. And now and again the audience was even treated to one or two of George's poems during the course of Simmel's lectures.

7. PC II, *p. 158.*

8. HJ, *p. 398.*

9. KG, *p. 274.*

10. Friedrich Gundolf, 'Gefolgschaft und Jüngertum' in *Blätter für die Kunst*, Series 8. The same attitude which is proclaimed here in a secular context is expressed by George in the poem 'Der Jünger'—Stefan George, *Vom Teppich des Lebens*, Verlag Georg Bondi, Berlin 1901.

11. MP, *p. 394.*

12. Friedrich Gundolf, *Friedrich des Grossen Schrift über die deutsche Literatur*, Verlag Rascher, Zürich 1957, p. 8.

13. Gilbert Cesbron, in *Albert Schweitzer, Études et Témoinages*, Édition de la Main jetée, 1951, p. 28.

14. Magnus C. Ratter, *Albert Schweitzer, Life and Message*, The Beacon Press, Boston 1950, p. 31.

15. Daniel Halévy, in *Albert Schweitzer, Études et Témoinages*, p. 264.

16. CY, *p. 22.*

17. Magnus C. Ratter, ibid., p. 93.

18. PC II, *p. 13.*

19. At the time of Schweitzer's birth (January 14, 1875) his father was curate in charge at Kaysersberg in Upper Alsace, but six months later he was transferred as vicar to Günsbach.

20. Diary of Lady Pauline Kirkpatrick, quoted by George Seaver in *Albert Schweitzer. The Man and his Mind, p. 134.*

21. CY, *p. 32.*

22. Ibid., *p. 57.*

23. Ibid., *p. 60.*

24. LT, *p. 36.*

25. Ibid., *p. 114.*

26. Rudolf Grabs, *Albert Schweitzer*, Steuben Verlag, Berlin 1949, p. 25, 2nd edition, *Albert Schweitzer, Gehorsam und Wagnis*, a biography, Verlag Richard Meiner, Hamburg.

27. CY, *p. 69.*

28. PC II, *p. 209.*

29. CY, *p. 89.*

30. Mark viii. *35.*

31. LT, *pp. 18–19.*

32. Albert Schweitzer, 'The Conception of the Kingdom of God in the Trans-

formation of Eschatology', epilogue to E. N. Mozley, *The Theology of Albert Schweitzer*, The Macmillan Company, New York, *p. 104*.

KANT

1. Albert Schweitzer, *Die Religionsphilosophie Kants von der reinen Vernunft bis zur Religion innerhalb der Grenzen der blossen Vernunft*, Verlag J. C. B. Mohr (Paul Siebeck), Tübingen 1899, p. V.

2. This lecture (July 29, 1908) was never published.

3. Theobald Ziegler, *Die geistigen und sozialen Strömungen des Neunzehnten Jahrhunderts*, Verlag Georg Bondi, Berlin 1901, p. 360.

4. PC II, *pp. 102–3*.

THE QUEST FOR THE HISTORICAL JESUS

1. Richard Kik, 'Eine Reise zu Albert Schweitzer nach Lambarene', in circular No. 10 for the Friends of Albert Schweitzer, December 1, 1956.

2. Cf. Günther Bornkamm, *Jesus von Nazareth*, Verlag W. Kohlhammer, Stuttgart 1956, p. 11. Rudolf Bultmann in his *Jesus*, Verlag J. C. B. Mohr (Paul Siebeck) 1951, gives no literary sources, and refers (p. 11) only to Schweitzer's: 'brilliantly written *Quest of the Historical Jesus*'.

3. *Das Abendmahl in Zusammenhang mit dem Leben Jesu und der Geschichte des UrChristentums*. Vol. I. 'Das Abendmahls-problem auf Grund der wissenschaftlichen Forschung des 19 Jahrhunderts and der historischen Berichte.'

Vol. II: *Das Messianitäts und Leidensgeheimnis*, a sketch of the life of Jesus. Both published by J. C. B. Mohr (Paul Siebeck), Tübingen 1901. The intended third volume: 'Geschichte des Abendmahls and der Taufe in der Frühchristliche Periode', never got farther than the manuscript for University lectures.

4. HJ, *p. 2*.

5. Friedrich Gogarten, *Entymythologisierung und Kirche*, Vorwerk-Verlag, Stuttgart 1953, p. 32.

6. Romano Guardini, *Das Ende der Neuzeit*, Werkbund-Verlag, Würzburg 1950, p. 32.

7. Cf. Georg Picht, *Bildung und Naturwissenschaft*, in Clemens Munster and Georg Picht, *Naturwissenschaft und Bildung*, Werkbund-Verlag, Würzburg 1955, p. 44. Also Georg Picht, 'Wahrheit und Gewissheit', in *Unterwegs zu neuen Leitbildern?*, Werkbund-Verlag, Würzburg 1957, pp. 9 et seq.

8. Ibid., p. 2.

9. HJ, *p. 2*.

10. Harnack's *Wesen des Christentum* appeared in 1900 and sold 70,000 copies.

11. HJ. Preface to the sixth German edition (1951), p. XVIII.

12. Ibid., p. IX.

13. HJ, *p. 396*.

14. 'The Gospels follow no order in recording the acts and miracles of Jesus, and the matter is not, after all, of much importance. If a difficulty arises in regard to Holy Scripture and we cannot solve it, we must just let it alone.' HJ, *p. 13*.

15. 'I was at last in a position to acquire the knowledge I needed in order to feel the firm ground of reality under my feet in philosophy.' LT, *p. 126*.

16. 'The thousand years between Plotinus and the Italian Renaissance just doesn't exist for Schweitzer', Rudolf Grabs, *Albert Schweitzer*, p. 392.
17. HJ, p. 553.
18. Ibid., p. 544.
19. Ibid., p. 518.
20. KG, *p. 9.*
21. HJ, *p. 338.*
22. Ibid., p. 554. Footnote No. 1.
23. Ibid., *pp. 356–7.*
24. Ibid., *p. 385.*
25. Ibid., *p. 310.*
26. KG, *p. 274.*
27. Albert Schweitzer, *Die psychiatrische Beurteilung Jesu*, Verlag J. C. B. Mohr (Paul Siebeck), Tübingen 1913.
28. KG, *p. 251.*
29. Ibid., *p. 275.*
30. Ibid., *p. 251.*
31. HJ, *p. 397.*
32. Ibid., *p. 334.*
33. Ibid., *p. 335.*
34. Sir Edwyn C. Hoskyns and F. Noel Davey, *The Riddle of the New Testament*, Faber & Faber 1936, *p. 15.*
35. HJ, *p. 341.*
36. KG, *p. 235.*
37. MP, *p. 189.*
38. Gunther Bornkamm, ibid., p. 111. Bornkamm rejects thoroughgoing eschatology, but (p. 203) he estimates Schweitzer's thesis that the figure and message of Jesus belongs not only within the framework of a different historical environment, but also of an apocalyptic historical picture which has become foreign to us, as 'a great discovery of decisive importance for the future of theology'.
39. KG, *pp. 34–5* & *p. 127.*
40. Cf. Bornkamm, ibid., pp. 155 et seq.
41. Gustav Frenssen, *Hilligenlei*, G. Grotesche Verlagsbuchhandlung, Berlin 1905, pp. 485 et seq.
42. KG, *p. 275.*
43. HJ, *p. 401.*
44. HJ, *pp. 401–2.*
45. LT, *p. 75.*
46. HJ, p. 636.
47. Oskar Kraus, *Albert Schweitzer, sein Werk und seine Weltanschauung*, Pan-Verlag, Charlottenburg 1926, p. 39.
48. PC II, *p. 210.*
49. MP, *p. 379.*
50. Sermon delivered at St Nicholas Church, Ascension Day 1906. Cf. Documents.
51. Cf. Friedrich Gogarten, ibid., p. 30.
52. HJ, p. 512.
53. GRW, p. 56

54. Fritz Buri, *Christentum und Kultur bei Albert Schweitzer*, Verlag Paul Haupt, Berne 1941, p. 130.

55. HJ, p. 641.

56. Schweitzer speaks sometimes of Jesus and sometimes of Jesus Christ in connexion with Pauline research; and in his sermons he also speaks often of Christ, but this does not imply any de-personalization of Jesus.

57. HJ, p. 524.

58. KG, *pp. 5–6.*

59. HJ, *p. 2.*

60. Sermon on the text Galatians v. 1 delivered at St Nicholas Church (1906) 'Stand fast therefore in the liberty. . . .'

61. Sermon delivered at St Nicholas on May 20, 1906, on the text Mark ix. 24. 'Lord I believe; help thou mine unbelief.'

62. HJ, *p. 398.*

63. Sermon delivered at St Nicholas on May 27, 1906.

64. LT, *p. 71.*

65. Albert Schweitzer, 'The Conception of the Kingdom of God in the Transformation of Eschatology', *pp. 104–6.* The original German text was published in February 1953 in the *Schweizerischen Theologischen Rundschau.*

66. Sermon delivered at St Nicholas on May 27, 1906.

67. Rudolf Grabs, *Albert Schweitzer*, pp. 9, 25.

68. Rudolf Grabs, *Albert Schweitzer. Denker aus Christentum*, p. 13.

69. Fritz Buri, *Albert Schweitzer als Theologe heute*, Verlagsverein 'Christ und Welt', Schaffhausen 1955, p. 31.

70. Fritz Buri, ibid., p. 24.

71. Oskar Kraus, ibid., p. 39.

72. Marie Woytt-Secretan, *Albert Schweitzer baut Lambarene*, Verlag Karl Robert Langewiesche, Königsstein im Taunus 1957, p. 59.

73. MP, *p. 379.*

74. LT, *p. 277.*

PAUL

1. LT, *p. 141.* The Bach edition is to include all his compositions for the organ. So far six volumes have been published: *J. S. Bach.* Complete Organ Works. A Critico-Practical Edition in Eight Volumes, G. Schirmer Inc., New York. The work is in three languages: German, French and English. Vols. I and II: *Preludes and the Fugues*; Vols. III and IV: *Preludes and Fugues*, 1913; Vol. V: *Concertos and Sonatas*; Vol. VI: *Various Choral Compositions*, 1954. Vols. I to V edited by Albert Schweitzer and Charles Marie Widor; Vol. VI edited by Edouard Nies-Berger and Albert Schweitzer.

2. LT, *pp. 142–3.*

3. *PI*, *p. V.*

4. MP, *p. 225.*

5. PI, *p. 138.*

6. Ibid., *pp. 197 et seq.*

7. Ibid., *p. 59.*

8. MP, *p. 204.*

9. Ibid., *p. 376.*

10. HJ, Preface to the sixth German edition, p. XVIII.
11. MP, *p. 379.*
12. Ibid., *pp. 381–2.*
13. Ibid., *p. 378.*
14. Ibid., *p. 396.*

ETHICS

1. PC I, *pp. 86–7* and *89.*
2. G, *p.* 16.
3. LT, *p. 172.*
4. Ibid., *p. 173.*
5. John Middleton Murry, *The Challenge of Schweitzer*, The Jason Press, London 1948, *p. 8.*
6. George Seaver, ibid., *p. 3.*
7. PC I, *p. 35* & *pp. 38–9.*
8. Friedrich Gundolf, *Rede zu Goethes Hundertsten Geburtstag*, Verlag Georg Bondi, Berlin, 1932, p. 9.
9. LT, *p. 179.*
10. Ibid., *p. 216.*
11. HJ, p. 521.
12. Ibid., *p. 401.*
13. Nicolai Berdyaev, *Das Neue Mittelalter.* Otto Reidel Verlag, Tübingen. New edition 1950, p. 36.
14. PC I, *p. 88.*
15. MP, *pp. 1–2.*
16. Quoted by Kraus, ibid., p. 38.
17. LT, *p. 1*
18. Ibid., *p. 176.* 'Civilization I define in quite general terms as spiritual and material progress in all spheres of activity accompanied by an ethical development of individuals and mankind.' (Ibid., *p. 232.*)
19. Ibid., *p. 67*
20. MP, *p. 302.*
21. LT, *p. 70.*
22. Oskar Kraus, ibid., p. 31.
23. PC I, *p. 98.*
24. LT, *p. 6*
25. Ibid., *p. 6*
26. PC II, *p. 197.*
27. PC I, *pp. 96–7.*
28. LT, *p. 233.*
29. PC II, *p. 9.*
30. Ibid., *p. 11.*
31. Ibid., *p. 9.*
32. LT, *pp. 187–8.*
33. Hubert M. Phillips, *Safari of Discovery*, The Universe of Albert Schweitzer, Twayne Publishers, New York, 1958, *p. 97.*
34. LT, *p. 279.*

35. PC II, *p. 216.*
36. Ibid., *p. 152.*
37. LT, *p. 187.*
38. Ibid., *p. 188.*
39. PC II, *pp. 189–90.*
40. Ibid., *p. 204.*
41. Ibid., *p. 200.*
42. LT, *p. 271.*
43. PC II, *p. 215.*
44. Ibid., *p. 223.*
45. Ibid., *p. 220.*
46. Ibid., *p. 111*
47. Ibid., *p. 221.*
48. Ibid., *pp. 216–17.*
49. Ibid., *p. 219.*
50. PC I, *p. 96.*
51. PC II, *p. 160.*
52. Ibid., *p. 211.*
53. Ibid., *p. 223.*
54. Ibid., *p. 224.*
55. Ibid., *p. 198.*
56. Friedrich Gundolf, *Goethe*, Verlag Georg Bondi, Berlin 1917, p. 165.
57. PC II, *p. 227.*
58. LT, *p. 272.*
59. PC II, *p. 228.*
60. George Seaver, *Albert Schweitzer. A Vindication*, James Clarke & Co. Ltd., London 1950.
61. The plan for the philosophy of civilization has in the meantime been reduced to three volumes. The writing of the third volume has gone so far that one may expect its publication, if not in Schweitzer's lifetime then from his literary remains.
62. Oskar Kraus, ibid., p. 40.
63. Hubert M. Phillips, ibid., *p. 117.*
64. Letter to the author, February 9, 1959.
65. LT, *p. 269.*
66. CW, *p. 18.*
67. LT, *p. 276.*
68. Ibid., *p. 259.*
69. Ibid., *p. 254.*
70. PC II, *p. 212.*
71. Ibid., *p. 185.*
72. Ibid., *p. 189.*
73. Ibid., *p. 212.*
74. Oskar Kraus, ibid., p. 38.
75. George Seaver, *Albert Schweitzer. A Vindication, p. 31.*
76. Cf. Rudolf Ehrenberg, *Metabiologie*, Verlag Lambert Schneider, Heidelberg 1950.
77. Hugo von Hofmannsthal to Carl J. Burckhardt, January 16, 1926.
78. Rudolf Grabs also points out that with regard to the problem of death

there is a 'gap in the religious utterances of Schweitzer'—*Albert Schweitzer. Denker aus Christentum*, p. 172.

79. PC II, *p. 11.*
80. LT, *p. 271.*
81. Ibid., *p. 189.*
82. Oskar Kraus, ibid., p. 49.
83. LT, *p. 271.*
84. George Seaver, *Albert Schweitzer. A Vindication, p. 45.*
85. John Middleton Murry, ibid., *p. 39.*
86. PC II, *p. 215.*
87. MP, *p. 297.* 'The ethical existence as the highest manifestation of spirituality.'
88. PC II, *p. 215.*
89. PI, *p. 59.*
90. LT, *p. 270.*
91. Letter to Charles R. Joy, quoted in G, p. 27.
92. HJ, p. 640.
93. 'That it [life] demands reverence is, according to Schweitzer, the first and last word of all ethics. . . . It is a matter of course that a theological ethic cannot go along with that.' Karl Barth, *Dogmatik*, Vol. III, Part 4, Evangelischer Verlag, Zollikon-Zürich 1957, p. 367.
94. Karl Barth, ibid., p. 398.

THE KINGDOM OF GOD

1. With regard to the relationship between Schweitzer's philosophy of Civilization and Christianity, see Fritz Buri, *Christentum und Kultur bei Albert Schweitzer*, pp. 29, 49, 104.
2. Albert Schweitzer, 'Die Idee des Reiches Gottes im Verlauf der Umbildung des eschatologischen Glaubens in den uneschatologischen', *Schweizerische Theologische Rundschau*, February 1952, p. 3.
3. PC II, *p. 244.*
4. Ibid., *p. 24.*
5. Fritz Buri, ibid., p. 36.
6. PC II, *p. 24.*
7. PC I, *p. 89.*
8. LT, *p. 274.*
9. Albert Schweitzer, *Die Idee des Reich Gottes . . .*, p. 18.
10. PC II, *p. 241.*
11. LT, *p. 270.*
12. MP, *p. 386.*
13. LT, *p. 68.*
14. Albert Schweitzer, *Die Idee des Reich Gottes . . .*, p. 16.
15. HJ, p. 638.
16. Fritz Buri, ibid., p. 113.
17. CW, *p. 83.*
18. Fritz Buri, ibid., pp. 16 and 108. In the meantime, under the influence of Carl Jaspers' existentialist philosophy, Buri has 'revised quite materially' his

judgement of the ethical ideology of Schweitzer. Cf. Fritz Buri, *Albert Schweitzer und Carl Jaspers,* Artemis Verlag, Zürich 1950, and *Albert Schweitzer als Theologe heute,* p. 23.

19. Albert Schweitzer, *Die Idee des Reich Gottes . . .*, p. 16.
20. HJ, *p. 19*
21. PC I, *p. 95.*
22. MP, *p. 389.*
23. Ibid., p. 384.
24. Albert Schweitzer, *Die Idee des Reich Gottes . . .*, p. 20.
25. MP, pp. *394–5.*
26. Albert Schweitzer, *Die Idee des Reich Gottes . . .*, p. 20.
27. CRW, *pp. 82–3.*

LAMBARÉNÉ

1. PF, *pp. 22–3.*
2. For example, A. Albers, *Münchener Neueste Nachrichten,* 1925, No. 12, quoted by Oskar Kraus, ibid., p. 30.
3. LT, *pp. 106–7.*
4. For example, 'Alte Leben-Jesu Leugnung', *Freiburger Katholisches Kirchenblatt,* February 1, 1959.
5. Rudolf Grabs, *Albert Schweitzer,* p. 175.
6. Albert Schweitzer, *Das Spital in Urwald,* Pictures by Anna Wildikann, Verlag Paul Haupt, Bern, and Katzmann, Tübingen 1948.
7. LT, *pp. 114–15.*
8. 'And so I learned to tie up parcels properly.'
9. Albert Schweitzer, *Briefe aus Lambarene 1924–1927,* Verlag C. H. Beck, Munich 1955, p. 139.
10. Ibid., p. 142.
11. Letter to the author, September 18, 1953.
12. Albert Schweitzer, *Ein Pelikan erzählt sein Leben*, Verlag Richard Meiner, Hamburg 1950.
13. PF, *p. 132.*
14. Ibid., *pp. 155–6.*
15. Schweitzer's most important observations on these questions can be found in his two books of African reminiscences; in the autobiographical *My Life and Thought*, and in the illustrated book by Charles R. Joy and Melvin Arnold, *The Africa of Albert Schweitzer,* The Beacon Press, Boston 1948; in an article in the *Contemporary Review*, 'Relationships between the White and Coloured Races', January 1928; and finally in the preface to the new French edition of *On the Edge of the Primeval Forest, A l'Orée de la Fôret Vierge*, Éditions Albin Michel, Paris 1952.
16. Schweitzer in *The Africa of Albert Schweitzer,* p. 151.
17. Ibid., p. 154.
18. PF, French edition, Paris 1952, p. 13.
19. The experiences of Schweitzer with the natives of French Equatorial Africa are confirmed word for word by his biographer George Seaver, who lived for five years as a District Officer in the triangle of land Zambesi, Luangwa and Lake Nyasa in East Africa in close contact with the natives.

20. Compare the judgement of an expert with the criticism that Schweitzer's hospital in Lambaréné is too primitive and that its usefulness is doubtful: 'The operating room is as good as any in Western Europe. Apart from highly specialized matters, such as endocardiac surgery, every form of surgical assistance is given here successfully. . . . Anyone who has seen Schweitzer working hour by hour in the operating room, anyone who has been fortunate enough to discuss medical questions relating both to the past and the future with him, including urgent problems of therapy or the interpretation of a post mortem, realizes very clearly that the Strassburg doctor of medicine, and the German honorary doctor of medicine (Münster 1958), is a very great surgeon too.' Prof. Dr Phil, Doctor Hermann Mai, 'Lambarene mit den Augen eines Artztes gesehen', in Circular No. 15 for the Friends of Albert Schweitzer, January 14, 1960, p. 20.

21. PF, *pp. 173–4.*

22. Ibid., *p. 174.*

23. Letter to the author, February 9, 1959.

24. LT, *p. 280.*

25. Letter of August 17, 1913.

GOETHE

1. G, p. 18.

2. Rudolf Grabs, *Albert Schweitzer*, p. 337.

3. Charles R. Joy in the preface to G, p. 13.

4. Wilhelm Flitner, *Goethe im Spätwerk*, Verlag Claassen & Goverts, Hamburg 1947, p. 114.

5. Letter to Charles R. Joy, quoted in G, *p. 14.*

6. The text of the award is interesting as evidence of the regard in which Schweitzer was held even a generation back: 'The Goethe Prize founded by the Town of Frankfurt is awarded this year to the friend of humanity, Albert Schweitzer; a man honoured by all confessions as a theologian and an investigator of religion; a man famous as a musician and writer on music far beyond the limits of the German language on account of his organ playing and his work on Johann Sebastian Bach; a man who gave up his professorial activity in favour of direct service to mankind as a doctor working in remote places against leprosy and sleeping sickness amongst the natives of the African jungle. It is awarded as some recognition of the example he has given in the Faustian transformations of his life, of his passionate devotion to the aims of human validity and elevation, of his share, furthering the heritage of humanitarian thought, in the Western struggle to fulfil the tasks of conscience set by civilization, and of his attempt in the spirit of Goethean thought to re-awaken the forces of life and world acceptance in the minds of all men.'

7. Schweitzer has made the following formal utterances concerning Goethe: Address on the occasion of the award of the Goethe Prize of the town of Frankfurt on August 28, 1928; Memorial address on the centenary of Goethe's death delivered in his place of birth Frankfurt on March 22, 1932; 'Goethe as Thinker and Man', text of a lecture delivered in Ulm in July 1932; 'Goethe, the man and his work', text of a lecture delivered in Aspen, in Colorado, on July 8, 1949; an article on Goethe the philosopher, written for *Europe*, Goethe Number, April 15, 1932. The addresses on Goethe were collected and published by

C. H. Beck, Munich, in 1950. An American edition published in 1948 before the German edition, contained the article written for *Europe*, but not the lecture delivered in Aspen.

8. The view that Goethe exercised no intimate personal influence on Schweitzer during the first half of his life is erroneous: Cf. Charles R. Joy, *Music in the Life of Albert Schweitzer*, Harper & Brothers, New York, 1951, p. 14.

9. Joy, Charles R., *Music in the Life of Albert Schweitzer*, A. & C. Black, London, *p. 5*.

10. G, p. 14.

11. José Ortega y Gasset, *Um einen Goethe von innen bittend*, Deutsche Verlags-Anstalt, Stuttgart 1932, p. 15.

12. CY, *p. 84*.

13. José Ortega y Gasset, ibid., p. 28.

14. G, p. 14.

15. G, p. 90.

16. G, p. 73.

17. G

18. G

19. Ibid.

20. Friedrich Gundolf calls him this. Speech on the centenary of Goethe's death, p. 19.

21. Cf. Arnold Bergsträsser, *Goethe's Image of Man and Society*, Henry Regnery Co., Chicago 1949

22. G, p. 82.

23. Letter to Lavater, December 28, 1773.

24. G, p. 39.

25. Wilhelm Flitner, ibid., p. 147.

26. Herman Grimm, *Das Leben Goethes*, Alfred Kröner Verlag, Stuttgart 1959, p. 197.

MUSIC

1. LT, *p. 82*

2. Albert Schweitzer, *Eugen Münch 1857–1898*, Verlag I. Brinkmann, Mülhausen 1898.

3. LT, *p. 170*.

4. Emilius Bangert, 'Albert Schweitzer und die Orgel', in *Gift of Friendship*, p. 179.

5. B, p. 445.

6. Albert Schweitzer, 'Mes Souvenirs sur Cosima Wagner', in *L'Alsace Française*, February 12, 1933, p. 124.

7. Martin Buber, 'Ein Realist des Geistes', in *Gift of Friendship*, p. 203.

8. KG, *p. 274*.

9. Albert Schweitzer, *Johann Sebastian Bach*, Le Musicien-Poéte, Paris 1905.

10. Philipp Spitta, *J. S. Bach*, Vol. I, p. 406.

11. B, p. 422.

12. Ibid., p. 401.

13. Ibid., p. 421.

14. The edition published in 1957 was 'newly revised'. A thorough revision

can naturally not be carried out by Schweitzer under the conditions imposed by his life and work in Lambaréné.

15. Apart from the French and German editions, there was an English edition in 1911 and an American edition published by the Macmillan Co., in New York in 1947. These editions in the English language are considerably altered and extended by comparison with the German edition.

16. B, p. 313.

17. LT, *p. 92.*

18. Albert Schweitzer, *Deutsche und Französische Orgelbaukunst*, Verlag Breitkopf & Härtel, Leipzig 1906.

19. *Internationales Regulativ für Orgelbau*, Verlag Breitkopf & Härtel, Leipzig 1909. A French edition was published in 1909 and an Italian edition in 1914.

20. LT, *p. 101.*

21. Preface to Bach, p. XI.

22. Cf. Charles R. Joy, *Music in the Life of Albert Schweitzer*, A. & C. Black, London.

EPILOGUE

1. HJ, *p. 397.*

2. Cf. Ethelbert Stauffer, *Jesus, Gestalt und Geschichte*, A. Francke Verlag, Berne 1957, p. 12.

3. Hans-Rudolf Müller-Schwefe, *Der Standort der Theologie in unserer Zeit'*, Verlag Vandenhoek & Ruprecht, Göttingen 1958, p. 24.

4. LT, *p. 74.*

5. Ethelbert Stauffer, *Die Botschaft Jesu damals und heute*, A. Francke Verlag, Berne 1959, p. 8.

6. MP, *p. 297.*

7. Letter to the author, February 9, 1959.

8. LT, *p. 113.*

9. Rudolf Grabs, in his book *Albert Schweitzer. Denker aus Christentum*, and the Norwegian Gabriel Langfeldt in his book *Albert Schweitzer*. Both devote special chapters to the problem. But neither gives a clear answer.

10. CW, *p. 53.*

11. 'Miles Christi Fidelis', Elogium of the University of Cambridge, on the award of an honorary doctorate in 1955.

12. MP, *p. 384.*

13. Letter to the author, February 9, 1959.

14. Sermon delivered at St Nicholas Church in Strassburg on May 20, 1906.

15. CW, *pp. 79–80.*

16. Goethe, *Marienbader Elegie.*

17. Cf. George Seaver, *Albert Schweitzer: Christian Revolutionary*, James Clarke & Co., London 1944. Cf. also Buri, Langfeldt and others.

18. HJ, p. 641.

19. Sermon delivered at St Nicholas Church in Strassburg on the eve of All Souls Day 1918.

20. Charles R. Joy and Melvin Arnold, *Albert Schweitzer's Africa*, p. 150.

21. The 'Three Appeals', first from Radio Oslo on April 20, 29, and 30, 1958, were subsequently published together under the title *Friede oder Atomkrieg* by C. H. Beck, Munich 1958.

22. Cf. Joseph Bernhart, *Franz von Assisi*, Verlag Hermann Rinn, Munich 1956, pp. 74 et seq.

23. Benoist-Méchin, *Un Printemps Arabe*, Éditions Albin Michel, Paris 1959, p. 371.

24. Sermon delivered at St Nicholas Church in Strassburg on June 6, 1905, on the text Matt. xviii. 3. 'Except ye . . . become as little children. . . .'

25. 'Humility is the crown of all virtues.'

26. CRW, *pp. 79–80.*

THE STORY OF THE QUEST FOR THE HISTORICAL JESUS

1. HJ, *p. 2.*

2. Let Bultmann confirm—as one piece of evidence amongst many—what significance this newly awakened urge to radical truthfulness had for Protestant theology: 'Those of us who came from liberal theology, would have been unable to become, or to remain, theologians if we had not encountered the solemnity of radical truthfulness in liberal theology; we felt the work of the orthodox university theology to be an affair of compromises in which we could have been only inwardly broken existences.' Rudolf Bultmann, *Glauben und Verstehen*, Collected studies, Vol. I. Tübingen 1933, p. 2.

3. HJ, *p. 4.*

4. Hase's first life of Jesus appeared in 1828; the last version, the *Geschichte Jesu*, appeared in 1876.

5. HJ, *p. 5.*

6. Ibid., Introduction to the sixth German edition. p. XVIII.

7. Cf. Gogarten, ibid., p. 12, and also Adam Fechter, 'Entmythologisierung, Methode und Manie' in *Wort und Wahrheit*, Monthly for Religion and Culture, December 1953, p. 906.

8. Adam Fechter, ibid.

9. Pius XII, *Divino afflante spiritu.*

10. Gerhard Szczesny, ibid., p. 119.

11. HJ, *p. 6.*

12. Friedrich Gogarten (ibid., p. 11) expressed the opinion that the Bible, both with regard to its origin and its content, should be treated as an historical book like any other, and goes on to say that 'during the course of the past two hundred years this has become a matter of course which no serious theologian can contest'. He adds that confidence in its evidence can be justified only 'by belief in what it evidences. But doesn't the creation of a relationship of belief lend a somewhat unusual character to such an historical source?

13. Its first representatives: Johann Jakob Hess (*History of the three last years of the life of Jesus*, 1768–72), and Franz Volkmar Reinhard (*Versuch über den Plan, welchen der Stifter der christlichen Religion zum Besten der Menschheit entwarf*, 1781).

14. Heinrich Eberhard Gottlob Paulus, *Das Leben Jesu als Grundlage einer reinen Geschichte des Urchristentums*, 1828.

15. Karl August von Hase, *Das Leben Jesu zunächst für evangelische Studien*, 1828. Friedrich Ernst Daniel Schleiermacher, *Das Leben Jesu*, 1864, after a lecture notebook copied in 1832.

16. David Friedrich Strauss, *Der alte und der neue Glaube,* Verlag S. Hirzel, Leipzig 1872, p. 78.

17. Johann Gottfried Herder, *Vom Erlöser der Menschen,* after the first three evangelists, 1796. *Von Gottes Sohn, der Welt Heiland,* after the Gospel of St John, 1797.

18. David Friedrich Strauss, *Das Leben Jesu für das deutsche Volk bearbeitet,* 1864.

19. Christian Hermann Weisse, Professor der Philosophie: *Die Evangelischen Geschichten kritisch und philosophisch bearbeitet,* 1838.

20. Christian Gottlob Wilke, *Der Urevangelist oder eine exegetisch-kritische Untersuchung der Verwandschaftsverhältnisses der drei ersten Evangelien,* 1838.

21. Bruno Bauer, *Kritik der evangelischen Geschichte des Johannes,* 1840.

22. Bruno Bauer, *Kritik der evangelischen Geschichte der Synoptiker,* 1841–2.

23. Ernest Renan, *La Vie de Jésus,* 1863. The book went into eight editions within three months. Within the space of a year no less than five different translations into German appeared.

24. Hugo von Hofmannsthal—*Carl J. Burckhardt, Briefwechsel,* Verlag S. Fischer, Frankfurt-am-Main, 1956, p. 34.

25. Adolf von Harnack, *Das Wesen des Christentums,* 1st ed., 1900. New ed. (77,000) with an introduction by Rudolf Bultmann, Verlag Ehrenfried Klotz, Stuttgart 1950, p. XIX.

26. Ibid, p. 23.

27. Johannes Weiss, *Die Predigt Jesu vom Reiche Gottes,* Göttingen 1892.

28. KG, *p. 274.*

29. HJ, p. 520. Foonote 1.

30. KG, *p. 235.*

31. HJ, *p. 2.*

32. Ibid., p. 517.

33. Ibid., p. 519.

34. Ibid., *p. 11.*

35. Ibid., Introduction to the sixth German edition, p. XV.

36. Ethelbert Stauffer, *Jesus, Gestalt und Geschichte,* p. 7.

37. Martin Dibelius in: *Theologische Rundschau,* p. 210. Similarly Rudolf Bultmann in *Kerygma und Mythos,* Evangelischer Verlag Herbert Reich, Hamburg-Volksdorf, Vol. I, 1954, p. 132 (147). Figures in brackets refer to the first edition. 'It is of the essence of kerygma tradition that one should not inquire into the authenticity of what has been passed down.' After the programmatic declaration of Dibelius it is astonishing how much historical substance he feels he is justified in taking from the sources when he sets out to write 'the history of Jesus. (*Jesus,* Göschen Collection, Berlin 1939.) On the other hand, according to Bultmann it is impermissible, for theological more than for exegetical reasons, to go to the Gospel texts for information about the life of Jesus. By doing so one would not only be untrue to what these texts are really trying to say, but one would condemn oneself never to encounter the real event of salvation. (Cf. Rudolf Bultmann, *Glauben und Verstehen,* I. pp. 180 & 208.)

38. Ethelbert Stauffer, ibid., p. 7.

39. Cf. in this connection HJ, pp. 376 et seq.

40. Martin Dibelius, *Die Formgeschichte des Evangeliums,* Verlag J. C. B. Mohr (Paul Siebeck), Tübingen, p. 15.

41. Ibid., p. 16.

42. Ibid., p. 102.

43. Ibid., p. 90.

44. Rudolf Bultmann, *Jesus*, Verlag J. C. B. Mohr (Paul Siebeck), Tübingen 1951, p. 11.

45. Ibid., p. 10.

46. Ibid., p. 12. This is, of course, of decisive importance for answering the question, very important for Bultmann, as to what Jesus wanted, cf. p. 11.

47. Ibid., p. 147.

48. Hans Werner Bartsch, *Christus ohne Mythos*, Stuttgart 1953, p. 66. What Bartsch has to say may be taken as an authentic if popularized version of Bultmann's views, since he was entrusted with the editing of the discussion on the chief theological theme of Bultmann, i.e., the entmythologization of the Gospels, in the publication series *Kerygma und Mythos*.

49. Hans Werner Bartsch, ibid., p. 83.

50. Rudolf Bultmann, 'Neues Testament und Mythologie', in *Kerygma und Mythos*, Vol. I., p. 21.

51. Cf. Hans Werner Bartsch, 'Die philosophische Bestreitung der Entmythologisierung', in *Kerygma und Mythos*, Vol. 3.

52. Hans Werner Bartsch, *Christus ohne Mythos*, p. 39.

53. Martin Dibelius, 'Die Formgeschichte des Evangeliums', p. 99.

54. Hans Werner Bartsch, *Kerygma und Mythos*, Vol. I., p. 80 (300).

55. Rudolf Bultmann, 'Zum Problem der Entmythologisierung', in *Kerygma und Mythos*, Vol. II, p. 207.

56. Rudolf Bultmann, ibid., p. 207.

57. Rudolf Bultmann, 'Antwort an H. Thielicke', in *Kerygma und Mythos*, Vol. I., p. 225.

58. Hans Werner Bartsch, *Kerygma und Mythos*, Vol. I., Appendix p. 80.

59. Hans Werner Bartsch, *Christus ohne Mythos*, p. 25.

60. Rudolf Bultmann, 'Neues Testament und Mythologie', in *Kerygma und Mythos*, Vol. I., p. 48 (51).

61. Rudolf Bultmann, ibid., p. 24.

62. Rudolf Bultmann, 'Zum Problem der Entmythologisierung', in *Kerygma und Mythos*, Vol. II, p. 184.

63. It must be specifically stressed that, of course, there is no intention in this framework to attempt any discussion of the highly complex theological-philosophical problems of Bultmann's de-mythologization programme, whose importance 'not only academically and theologically, but as an event of importance to the Church' (Thielicke) is not questioned. But without a knowledge of it, which would take us far beyond the limits of this study, it is impossible to appreciate fully Bultmann's contribution to Jesus research. For those who may wish for a more detailed treatment of Bultmann's theological programme there is the work of the French Jesuit René Marlé, *Bultmann und die Interpretation des Neuen Testaments*, Verlag Bonifacius-Druckerei, Paderborn 1950. Bultmann himself has formally recognized that Marlé has clearly understood his theology, and the examination carried out by Marlé is, in fact, an exemplary performance, displaying both a sovereign mastery and an objective understanding of its subject.

64. Rudolf Bultmann, 'Die Entmythologisierung der neutestamentlichen Verkündigungen als Aufgabe', in *Kerygma und Mythos*, Vol. I, p. 17.

65. Rudolf Bultmann, ibid., p. 18.

66. 'My attempt at demythologization is undertaken in order to remove the obstacles which exist for the modern man because he lives in a world whose outlook is determined by science.' Rudolf Bultmann in *Karl Jaspers—Rudolf Bultmann, die Frage der Entmythologisierung*, Verlag R. Piper & Co., Munich, 1954, p. 61.

67. Ethelbert Stauffer, 'Entmythologisierung oder Realtheologie?' in *Kerygma und Mythos*, Vol. II, p. 19.

68. HJ, *p. 111*.

69. Helmut Thielicke, 'Die Frage der Entmythologisierung des Neuen Testaments', in *Kerygma und Mythos*, Vol. IX, p. 161 (179).

70. In connection with this very difficult problem for the layman in natural science the popular study by Hedwig Conrad-Martius 'Wissenschaft, Mythos und Neues Testament' in *Hochland*, October 1955, and particularly p. 7, is recommended.

71. Julius Schniewind, 'Antwort an Rudolf Bultmann' (Theses on the problem of de-mythologization) in *Kerygma und Mythos*, Vol. I., p. 105 (116).

72. Rudolf Bultmann, 'Zum Problem der Entmythologisierung', in *Kerygma und Mythos*, Vol. II, p. 184.

73. Ibid., p. 191.

74. Ibid., p. 207.

75. Regin Prenter, 'Mythos und Evangelium', in *Kerygma und Mythos*, Vol. II, p. 76.

76. Friedrich Gogarten, ibid., p. 32.

77. Fritz Buri, 'Entmythologisierung oder Entkerygmatisierung der Theologie' in *Kerygma und Mythos*, Vol. II, p. 88.

78. HJ, *p. 396*.

79. Martin Kaehler, *Der sogenannte historische Jesus und der geschichtlich-biblische Christus*, newly re-issued by E. Wolf, Verlag Chr. Kaiser, Munich 1946, p. 21. Unfortunately Schweitzer omitted to deal with this important study, which is still of influence even today.

80. David Friedrich Strauss, *Der alte und der neue Glaube*, p. 76.

81. 'No one is any longer in a position to write a life of Jesus', Günther Bornkam, ibid., p. 11. 'The ideal of the nineteenth century which was to produce a biography of Jesus—today we know that it is unattainable,' Ethelbert Stauffer, *Jesus, Gestalt und Geschichte*, p. 12.

82. Günther Bornkamm, ibid., p. 6.

83. Although Kaehler pushes the historical basic questions of Jesus research into the background, he is nevertheless constantly occupied with this picture. Cf. ibid., pp. 55, 68, 69, 72, 77 and 84. Dibelius is also (*Jesus*, p. 7) unwilling to do without this picture.

84. Rudolf Bultmann, *Jesus*, p. 11.

85. Ibid., p. 15.

86. Martin Kaehler, ibid., p. 69.

87. KG, *p. 250*.

88. Martin Kaehler, ibid., p. 19.

89. Hans Werner Bartsch, *Christus ohne Mythos*, p. 19.

90. Cf. Heinz Zahrnt, *Es begann mit Jesus von Nazareth.* Die Frage nach dem historischen Jesus. Krunz-Verlag, Stuttgart 1960, p. 124. An excellent popular representation of the present stage of the quest of the historical Jesus.
91. In this connection see also Julius Schniewind, ibid., pp. 108 and 113.
92. HJ, *p. 398.*
93. Sir Edwyn C. Hoskyns and F. Noel Davey, *The Riddle of the New Testament* [with a preface by Gerhard Kittel and Julius Schniewind, Verlag W. Kohlhammer, Stuttgart 1938, *p. 248*].
94. Hoskyns & Davey, ibid., *p. 10.*
95. De-mythologization is simply not interested in where the line runs between the historically reliable and the historically untenable,' Hans Werner Bartsch, 'Die neutestamentliche Theologie in der Entscheidung', in *Kerygma und Mythos*, Vol. II, p. 35.
96. Rudolf Bultmann, 'Zum Problem der Entmythologisierung', in *Kerygma und Mythos*, Vol. II, p. 191.
97. Hoskyns & Davey, ibid., *p. 209.*
98. HJ, *p. 338.*
99. Martin Dibelius, *Die Formgeschichte des Evangeliums*, p. 5.
100. Ibid., p. 15.
101. For example, Rudolf Bultmann, *Jesus*, p. 11. Bornkamm (ibid., p. 20) though he fully appreciates the value of form-historical investigation, points out that 'evangelical tradition is after all very interested in the pre-Easter story of Jesus'.
102. Cf. Otto Michel, 'Albert Schweitzer und die Leben-Jesu-Forschung heute: Apokalyptik und Qumran', in: *Albert Schweitzer. Sein Denken und sein Weg.* Herausgegeben von Dr H. W. Bahr, Verlag I. C. B. Mohr (Paul Siebeck), Tübingen 1962, pp. 125 et seq.
103. Günter Bornkamm, ibid., p. 2.
104. Hoskyns & Davey, ibid. cf. Footnote 93. The editors of the German edition of this book, Gerhard Kittel and Julius Schniewind, are in agreement that they 'know no other book which so fully and impressively describes the position of New Testament exegesis after a century of historico-critical research'. Sir Edwyn Hoskyns, Bishop of Southwell and Canon of Corpus Christi College, Cambridge, died in 1937.
105. Hans Werner Bartsch, in *Kerygma und Mythos*, Vol. I, Appendix, p. 60 (280).
106. Cf. HJ p. XI. 'The historical problem confronting the scientific student of the life of Jesus may be said to be solved in its essentials. . . .'
107. Even in the circle of Bultmann followers it has in the meantime been recognized that an implicit Christology is contained in Jesus eschatology. Cf. James M. Robinson, Professor of Theology and New Testament at the Southern California School of Theology in Claremont: *Kerygma und historischer Jesus.* Zwingli-Verlag, Zurich/Stuttgart 1960, p. 125.
108. Heinz Zahrnt, ibid., p. 131.
109. Heinz Eduard Tödt, *Der Menschensohn in der synoptischen Überlieferung.* Gütersloher Verlagshaus Gerd Mohn 1959, pp. 314, 265. This work, which derives from the Bultmann school, may be regarded as one of the most important contributions to the quest of the historical Jesus in recent years.
110. Heinz Zahrnt, ibid., p. 127.

111. Georg Picht. *Unterwegs zu neuen Leitbildern?*, p. 15.
112. Hoskyns–Davey, ibid., *p. 260.*
113. Hoskyns–Davey, ibid., *pp. 259–60.*
114. Ethelbert Stauffer, 'Entmythologisierung oder Realtheologie?' in: *Kerygma und Mythos*, Vol. II, p. 17.
115. Hoskyns–Davey, ibid, *p. 66.*
116. Schweitzer 'was confirmed to an extraordinary extent' by recent investigations of the apocalyptic ideology of Neo-Judaism, which were based on much richer source material. Otto Michel, ibid., p. 127.
117. C. F. Robinson, ibid., pp. 141, 94.

THE SERMONS

These sermons of Albert Schweitzer are to be regarded from the standpoint of the spoken word. The manuscripts were never revised for print. Further, they are mere sketches. Schweitzer always preached more or less extempore and never felt himself bound to any prepared text.

INDEX